KU-593-698

Major Dudes

A Steely Dan Companion

Edited by Barney Hoskyns

Constable • London

CONSTABLE

First published in Great Britain in 2017 by Constable

1 3 5 7 9 10 8 6 4 2

Copyright © Backpages Ltd., 2017

The moral right of the author has been asserted.

All rights reserved.
No part of this publication may be reproduced, stored in a retrieval system,
or transmitted, in any form, or by any means, without the prior permission in
writing of the publisher, nor be otherwise circulated in any form of binding or cover
other than that in which it is published and without a similar condition including
this condition being imposed on the subsequent purchaser.

A CIP catalogue record for this book
is available from the British Library.

ISBN: 978-1-47212-756-3 (hardback)
ISBN: 978-1-47212-755-6 (trade paperback)

Typeset in Minion Pro by SX Composing DTP, Rayleigh, Essex
Printed and bound in Great Britain by Clays Ltd, St Ives plc

Papers used by Constable are from well-managed forests
and other responsible sources.

Constable
An imprint of
Little, Brown Book Group
Carmelite House
50 Victoria Embankment
London EC4Y 0DZ

An Hachette UK Company
www.hachette.co.uk

www.littlebrown.co.uk

For Tony Keys, the most ardent of Dan fans . . . and without whom Rock's Backpages would never have been possible.

Contents

CONTENTS

MAJOR DUDES

Acknowledgements

With many thanks to Constable's Andreas Campomar and Aitken Alexander's Matthew Hamilton – major dudes and Dan fanatics both – for making this bodacious compendium happen. Thanks to Claire Chesser and Lucian Randall at Constable and to Mark Pringle and Tony Keys for sourcing pieces from the Rock's Backpages archive. Thanks to Louise Stakem at *Time Out* for her assistance. Thanks to all the contributors to this anthology: Richard Cromelin, Daryl Easlea, Andy Gill, Mick Gold, Geoffrey Himes, Chris Ingham, Jonh Ingham, Dylan Jones, Mark Leviton, Gavin Martin, Charles Shaar Murray, Ian Penman, Bruce Pollock, Ira Robbins, Wayne Robins, Steven Rosen, Bud Scoppa, Fred Schruers, Sylvie Simmons, Rob Steen, Adam Sweeting, Chris Van Ness, Michael Watts, Chris Welch and Richard Williams. Also to Bill McCormick for granting permission to use the pieces by his late brother Ian MacDonald; Jim Smith for the *Aja* review by the late Richard C. Walls; Augusta Palmer for the piece by her late father Robert; and Dan Valentine for the piece by his late mother Penny.

A squonk's tears:
Steely Dan at forty-five

'If we were ahead of our time, it was simply because we grew up with a certain natural ironic stance that later became the norm in society.'
Donald Fagen, 1991

1 Live at the HMV Apollo, vol 2

7 July 2007: Old bald white blokes are standing about in striped shirts, clutching plastic cups of tepid lager. Some may be here at the old Hammersmith Odeon – now rebranded as the HMV Apollo – to rekindle memories of seeing Steely Dan at London's Rainbow Theatre in May 1974, shortly before the group's Walter Becker and Donald Fagen quit touring and retreated to the hermetic insulation of southern California's plushest recording studios.

Back then, these old blokes would have been lone groovers in loon pants, habitués of import record stores who'd heard the Dan's *Can't Buy a Thrill* (1972) or *Countdown to Ecstasy* (1973) and quickly concurred with Ian MacDonald of the *New Musical Express* when he asked where else a 'deafened connoisseur' could 'get his shots of lyric succinctness matched with thoroughly coherent musicality'. Writing in *Creem* that year, MacDonald's fellow rock critic Wayne Robins noted that the typical Dan fan could be 'found often in unlikely places, following no discernible pattern except walking slow, drinking alone, and moving swiftly through the night . . . ' (the piece is included in this anthology in its *NME* reprint).

Robins, as it happens, had known jazzbo misanthropes Becker and Fagen at 'funky and fragmented' Bard College, upstate from Manhattan on the Hudson, in the late '60s. 'Reelin' in the Years', the second hit from *Can't Buy a Thrill*, was, for him, 'probably the best song ever written about the pseudo-poetic, preppie-hippie assholism that dominated Bard and other joints of its kind'.

At the HMV Apollo, Fagen reels in his sixty-one years, planted behind his Fender Rhodes electric piano like some Hebraic Ray Charles with a mouth like *The Simpsons'* Moe the Bartender. The theatre is, he declares, 'one of the many fine toilets we'll be playing' on a European tour that's already taken in Amsterdam, Brussels, Edinburgh and Birmingham and will include more cosmopolitan stops in Paris, Rome, Milan and Monte Carlo. When occasionally Fagen gets to his feet, hunched and clutching a melodica – Augustus Pablo eat your heart out – he patrols the stage like a kind of king penguin.

The last time I saw Steely Dan live it was at Wembley Arena in September 2000, when they offered two amiable fingers to anyone who still lumped them in with all the tepid funk-lite the duo inspired in the '70s and '80s. Backed by such *simpatico* stalwarts as drummer Ricky Lawson and chameleonic guitarist Jon

Herington (still a member of their touring band), they invested ageless vignettes like 'The Boston Rag' and 'Hey Nineteen' with vim, humour, and slick Jewish soul. 'This is no one-night stand,' Fagen drawled on *Gaucho*'s insidiously slinky 'Babylon Sisters'. 'This is a real occasion.'

It was.

2 Fabriani and Mahler were here

Twice I've been granted audiences with Becker and Fagen; twice they've come on like a comic double-act – Walter Matthau and Jack Lemmon via Larry David or Garry Shandling. Transcriptions of conversations with them read more like Marx Brothers scripts than music-press interviews. It's not hard to imagine the merciless wit they must have wielded at Bard, where – as *Can't Buy a Thrill*'s scornful 'Only a Fool Would Say That' made plain – they were as removed from the general hippietopian vibe of the times as Randy Newman or Frank Zappa or the Velvet Underground. 'We were a little younger than the '60s bands,' Fagen told me in 2000. 'A lot of the '60s foundation was starting to collapse by the time we put out our first record.'

Jay Black, who hired the young Don 'n' Walt to play in his mob-backed Top 40 group Jay & the Americans, referred to the duo as '[Charles] Manson and [Charles] Starkweather'. Tickled by their unusual mixture of erudition and subversion, Black joked that they were like 'librarians on acid'. The pair saw themselves not as rock stars but as backroom boys, Leiber and Stoller for longhairs, the logical late-'60s successors to Barry and Greenwich (or Bacharach and David or Berns and Ragovoy). The pair haunted Manhattan song-hive the Brill Building in hopes someone might mistake their quirky, cryptic little songs for

actual hits. (Fat chance, given the extreme strangeness of compositions such as 'Yellow Peril', 'Brain Tap Shuffle' and 'The Roaring
of the Lamb' – though early stabs at 'Brooklyn' and 'Barrytown'
should have caught the ear of any half-decent A&R man.)

Kenny Vance, manager of Jay & the Americans, bankrolled
Becker and Fagen's demos; a cover of 'I Mean to Shine' even
wound up on Barbra Streisand's 1971 album *Barbra Joan
Streisand*. But thanks to the intercession of producer Gary Katz
(a.k.a. Kannon), Becker and Fagen left New York for Los Angeles,
brought into the desperately unhip fold of ABC-Dunhill Records
as staff writers for such fundamentally unsuitable acts as the
Grass Roots and Steppenwolf's John Kay. (Exceptions to the rule:
Thomas Jefferson Kaye's versions of the glorious 'Jones' and
'American Lovers' from his great 1973 album *First Grade*.) There
the dyed-in-the-wool east-coasters strove to make satirical sense
of miasmic southern California. The common ground the duo
might have felt with a local satirist like Randy Newman brought
them no closer to the calico mafia of Laurel Canyon or the hegemony of Lenny Waronker's Warner-Reprise roster in Burbank.

Summer 1972 saw the release of the Dan's debut LP, kicked
off by the slinky, addiction-themed hit 'Do It Again'. 'The newly
formed amalgam [of Steely Dan] threatens to undermine the
foundations of the rock power elite,' Tristan Fabriani (Fagen)
wrote drolly in *Can't Buy a Thrill*'s sleevenote. The band, he
added, 'casts a long shadow upon the contemporary rock
wasteland . . . struggling to make sense out of the flotsam and
jetsam of its eclectic musical heritage.' (Little wonder that Fagen,
a pop intellectual, wrote a column for the movie monthly
Premiere in the eighties and later authored the shrewd and
amusing *Eminent Hipsters*.)

Though Steely Dan were never a critics' band per se – not like the Velvet Underground or Big Star were – Becker and Fagen talked about music like critics talked about music (for instance, inserting the notorious line 'Even Cathy Berberian knows there's one *roulade* she can't sing' into *Countdown to Ecstasy*'s 'Your Gold Teeth'). In the long run this may have counted against them, since critics rarely embrace anything as cerebral or egg-headed as, well, critics.

Offsetting the clever-clogs component on *Thrill* were the pure melodic pleasures of 'Dirty Work', 'Kings', 'Reelin' in the Years', 'Brooklyn' and 'Change of the Guard'. Drilling a hastily-assembled LA band (guitarists Jeff 'Skunk' Baxter and Denny Dias, an old collaborator from the east coast; drummer Jim Hodder; temporary second singer David Palmer and some auxiliary session men), Becker and Fagen made everything count in the playful precision of their chords and harmonies, every last fill exact and satisfying. 'Midnite Cruiser', all sun-kissed vocals and liquid twin guitars, wasn't far from the creamy freeway rock of LA contemporaries the Eagles, a band later wryly namechecked on *The Royal Scam*'s 'Everything You Did'. (The Eagles, who shared management with the Dan, returned the namecheck compliment in a line about 'steely knives' on 'Hotel California'.)

Can't Buy a Thrill was where Becker and Fagen set out their stall: a suite of singalong songs that sounded both personal and conversational – almost short-story-esque – while being still essentially ambiguous and mysterious. Listening to 'Fire in the Hole' and 'Turn that Heartbeat Again' – as to 'Razor Boy' (*Countdown to Ecstasy*), 'Any Major Dude Will Tell You' (*Pretzel Logic*) and 'Bad Sneakers' (*Katy Lied*) – was like hearing Thomas Pynchon's *The Crying of Lot 49* set to rock music.

3 Faux-luxe interiority

William Gibson, whose precocious novels from *Neuromancer* onwards were a clear influence on Fagen's 1993 solo album *Kamakiriad*, once suggested to me that 'a lot of people think of Steely Dan as the epitome of boring '70s stuff, never realising this is probably the most subversive material pop has ever thrown up.'

Cyberpunk king Gibson saw all too clearly how Becker and Fagen had camouflaged their beat-influenced mischief and drug references so subtly that they went straight over the average rock fan's head. As the *LA Times*' Richard Cromelin wrote on the release of *The Royal Scam* (1976), 'The amorphous nature of Steely Dan, furthered by the mysterious *outré* world their music creates and by wry Walt and doleful Don's resolute reclusiveness, has bred widespread indifference among the public at large and unceasing fascination among aficionados of the Steely Dan mystique.'

Hearing 'Show Biz Kids' – that most withering dissection of Californian narcissism – on John Peel's Radio 1 show was thoroughly disorienting for my fourteen-year-old self. Who *were* these people? Were they Yanks or Brits? White or black or brown? Why were the backing vocalists urging us to go to Las Vegas? (They weren't, as it turned out: Wayne Robins elucidates further in the 1974 *NME* piece included in this collection.) And was the singer consciously filching the vocal line from Harry Nilsson's 'Coconut'? In 1973 there was no frame of reference for music so funky or coolly cynical. Who else would have slipped the phrase '*coup de grâce*' – or, indeed, the name of their own band – into a song?

Some get the point of Steely Dan but reject the idea that a rock group can sound so slick and put such a premium on the chops of top session musicians. For them, rock should be raw and untamed – 'guts and fire and feeling,' in the words of Dan fan Nick Hornby, 'not difficult chords and ironic detachment'. Even William Burroughs, after whom they'd named themselves, thought Steely Dan 'too fancy . . . doing too many things at once'.

The *NME* stayed loyal to the duo even after punk toppled pomp-rock, but it wasn't easy to defend the extended jazz-funk-rock pieces on 1977's huge-selling *Aja* when the prevailing musical mood was so bluntly reductive. Joni Mitchell came up against the same jazzphobia when she released *Court and Spark* (1974) and *The Hissing of Summer Lawns* (1975), albums featuring some of the session men (Tom Scott, John Guerin, Victor Feldman et al.) whom Becker and Fagen employed.

With punk, naturally, came a deep suspicion of perfectionism – and Fagen, for one, was so neurotically perfectionist in the studio that people referred to him as 'Mother'. Turning away from rock's fake guitar bravado – as from the fake bonhomie of on-the-road band democracy – Steely Dan fashioned a new sound with the assistance of maestro engineer Roger 'The Immortal' Nichols: crisply funky, glisteningly elegant, clinically cushioned. On the non-album song 'FM', theme track for their manager Irving Azoff's 1978 film of the same name, Fagen sang the immortal line 'Give her some funked-up muzak, she treats you nice . . . ' If you'd wilfully invented a genre that was diametrically antithetical to punk rock, funked-up muzak would probably be it.

Becker and Fagen were deeply smitten by the artifice of studio sound, particularly the way disco records were being produced in the '70s. Hence the fetishising of such luminaries as guitarist Larry Carlton and drummer Steve Gadd, plying their tasty trade in the perma-twilight of New York's and LA's most well-appointed studios.

In 2000 I asked Becker and Fagen why they felt so at home behind the recording console. '[It's] all about the idea of the set-up,' Fagen offered. '[It's] a room where you have all this technology to help you and where you have some toys. And you need air-conditioning and a book with menus in it. It's about that space-age bachelor-pad vibe. The studio satisfies a lot of those urges.'

4 Got them old Deacon Blues again, mama

Even Fagen thought he and Becker had gone too far on *Gaucho*, 'trying to realise a technical perfection that started to deaden the material' (Robert Palmer – whose 1981 *Rolling Stone* piece on the duo is included in this book – opined that Steely Dan's music sounded like it had been 'recorded in a hospital ward'). It's interesting, therefore, to note how many *Gaucho* songs are trotted out tonight at the HMV Apollo.

'Time Out of Mind', an oddly cheery junkie classic written in the full flow of Becker's turn-of-the-decade addiction, is the second song up. 'Hey Nineteen' remains the wittiest observation ever penned about comely young women and older male predators. The smooth-jazz anomie of 'Babylon Sisters' is followed seamlessly by the jet-set coke anthem 'Glamour Profession'.

At Hammersmith there's plenty from *Aja* and *Katy Lied*, less from *Countdown to Ecstasy* and *Pretzel Logic*; a song apiece from *Can't Buy a Thrill* and *The Royal Scam* and *Two Against Nature*; and nothing at all from *Everything Must Go* or the Becker and Fagen solo works (Fagen's 1982 album *The Nightfly* incidentally being as good as anything Steely Dan ever recorded). The black jazz-virtuoso feel of so much Dan music doesn't alter the fact that the only African-American faces for miles around belong to bass guitarist Freddie Washington and the trio of backing-vocal honeys, one of whom turns out to be Tawatha Agee, baby-doll siren of Scritti Politti's *Cupid and Psyche '85*. Picture the Sweet Inspirations resurrected as the Babylon Sistas: 'You got to shake it, baby, you got to shake it, baby, you got to shake it . . . ' That Steely Dan has been sampled by hip hop artists from De La Soul ('Peg') to Kanye West ('Kid Charlemagne') is an irony they must relish when they look out over the seas of Caucasian faces that flock to their concerts.

Several songs ('Reelin' in the Years', 'Show Biz Kids' et al.) are all but unidentifiable in revised guises. Becker and Fagen are truer to 'My Old School' – one of their most purely hummable songs – and to the dark boogie of 'Black Friday'. 'Aja' is magnificent, drummer Keith Carlock pulling off uncanny simulacra of Steve Gadd's awesome fills on the original album of that name. Generally the sound is a little thin and boxy, with the jazz overlay sometimes crimping the glossy succulence of *Aja* and *Gaucho*, but the gloopy Fender Rhodes keyboard remains a trademark signature of what Becker at one juncture refers to as 'the deep '70s'. Walter's limited palette on the Stratocaster hasn't changed much; then again, let's be thankful we only have to hear his undulcet vocal tones the once, on 'Daddy Don't Live in That New York City No More'.

It's hard to believe Becker was ever a major dope fiend or that his girlfriend Karen Stanley actually died of an overdose back in 1980: but then has any band *ever* been so cryptically allusive about class-A substances? 'He was kind of leaping toward destruction,' Fagen said of his partner in the *Gaucho* era. 'When he was having a really hotcha swell time, you know, he'd be late for sessions and was not that easy to deal with.'

'Deacon Blues' recalls not only the spate of '80s bands who cited Steely Dan as an antecedent – Danny Wilson, Prefab Sprout,

Hue and Cry and, natch, Deacon Blue – but the long-term damage arguably done to the duo's credibility by such Brit disciples. '[Our songs],' Fagen conceded, 'had some of the irony that became the lingua franca of the '80s.' Though Danny Wilson's Gary Clark had a voice like Donald Fagen crossed with Dan-sideman-turned-Doobie-brother Michael McDonald, the artfulness of such groups was soon shunted aside by Madchester and then by grunge.

Guitarist Elliott Randall, who played so blisteringly on *Can't Buy a Thrill*, enters stage right for a more orthodox 'Reelin' in the Years' – the night's first encore – and is the same shamblingly happy figure I recall jamming with Fagen in 1993 in the latter's long-forgotten New York Rock and Soul Revue. The final song is 'Kid Charlemagne', that glorious paean to a sometime drug king-pin whose 'patrons have all left you in the red'.

Does one get more – or just a different – pleasure from hearing and seeing Steely Dan live? At a time when prices are sky-high for live music, wouldn't you rather hear 'Aja', always predictably perfect, on your own faux-luxe sound system? Weren't Steely Dan one of those bands it was always better to imagine than actually watch?

5 Mildly Humorous Yet Palatable

That Steely Dan was one of the defining acts of the deep '70s is as indisputable as the fact that Walter Becker and Donald Fagen are the greatest duo of their kind – think Sparks, Pet Shop Boys, and other ironic subverters-from-within – that pop-rock ever produced. It's hard not to yearn for days when a brainy and not terribly pretty band like Steely Dan could be given a serious shot at realising their arena dreams.

But would it ultimately have been better – cooler – for Becker and Fagen to disappear almost completely from view, as they did for the best part of a decade after parting ways in June 1981? Donald himself would later concede to Richard Cromelin that Steely Dan 'may be inseparable from its time' and that 'the way we looked at things and what was going on at the time gave it a specific character which I don't think it could ever have [again].'

When the duo resurfaced against all expectation to tour in 1993 – releasing the lukewarm *Alive in America* as a memento – the astringent cynics of the '70s sounded almost avuncular. And though their lyric powers on *Two Against Nature* and *Everything Must Go* (as on Fagen's subsequent solo albums) were undimmed by the reeled-in years, the music had lost more than a little of its edge. Middle-aged boffins competing in a world of midriff display and what Becker called 'nominal generational anger', Steely Dan were themselves less furious at (and more accepting of) the world. One could also posit the theory that America – or at least US television (*Seinfeld, The Simpsons* et seq.) – had caught up with the Dan brand of irony, forcing them to adopt the stance of what Fagen termed 'pseudo-post-irony'.

'I think what happens with a lot of people is that after that initial youthful spurt, they never come out of it,' Fagen said to me in 2000. 'They either succumb to despair or intoxicants. Part of it is that you have to throw off the narcissism of youth, which is your energy when you start. When that's gone, you have to find another source.'

Three years later, Becker expounded on roughly the same theme to me. 'Donald and I have been moderately successful at reconciling our sense of alienation with the actual need for survival,' he told me. 'It's been more or less accommodated by the world and by our wives and partners and by the physical realities of our bodies and so on, so that we can still sort of live in these fantasy bubbles of art. We spend most of the day planning our revenge without actually walking out into the middle of the traffic.'

Thank the Lord for that.

Bernard Purdie, self-proclaimed World's Greatest Drummer and star of *Aja*'s 'Home at Last', said Steely Dan were 'the closest thing to genius I've ever seen'. Other Dan collaborators would agree. Personally I contend that whatever age you are – and however nominally angry – it behoves you to acquaint yourself with what former *Time* critic Jay Cocks called 'the lithe inflections of the Becker-Fagen melodies . . . a grace that is both sensuous and sinister'.

When I last met the indomitable duo, in a swish hotel suite in Santa Monica in 2003, I asked if it was ironic that some regarded Steely Dan as old farts when actually they were writing more trenchantly about the fucked-up virtual world of the early twenty-first century than anyone else in rock music.

Becker paused to think about it – or at least about how Steely Dan came to 'subvert from within' in the first place – before replying. 'I think part of the reason that we were able to slip through the cracks or get in the door was because you could see what we did at that level and it was mildly humorous yet palatable, and it wasn't necessary to know or be troubled by anything beyond that level.'

'It was lucky that we had these populist tastes,' added Fagen. 'Kind of *bad* taste, in a way.'

'We've been able,' Becker concluded with an owlish look, 'to combine high vulgarian stuff with low highbrow stuff.'

Fagen glanced at his old college buddy for a moment before saying, in a cod-English accent I had to assume was partly for my benefit, *'Or whatever . . .'*

The Dan in Coldwater Canyon, Los Angeles, September 1972. Clockwise from top left: Jeff 'Skunk' Baxter, Denny Dias, Jim Hodder, Donald Fagen and Walter Becker.

Ed Caraeff/Morgan Media/Getty Images

ONE: Thrill Seekers

'We were like mouldy figs before we were born'

Donald Fagen, 2000

1

Rock and roll via Third Stream

Chris Van Ness, *Los Angeles Free Press*,
27 October 1972

It all started with one of the most casual hypes I have ever gotten. It came in the form of an advance tape of an album by a new group called Steely Dan.

'Listen to it. I don't know anything about the group, but I'm told they're pretty good,' was what the press agent said. He was either pretty shrewd in trying to make me think he hadn't done his homework or he had my tastes down and knew I would react favourably.

But the favourable reaction was not immediate. If the hype had been a record, I would have taken my own good time to listen to it but, since it was a tape, I realised that someone must think this group was something special or they wouldn't have gone to the trouble. I listened to the tape.

My reaction was one of reserve. I could tell the group was better than average, and there were two songs ('Midnite Cruiser' and 'Reelin' In The Years') that I liked instantly, but I was not ready to make any major commitment. That came later, after I heard them play live.

I will admit my interest was high, because I readily agreed to drive all the way out to Glendale to hear the band play their first live gig ever. The place was called the Ice House, and the band was on when I arrived. That's when I started to get a little crazy behind this group.

Six people: keyboards, drums, bass, vocalist, second lead guitar and lead guitar who also doubled on steel and congas – and more pure rock'n'roll energy than the J. Geils Band and the Faces put together.

An interview follows:

How was the band put together and is it correct to assume the band was put together around you?
Walter Becker: In a way it was put together around us. It was put together by Gary Katz, who's our producer. When he came to work for Dunhill, we'd been working with him as musicians and writers. And a couple of other people he'd been working with were Jeff Baxter, our guitarist, and Jim Hodder, our drummer. He sort of put it together around the four of us and then we added Denny Dias, the second guitar player, whom we'd worked with before, and Dave Palmer, the singer, was the last member to join the group. He joined the group, actually, when we were half through with the album.

Oh, so that explains why everybody else sings on the album and Dave does all the vocals in live performance.
Donald Fagen: Yeah, he would have done more, 'cause he sings better; but we got him late. But he'll be doing most of the singing.

I guess the obvious question is: Why is the band happening right now? You guys were writing together for a number of years before Steely Dan happened, right?

WB: Right. We met in college four years ago, and we've been writing for a while.

DF: We had a lot of strange material that no one could do. Until just now, when we found these people who were able to play it and make it sound like music. For some reason, we had a lot of trouble finding musicians all those years.

Why do you classify it as strange material?

DF: It used to be stranger. I think it was a compromise both ways: we compromised on the material, to a certain extent, in making it easier to respond to, and I guess that's why we now have musicians.

How was the material different?

DF: It was more complex – more sophisticated, to a certain extent – harmonically. And lyrically, too.

What songs that you do now come closest to your older strange material?

WB: Maybe 'Fire In The Hole', that's an old one. Or 'Turn That Heartbeat Over Again'. We used to have a lot of songs like that, but after you've written a song and had it sitting around for a couple of years, you're more eager to do fresh material – do the things you're learning now.

DF: We've simplified. I have a feeling that, whenever we look back on some of the songs we used to write, aside from being more complex and sophisticated they're also a little more pretentious. So I think the simplification, in fact, made it better.

I remember the first night I heard the group live, there were some things happening musically that told me somebody was into some heavy jazz. Is that what you mean by 'more complex and pretentious'?

WB: It wasn't really jazz, but you're quite right that Donald and I are really jazz fans.

DF: There's a lot of jazz harmony.

WB: But the older music was more jazz-influenced than, let's say, what we do now. I know the particular tune you're referring to. That was one we wrote about three years ago, and even that one used to be a lot weirder than it is now. We straightened that one out.

DF: I guess what we used to write is what you might call classical and jazzical – third stream. It's the same kind of thing, only it was rock-and-jazz and we didn't feel it really worked. It was a very unstable combination.

Are you happy with where the music is right now?

DF: Yeah, I think it's good and it'll get better. I think we'll start working toward more ambitious musical things.

Right. You answered the hidden question there.

WB: Yeah. The thing is: When you start to work with a group of musicians . . .

DF: We didn't want to scare them.

WB: . . . things evolve. To really play that kind of more complex music, there has to be a greater rapport, and that just takes time.

Do you feel that your music now – well, let's take the album – is commercial?

WB: I think a lot of it is. I think 'Do It Again' is commercial – without being compromised in any way.

DF: We're going to do an edit to make it shorter for the single.

WB: And that'll be the only compromise, really. But I'm glad that 'Do It Again' was picked; that was my favourite cut on the album. And I think it's a very good blend of commercial potential without being silly.

Is that what you're going for right now? Do you feel that you need a good commercial hit to get you off the ground?

DF: It can't hurt.

WB: It would help, but I don't really think we need it.

DF: That's the whole thing. What we used to do was try to widen the public's appreciation of some more interesting rock'n'roll than they'd been hearing. And for years we couldn't get a bite until we did something like 'Do It Again', which I think is very good, but we'd like to start working from there.

Do you feel the album represents where the group is right now?

DF: It's the state of the art.

Do you feel the group is better represented in live performance?

DF: It will be very shortly, if it isn't now. I can see the way it's going and it's growing very satisfactorily into what we'd like it to be.

WB: There's a certain excitement that's in the live performance visually – especially because Dave is the singer on stage, whereas he only sang two cuts on the album. I think that gives it a different appeal. We're just starting to experiment, but I like it.

Do you feel, as the group's only writers, that Steely Dan is your band? And if so – or if not – can you keep those six people together?

WB: Well, when we started out, because all the material was ours and Donald was doing most of the singing, it was our band. But as we play together more, I think it becomes a group effort more fully. And because of that, I think it's a sure thing these six people will stay together.

DF: Especially as far as arranging goes. As far as material goes, yeah, I suppose it is our band and we'll always write the material. But as far as arranging goes, everyone makes a contribution.

WB: And so far it works pretty good. The six people involved are not nearly as egotistical as they might be, and they really want to work.

DF: They're professional.

I don't know if any of what I have said has gotten back to you, but I think the group is one of the most exciting new bands I've heard in a long time.

DF: I'm glad you like it. That's the point, you know.

WB: We've sort of felt all along – although perhaps we're deluding ourselves – that what we do would probably appeal to critics even if it didn't get any airplay or any immediate public response. I don't know whether it has . . .

It has, but I think that's almost a backwards way to look at it.

WB: It is, but somehow it made sense to me. I knew that if I were a critic . . .

DF: Not that we cater to critics . . .

WB: Not at all. It just seems to me that a person with a fairly extensive musical background would be able to immediately appreciate what we did.

It's that rare combination of a group that's obviously versatile, obviously has more musical ability than most – I happen to think you guys are great writers – and yet, on another level entirely, it's an exciting rock'n'roll band.

DF: Thank you. That's what we're trying to do, and I think we're heading in the right direction. I think we've got a good start.

2

Review of
Can't Buy A Thrill

Andrew Tyler, *Disc*,
20 January 1973

This one's already speeding up the *Billboard* and *Cashbox* charts – currently around the 30 mark and likely to jump about twenty places by next week. Quite understandable and justified, let it be said.

Still only a few months together, the band produce a remarkable range of sounds in the medium-to-heavy bracket – lots of excellent piano from Mr Jeff Baxter [*sic – Ed.*] and many powerfully melodic and lyrical songs from the founding duo of Donald Fagen (also on keyboards) and Walter Becker on bass. The pair met at college and later played for a couple of years with Jay & the Americans. They were soon hustled off to the West Coast by producer Gary Kannon for a staff writing job with ABC-Dunhill. Putting together a band was the next logical step, so in addition to Baxter, Kannon brought in Dave Palmer on vocals, James Hodder on drums and Denny Dias on guitar.

'Reelin' In The Years' is the most instantly likeable of the package and would have made a strong single. They settle, instead, for a compacted version of 'Do It Again', which has a crispy-crunchy Latin feel and some nice changes.

Comparisons are always difficult and usually invalid but, if you were to imagine a combination of CSNY and Chicago, you'd still be miles off but headed in the right direction.

It's fair to say that Steely will have a place on the nation's turntable for as long as they produce music of this magnitude. And word is that they might well visit our shores in February or March, depending on how the single and album make out.

Get Your Thrills Here

Penny Valentine, *Sounds*,
10 March 1973

The most exciting new band to break from the States this year is Steely Dan. *Can't Buy A Thrill* is the lie of a title they chose for their first album. By parting with your hard-earned currency and acquiring this collection you are faced with a combination of startling and – not the least – highly pleasing music. Complex, but still direct enough to hand gently round the ears; smooth without being laid-back in cotton wool . . . Steely Dan prove that you *can* buy a thrill, and a lot more besides.

So who are they – these tinglers whose name was born from a chapter in William Burroughs' *Naked Lunch*, and who treat interviews with a kind of tongue-in-cheek cynicism? They have, in fact, been around quite a time (maybe that explains it!).

Six guys – Walter Becker, Donald Fagen, Dave Palmer, Jeff Baxter, James Hodder and Denny Dias – formed themselves into Steely after years of playing as session musicians on the East Coast and various stints playing backup across country for Jay & the Americans. A period which Becker and Fagen describe fluently as 'a long horrible time – more or less images of toilets interspersed with arenas'.

It's Becker and Fagen who are really the backbone of Dan. It's their work as songwriters – stemming from their time together at college – that the rest of the band are only too glad to enthuse about. According to guitarist Denny Dias, whom I spoke to last week around 2 a.m. Los Angeles time, he had such faith in Becker and Fagen's genius he 'hung around for two years doing odd jobs like being a car wash boy' until the band looked likely to be formed and he was summoned out to the West Coast to join up.

'I met Donald and Walter back in '69 and recognised straight away they were real geniuses,' Denny said. 'At that time, they were trying to sell themselves to someone who would put money behind them – like a record company. But nobody was interested until Gary Kannon got to Dunhill.

'When we started together, there was no real reason to call it a band as such. There was no money to hire proper equipment or a place to rehearse. There was all this potential but nothing happened until last year. Believe me, it was pretty frustrating getting your hopes high each day and then nothing happening.'

With some of the band culled from an amazing East Coast set-up under the auspices of Ultimate Spinach – described by Denny as 'one of those groups whose leader was taking them through a "spiritual trip" of loud noise' – Steely Dan as a unit finally broke the fate barrier and got into the studio late last year.

'We went into the studio in early September, and three weeks after that the album was finished. I guess the people who say it sounds thrown together are right – it was. Equally, the ones who like it – well, I guess it's fairly decent by any standards. Really we had just started learning to play together at that time.'

If Dias's conversation isn't exactly exuding the ultimate in breathless enthusiasm, then really it's because he feels that, having finally broken into the recording complexes and got some finance behind them, the next Steely Dan album will show what they're really about.

'I guess I am a perfectionist, but *Can't Buy A Thrill* is the worst album we'll ever make. Some of the songs on the album were written years ago and I think the older stuff tended to be stronger. I think Donald and Walter wrote the other numbers – the more commercial stuff – to get the record companies interested. I've always felt the writing was better on the more sophisticated numbers like "Turn That Heartbeat" and "Fire In The Hole". That's going to be the bone of tone [*sic – Ed.*] of the next album.

'For me, this band is the end of two years of hanging around. I had faith in it finally coming together, but to tell the truth I was just about ready to give up the waiting when they phoned and said come out to LA.'

4

Counting Down to Headline Status

Steven Rosen, *Los Angeles Free Press*,
August 1973

O n 2 September, Steely Dan perform their first concert as
headliners, that status which lifts the working-class band
from the ranks of the bourgeois and places it in the stead of the
nobility groups. After only two albums, the quintet has risen
from a third-on-the-bill opening band to a commercially structured rock'n'roll outfit responsible for several Top 10 records
during the past year.

Founded in the writing talents of Walter Becker and Donald
Fagen, the Dan have proved that rock music is capable of diving
much deeper than the basic twelve-bar format. Their second album
has just been released and, while it is a much stronger statement
than their debut record, it still seems to lack any real direction.
But according to Jeff Baxter, the 'song' itself is the pipeline.

'It's hard to understand what people mean by direction. There's
a lot of bands that play the same kind of music, if that's what you

mean. But since there's so many different ways and everybody in the band plays so many different styles of music, you might as well take a song and do a tango here, a rock tune there, a country song here and a ballad there. The focal point is Donald and Walter's material. What they write about, and their lyrics, are pretty much the focal point of the whole band. And then we just arrange around it. It's a guitar band.'

The process of writing a song is a simple one: a fragment of the song is presented (either a lyric or chorus); this segment is expanded on by the various members of the group, and if a strong idea doesn't materialise in ten minutes, the entire concept is thrown away. It is this spontaneity of sorts which is probably the most important asset the group has, an element which prevents them from working on anything forced or unnatural.

Last spring, part-time vocalist David Palmer was ousted because he didn't present a happy working musical marriage with what the band was trying to do. Like their songs, Steely felt Palmer was an unnatural element and consequently was rid of him. David joined the band when they were two-thirds finished with *Can't Buy A Thrill* (their first LP) and, while many people may have thought otherwise, it was Donald Fagen's voice adorning the early hits (including 'Reelin' In The Years' etc.). Their newest album, titled *Countdown To Ecstasy*, is a much more energetic piece than *Thrill* and showcases the band in their unique use of standard music styles and figures embellished with the Dan touch.

The album includes a back-up chorus of vocalists (with Palmer, who was still in the band at the time, singing on one song) added to enhance the usually rousing lyric line in each Dan song. For the most part, an ordinary Fagen/Becker composition would include a song lyric line, a vigorous chorus, a clever transitional bridge and a gang-war instrumental break. All standard pap for a rock song, but it is the creativity of Steely which allows them to take these basics and transform them into a spiritish-sounding tune such as 'Bodhisattva' on the new album.

The band also has just added a couple of female back-up vocalists to bring the vocal strength of the band up to the instrumental power of the band. Gloria Granola and Jenny Soule (names are approximate), aside from contributing substance to the vocal side, have added another dimension to the visual punch of the band. Their presence onstage relieves some of the pressure of the band in having to go through the expected moves of the outfit. The Steelies' vocals tend to fly somewhere in the highest range for male voices, so the girls' natural reach in those areas has helped the band to concentrate more on their instrumental duties.

But the group's creativity and experimentation doesn't stop in the concert hall. Every member of the band has logged countless hours in the studio (from Baxter's work with Ultimate Spinach to Becker's and Fagen's work with Jay & the Americans) and, where the first album was a piecemeal affair, *Countdown* shows a technical feel for the studio consummated only after years of recording experimentation. They are in the process now of synthesising their own style of studio work, and certainly the rewards will be present on their next album.

The Dan's two albums show a progressive sophistication in their approach to material and their ability to play together as a unit. The reward of their dedication will be mirrored on the first Sunday of September, when they will appear as the headlining band at the Santa Monica Civic Auditorium. Surely this is the ultimate goal of any band, to ply your music at a concert where the people have (for the most part) come to see and hear you?

'No, it really doesn't mean anything to me,' candidly admitted Walter Becker. 'It just means we go on a little later. Personally, I enjoy opening shows, because the audience is really fresh and you have a bunch of people out there who are in the tradition of being very pleasantly surprised.'

Does the elevation of status put any added pressure on you? 'No, it's added a coupla minutes to our show. See, we haven't done any yet, but I imagine we'll find out . . . [maybe we'll get] better dressing rooms and lots more beer.'

This new level of performing has sort of offhandedly opened the doors for more television work. Friday evening on 31 August, the band will be appearing on the *Midnight Special* taping, as well as a previous appearance on the *In Concert* programme. Plans are also under way for the group to start work on some TV commercials, but as yet no plans have been confirmed.

With more prominent coverage, a larger audience and better paying engagements, Steely Dan could find itself falling into the same trap that so many other outfits have walked into: the 'Success Syndrome'. A group will work its proverbial balls off trying to break into the shifting record market. Once they have landed a contract, they continue to work and turn out creative product for maybe a couple of albums and, once they find themselves with records in the Top 10 and more bullets than the Lone Ranger, their musical drive stops. Stagnation sets in and a once top-rank ensemble contents itself with releasing albums that even Tolkien's Gollum wouldn't listen to.

But in the case of Steely Dan, the situation is reversed. Their first album was a hotsy and, if anything, they had to steer away from music which may have borderlined on the teeny. 'We may have been typecast from our first album,' Becker says, 'but I don't think I know or anybody else knew what kind of group that was. The diversity of material on the first album is rather great and it was intentionally put together that way. You know, it's funny how you put something together like an album and people see some coherent strain running through it that was never intended or conceived or that we don't see that way. I mean, I've noticed quite a few people really don't know what kind of music to call it. I don't know, but certainly it's not too well-defined in my mind.'

Oddly enough, the second album does project the band's music more vividly in terms of material and production (they haven't fallen into the 'Syndrome' trap . . . yet), but *Countdown* doesn't do anything to define where the band is headed.

'I'm not particularly anxious to narrow it down,' conceded Becker. 'I think the diversity makes it much more interesting for us and hopefully for the people who buy the albums. There's a lot of things you can grab on to, but that doesn't mean the band has to be so predictable and familiar that you can instantly associate one cut with the next. I don't think the diversity harms that at all.'

'I'd rather have people looking forward to a song they don't know anything about,' voiced guitarist Baxter, 'than looking forward to a song they know is gonna sound the same as the last song. I think that's a big mistake.'

'Planned diversity' is the term Walter used to describe the band's music. While material has been written for the next album, there is still no clear-cut definition of what their music is like. In the works is a Guitar Club (Institute for the Advancement of the Electric Guitar), which presently includes Jeff Baxter and Denny Dias of Dan, Elliott Randall and Rick Derringer and will shortly include a couple other 'name guitarists'. 'It's not a guitar band the way Rolling Stones is,' says Becker. 'The music is written on piano and it's more sophisticated chord changes than guitar players usually come up with.'

'Most of the music is made by electric guitars,' explained Baxter. 'The padding, the solos; but it's not like "Stick Shift" by the Duals.'

The Guitar Club has already set in the works an album which will be composed of seven or eight players in the organisation, with the rhythm section to be supplied by the Dan. Whatever is in store for Steely Dan, rest assured it will be handled with the finesse of a tightly and creatively structure. 'What seems to be happening is that every album we've done hasn't been different [within itself] as one from the other. So we try to put together a live show that matches the album. We'll probably be changing our live show, adding personnel, except for the five basic members of the band.'

5

Review of *Countdown to Ecstasy*

Mick Gold, *Let It Rock*,
December 1973

Steely Dan is a vehicle for the songwriting talents of Donald Fagen and Walter Becker, who entered the music world via a two-year gig with Jay & the Americans. They say they don't regret that period, but since they've lifted their name from *Naked Lunch* they've clearly been through a few changes. Not that this album displays any of *Lunch's* aggressive weirdness.

Fagen and Becker have a gift for weaving songs out of American place names, fragments of conversations and fag ends of dreams. They describe their songwriting as junk sculpture and I won't argue. Trouble is that the rhythm section is so well-oiled, and the lyrics are so fragmentary, that Side One just glides over me. The songs don't have the hooks or barbed ends necessary to grab the casual ear.

Side Two is much more interesting. It kicks off with the Dan's last single, 'Show Biz Kids', featuring the most insidious chorus

I've heard since 'Drift Away'. They paint a picture of kids who've stepped out of school into stardom, one that's both cruel and sympathetic, and all done to a highly infectious rhythm. Should have been a hit. And the other songs are almost as good. 'My Old School' turns memories of adolescent hassles into a bittersweet requiem for dead relationships, with unexpected bits of poetry ('She said, "Oh no/Guadalajara won't do"') surfacing and sinking again. 'Pearl of the Quarter' is a rather schlocky tribute to a hooker with a heart of gold who prowls around New Orleans singing '*Voulez-vous*'. I have a suspicion the tune is cribbed from The Band's 'In A Station', and I pass on to the final number, 'King of The World', which is a real novelty item: a stirring ballad for survivors of an atomic holocaust: 'No marigolds in the promised land/There's a hole in the ground where they used to grow'. The song doesn't quite lift off but the lyrics are amusing in an eerie way.

I don't feel like recommending an album with eight songs on it, four of which managed to pass through my head without producing any noticeable effect. But 'Show Biz Kids' really is a great song and there's a lot of low-key intelligence at work on this record. Look for the single or pick up the album cheap.

6

Walking Slow, Drinking Alone and Moving Swiftly Through the Night . . .

Wayne Robins, *New Musical Express,*
23 February 1974

NOTE: Wayne's piece, originally published in Creem, *has been reworked in order to edit out substantial quotes from Steely Dan lyrics.*

I'm sitting drinking Campari in the Angry Squire on Seventh Avenue on a dull, sultry Sunday night in Greenwich Village, watching the sippers and swallowers drift through a brew or two, then buzz out somewhere else.

A swarthy New York street cowboy saunters in, locking his Honda bike to the hitching post outside. He orders a Whitbread Ale (on tap), takes a poke, then moves to the juke. A song about a guy with 'murder in his eyes': it's 'Only a Fool Would Say That', the B-side of the Steely Dan hit 'Reelin' in the Years'.

I nodded to the guy in the cowboy hat, but he didn't see me. That was cool. But when another obscure Steely Dan B-side, 'Fire In The Hole' (the flip of 'Dirty Work'), came on under his quarter, I decided to walk over and ask him what his motives were.

But before 'Reelin' In The Years' went through its remarkable Elliott Randall guitar solo, the urban cowboy was out of the door. To me it kind of indicates where the Steely Dan cult is at: found often in unlikely places, following no discernible pattern except walking slow, drinking alone and moving swiftly through the night. It's strange that a band with such an unfashionably enigmatic lyric sense, rich in a bittersweet vision of people and places both familiar and remote, would turn out to be a Top 40 hit act rather than a 'critic's band'. Especially considering they took their name from a dildo in William Burroughs' *Naked Lunch*.

'We always felt we would be a hit with the critics, if not with the public,' muses Walter Becker, who with Donald Fagen makes up the songwriting nucleus of the Dan. 'But rock'n'roll reviewers adapt to the times and, if the times happen to be unsophisticated, that's what happens.'

Whether or not you agree with Becker, it's true that the Dan are indeed sophisticated for these times. Musically, they combine deceptively simple Latin-Caribbean rock'n'roll riffs with melodies that *can* buy a thrill. But Steely Dan go much deeper than that, especially if you're one of the six hundred or so people on the planet who each year attended funky and fragmented Bard College in Annandale-on-Hudson, New York, in the late '60s, where Fagen, Becker, and myself got certain parts of their schoolin'.

I recognised Fagen and Becker as fellow Bardians when I saw Steely Dan perform in 1972 as the guest of Robert Christgau. I had been introduced to the Dean of American Rock Critics at a lavish CBS Records party for West, Bruce & Laing at Rockefeller Center's Rainbow Room. Christgau was at the time the rock critic for the massive Long Island, NY, newspaper *Newsday*, which had been my hometown paper growing up. He invited me to come along to Westbury Music Fair the following week, where Steely Dan, still the original aggregation with David Palmer as the putative lead singer, was the opening act. For Cheech & Chong.

I had seen Becker and Fagen around campus, most likely in the coffee shop, but never spoke to them beyond a brotherly 'What's up?'

The kids who went to Bard were generally of the same breed that went to any of the schools with which it's been associated; hotbeds of social permissiveness and intellectual stimulation like Goddard, Antioch, Franconia and Reed.

Fagen and Becker began playing together at Bard. 'Whenever there was a social function that demanded a cheap rhythm section, we were there,' says Becker, who looks the bespectacled silent type – with or without his bass – but is really verbal and articulate. 'Actually, there were two branches – the New York branch, and the Boston branch.'

Out of the Boston branch came Jeff 'Skunk' Baxter, erstwhile guitar and steel player, who was once a member of Bosstown sound pacesetters Ultimate Spinach.

'I joined the band [Spinach] after their first guitar player got too psychedelic,' says Skunk.

'You mean 13th Floor Elevators psychedelic or dangerous psychedelic?'

'No, this was different. This was real drugs. Lots of drugs.'

Skunk doesn't want to talk anymore about Ultimate Spinach. He's far too modest about their place in the rock pantheon.

During the interview, which took place at a rehearsal studio on Yucca Street in Hollywood, a few blocks off Sunset and Vine, we kept coming back to Bard. References to the school run through much of Steely Dan's two albums. 'Reelin' In The Years' is probably the best song ever written about the pseudo-poetic, preppie/hippie self-consciousness that dominated Bard and other joints of its kind in the late '60s.

On the second album, *Countdown To Ecstasy*, there's even a tune called 'My Old School'. It is possible that in part it chronicles one of the annual Bard busts, in which the Dutchess County Police, under Sheriff Quinlan and an assistant DA named G. Gordon Liddy, would deputise every townie bowling at the 9-G Lanes and carry off ten to twenty per cent of the student body.

There were plenty of fitting human subjects for songs at Bard, people who left themselves permanently imprinted in the Bard collective unconscious. Dudes like Marcus Aurelius Greenberg, an R&B oldies fanatic, greaser and part-time (most of the time) junkie, who was once roused out of a serious smack'n'Seconal OD at 3.30 a.m. to write a twenty-page paper on Nabokov that was due the next morning. (He got an A minus.)

Of course, Steely Dan aren't the first ones to write specifically about Bard in their music. When we were there, old Bardians swore that the busted pump down the road near Adolph's bar (legendary Bard hangout) didn't work ''cause the vandals took the handles', and that Dylan wrote that song ('Subterranean Homesick Blues') on the walls of the graffiti-famed Potter dorm shit-stalls. I take this to be myth.

After Bard, Steelies Fagen and Becker made their way back to New York. They did an album on Spark Records under the name *The Original Soundtrack*. The album itself *was* a soundtrack, for the famed Zalman King movie *You've Got to Walk It Like You Talk It (or You'll Lose That Beat)*. It featured a really killer Fagen and Becker song called 'Dog Eat Dog', one of those early attempts at pop tunes that was just too odd for Top 40 radio.

After the soundtrack (the movie lasted in release about fifteen minutes), Fagen, Becker and Denny Dias formed a rehearsal band that played in Denny's basement in Hicksville, Long Island. The drummer happened to be Jay & the Americans' road drummer, and all of them soon found themselves on the road with . . . Jay & the Americans.

'Mostly it was playing sleazy little night clubs in Queens and the Bronx,' recalls Walter Becker. 'It was a very compact operation . . . it also paid the rent.'

After a year or so, the circuit began to get tedious. Fagen and Becker – and Denny and Skunk – were sort of hanging around when an old friend, Gary Katz, became a staff producer at ABC-Dunhill in Los Angeles. Katz got Fagen and Becker jobs as staff writers at Dunhill, and that's where the modern Steely Dan saga takes off.

'They gave us somebody else's office with a terrible piano in it,' said Walter, 'and we started banging out the hits. It didn't take us too long to find out that it wasn't going to work, because the "hits" we were coming up with were really too weird or too cheesy for anyone to record.'

'A staff writer is supposed to be a researcher of radio as well as a creative person,' adds Donald. 'It's essentially imitating whatever you hear on the radio and putting it out eight or ten months later.'

The first Steely Dan album, *Can't Buy A Thrill*, was recorded in June 1972, after six fruitless months on the song squad. Both the

Dan's hit singles ('Do It Again' and 'Reelin' In The Years') are here, as well as a few songs that could've been hits if the band were greedy. LA songs like 'Midnite Cruiser' and 'Turn That Heartbeat Over Again'. New York nostalgia moves like 'Brooklyn (Owes the Charmer Under Me)' and the brilliantly pop-ish 'Dirty Work', which Birtha are trying to break out with.

A few personal changes have ensued. Vocalist David Palmer, who sang on neither of the band's hits, is gone. To add spice to the vocals and the visual situation (the band don't exactly look like they just jumped out of *Modern Romance* magazine), two foxy lady vocalists have been added. Their names are either Porky and Bucky, or Chip and Dale, or Gloria Granola and Jenny Soule.

The second album, *Countdown to Ecstasy*, was my most played album throughout the past summer, and remains a steady favourite. The sound is deep and well-strung with patterns constantly shifting under the melodies and rhythm.

The scenarios are elliptical. There are women in cages in 'Razor Boy', which always reminds me of David Bowie's haircut. In 'The Boston Rag' there's a character named 'Lonnie the king-pin'. Another Bard reference, this one widely shared: Lonnie was the sandwich man who would visit the dorms late at night, just as the munchies were making us ravenous, selling delicious ham and cheese sandwiches, potato chips and cola beverages that quenched our weed-parched throats.

'Show Biz Kids' is the band at their weirdest, and possibly most accessible. It's a strange follow-up to two gold singles, considering it's a hypnotic, enigmatic musical piece based around the world's oldest Las Vegas joke. The girls sing 'Go to lost wages, lost wages', a 1950s American lounge comic's reliable pun for Las Vegas. There's a line about fans wearing Steely Dan T-shirts, which I took as an inside joke, because Steely Dan didn't have T-shirts yet, as far as I knew. There may be yet another Bard reference, to a character named 'El Supremo', perhaps a bandito stoner in a dormitory mural, though I'd never seen it.

A more likely single might turn out to be 'Pearl Of The Quarter', with its lazy Louisiana steel guitar, soft as a 'Cajun smile' and cynical as 'she loves the million-dollar words I say'. Fine drumming, as always, from Jim Hodder, who appears in this article for the first time.

The real Steely Dan heartbeat is 'King of the World'. It moves from nostalgia for childhood, with imagery ranging from ham radio to Saturday afternoon westerns. Says Walter Becker: 'Typical devastation. Like, what do you do at the end of the world? The sense of doom is overwhelming. We wrote it after watching Ray Milland in *Panic in Year Zero*!'

Cha-cha-*cha*!

Donald Fagen at the piano and Walter Becker on bass during a session for *Katy Lied*.

Michael Ochs Archives/Stringer/Getty Images

TWO: Dark Companions

'We're hoping that we're going to make some sort of miracle sweep and just sort of worm our way into the hearts of America'

Donald Fagen, 1975

1

Review of *Pretzel Logic*

Ian MacDonald, *New Musical Express,*
9 March 1974

A fine record. And that sentence goes first because the fact that a band as perfectly poised as Steely Dan can reach their third album without apparently causing more than a ripple on the surface of the British rock public's awareness is a disturbing phenomenon that demands flags flown against its continued persistence.

After all, with The Band locked up in label-swapping, Dylan-hopping and nostalgia-dropping, where else can a deafened connoisseur get his shots of lyric succinctness matched with thoroughly coherent musicality? The Dan's brand of ruthless cool is so vital to rock right now that we can't afford to leave things like *Pretzel Logic* solely in the hands of discerning cliques in the import shops.

So don't.

And now, extending the backward progress of this admittedly slightly crazed review, we go from the conclusion to the premise.

Pretzel Logic is a pretty surprising piece of work, considering the development discernible from *Can't Buy A Thrill* to *Countdown To Ecstasy*.

Thrill was recorded soon after the group formed and sticks closely to Becker and Fagen's song-arrangement concept, keeping guitarists Dias and Baxter on a fairly tight rein. On *Ecstasy* the numbers are chordally simpler, more open and less orientated to the instrumental 'fill' techniques and timbre effects of the initial outing. Solos are longer and lyrics generally less opaque – even subservient to the maintenance of the groove the band obviously hit through live experience.

Pretzel Logic unexpectedly about-faces the trend towards spaciousness and single-line thinking. On the new album, Becker and Fagen have pulled in the reins once more, produced ten of their most commercial songs yet and constrained their twin-guitar virtuosi to become part of the overall picture again, on several numbers beefing up the sound with additional horns and strings.

As if it was a natural consequence, the words have returned to the hermetic, collegiate inscrutability of the majority of *Can't Buy A Thrill*, and I haven't yet listened to them enough to penetrate what the LP's about lyrically.

On the other hand, I may not get around to that for some time, since the tunes and settings are so maturely attractive and the performances so impressive that they satisfy on their own.

Try, for example, the opening cut 'Rikki Don't Lose That Number', a sepia-tone bossa-nova by 'Razor Boy' out of Wayne Shorter's 'Tom Thumb'. Poignant Fagen vocals haunt the verse before the full harmony team swings in on an irresistible chorus. A hit single, if this was a half-reasonable world – as would be 'Barrytown', a Dylanesque filtering of McCartney's 'Tell Me What You See' that skilfully skirts the schmaltz of such as

'Midnite Cruiser' and the David Palmer tracks on *Thrill* without losing any sweetness.

Then there's the tough, stuck-in precision-funk of 'Night By Night' and 'Monkey In Your Soul'; the reflective grace of 'Any Major Dude Will Tell You' and 'Through With Buzz' and the skeletal nakedness of 'Charlie Freak' and the title-song (which is nearly a straightforward blues).

Rounded off with distant jazz echoes on 'Parker's Band' and Duke Ellington's 'East St Louis Toodle-Oo', *Pretzel Logic* exhibits far more range, depth and flexibility than its forebears and hopefully points to a fourth album that will come within striking distance of standards set by *The Band* and *Big Pink* – without infringing in any way on the sound or cultural roots of Robertson's combo.

This is, after all, slick, Big City music, not grainy rural wood-shedding and, although the two groups have a certain fastidious understatement in common, their ultimate concerns could hardly be more different.

Providing they can hold it together (which depends largely upon how Dias and Baxter take to being manoeuvred by the two songwriters), Steely Dan must surely make their breakthrough to the wider audience soon and, sometime in the future, cut one of rock's definitive albums.

Pretzel Logic is a big step in that direction and you'd be well-advised to pick up on it now.

2

Band Breakdown

Chris Welch, *Melody Maker*, 1 June 1974

Steely Dan, in their short time together, have been hailed as one of the best bands to emerge from America in a long time. They have set the US rock scene back on a road to musical creativity and helped free it from the dominance of British bands established over the past six years. And they have done all this within the framework of pop songs – no more, no less.

The main members of the band are Walter Becker and Donald Fagen, who write all their material and started out their career as staff writers for a record company. Steely Dan is really their orchestra, designed to present the songs on stage and record in the best way possible. As a result they have been through a few personnel changes, but the basic five are still together as they were on the first album *Can't Buy A Thrill*.

They have built something of a cult following in Britain since the beginning of last year, with DJs playing great compositions like 'Do It Again', 'Reelin' In The Years' and, more recently, 'Rikki Don't Lose That Number'. The songs have a depth and a 'finished' quality that gives Dan the edge over other bands.

The band also sport some fine instrumentalists, Donald Fagen being an accomplished pianist with a sophisticated jazz and classically trained background, whose introductions to some of the numbers provide one of the high spots of their show. And there is Jeff 'Skunk' Baxter, who has been received on the band's recent tour of England as a new guitar hero. Jeff also plays pedal steel guitar and conga drums, while Donald's co-writer, Walter Becker, is usually found at the back of the band, hidden away playing bass guitar.

Denny Dias plays a lighter guitar style to Baxter's funkier approach, while Jim Hodder is the original drummer, joined on stage by Jeff Porcaro. Other additions to the stage act have been Royce Jones, a soulful balladeer with an appealing style who helps out on percussion, and Mike McDonald on Fender Rhodes piano.

One of the reasons for the various additions – two drummers, two guitarists – has been the quest for powerful stage sound to match the albums, which have incorporated session musicians from time to time. For example, on the first album, Elliot Randall, the blues guitarist, was added and played lead on 'Reelin' In The Years', and there were seasoned jazzmen like Victor Feldman, Jerome Richardson and Snooky Young involved. Also, Donald was not happy at being the main lead singer, although he has an outstanding voice.

Steely Dan (the name comes from some strange New York phallic device) are a fairly hard-bitten bunch, capable of being sardonic and demanding off-stage. They give the impression of being used to the pressures of hustling in the big city for a long time before success came their way, and there is less of the laissez-faire to their personalities than one might expect to find in the average English band. But once they have relaxed, they are amenable and talkative.

The future will probably see more changes in the line-up and they are cagey about a next album. But whatever they do next they have, in a brief career, produced some satisfying and memorable music. You can't ask for more.

Donald Fagen

Donald is a dark-haired, serious young man for whom Steely Dan is his orchestra – and life. But he has a sense of sardonic humour that is reflected in his oft-quoted remark that 'our songwriting process is not unlike the creation of junk sculpture.'

Like his cohort, Walter Becker – they went to college together – he is quick-witted, sharply spoken and keen to talk in pungent and forthright fashion.

At the fashionable Blake's Hotel in London, where the hippest musicians tend to congregate, Donald was deep in conversation with Jeff Baxter about the mysteries of the Third Reich, and both had been fascinated by their visit to Radio Luxembourg's studios, which were Gestapo headquarters during the last war.

Black magic aspects of the Nazi creed were also under discussion, but it seemed healthier by far to talk on the subject of Dan, Steely, and their many compositions. What by the way, had led them to record Duke Ellington's 'East St Louis Toodle-Oo' on the *Pretzel Logic* album?

'There are about four recorded versions of "East St Louis Toodle-Oo",' said Donald, crouching in a settee over a cup of tea. 'We took the best part of each and made a composite version. We changed horn parts to a piano solo, but we didn't change it very much. It was Duke's birthday recently and I sent him a copy of the record, and I would have been very flattered if he had heard it. But I don't know if he did.

'Walter and I are both jazz fans, and as a composition this one stood up so well, we wanted to hear it with all the expertise of modern hi-fi. Most of the great jazz compositions have been neglected. There is no jazz in America now. There is a considerable amount of electric experimenting, but that doesn't interest me and their improvisation is strictly modal – and boring. John Coltrane was a fantastic player, but he was responsible for leading people into making a terrible mistake. I like more changes in music and, anyway, I preferred John before his modal period, when he was with the Miles Davis Quintet.

'So there is no jazz of note in the States now. Most of the stuff played is nostalgic '50s arrangements with good soloists. And of course Miles Davis has gone over the edge. I like to think we are a rock'n'roll band – with class. My bass player and I write all the material, but the solos and arrangements come from the group. Walter and I think it out in advance and then we go into the studios and work on the tunes from there. I think of them as compositions rather than songs. They are structured, but there is room for improvisation.

'We're a strange band, y'know. The music is all *wrong*. We all sat around in our living room and came up with this way of playing. It's all very weird. Then there is the "imminent break-up". Quote, "We're about to break up", unquote. That's all ridiculous bull. We're more or less fairly stable now as the five humanoids that started this thing.'

Walter Becker

Walter, the mystery bass player who keeps well-hidden at the back of the stage, usually perched in the shadow of Jeff Porcaro's drums, is a cheerful jester with a quick line in verbal badinage. But despite his public reticence, he is a vital founder member of the Dan, who co-writes those amazing songs with Donald Fagen, and for whom quality rather than commercialism is the most important factor.

'Our sound system is designed for small halls like the Palace Theatre at Manchester, and we'd rather work in those situations than sacrifice the sound quality in a bigger venue. Dinky Dawson designed our sound system and he's brilliant. He's worked with us from our first gigs when we used to support the Kinks and the James Gang. That was terrible – bands used to play tricks on us in those days. Like not letting us onstage for a soundcheck, or turning the lights off. When Dinky first joined us to do the sound, I couldn't understand a word he said, but I knew he was an intelligent, professional guy.

'In our early days, we had some terrible disasters. I remember a press party we were supposed to play, when the equipment wasn't set up properly and nobody could hear a note, and the lead singer picked up a can of beer, missed his mouth and poured it all over himself. That was our press reception. A heavy bummer! The singer was David Palmer. That was when Donald didn't want to be lead singer – no way. Now Dave is a co-writer with Carole King, which shows where we were at. I didn't even know he could write.

'Sure, there have been some personnel changes. First there was the six and then there was the five and now we have three extra guys, including Royce Jones on percussion and vocals. We had two girl singers on our last tour, one of whom was known as Porky and is here with David Cassidy now.

'Ostensibly we're an eight-piece now, but that doesn't mean we won't change it. But all the main five have worked on all the LPs. Incidentally, we record every show we play live on tape – I'm not kidding. If we wanted to, we could put out a live LP, but there is only one song we play on the road that hasn't been recorded before, and that's "This Mobile Home", which is a song about a trailer. You'll have to hear the lyrics. We tried to record it for *Countdown To Ecstasy* and *Pretzel Logic* and, if it had been like it is now, we might have succeeded. We're not that interested in live recordings, though, because there is a gross overkill in that department.'

How did Donald and Walter get together?

'We've always written songs together, from when we started at college. But people wanted Mickey Mouse stuff, and the things we were writing were so *outré*. They were all four-minute songs – miniaturisation, as Donald would put it – but someone compared them to German art music. When we do an LP we like to get fourteen/fifteen songs on it, without sacrificing the recording quality. We just don't have room for any more ambitious writing, until we do LP sets and, anyway, it doesn't do to get too heavy.

'The Who invented the concept LP with *Happy Jack*, right? I think that was very successful, along with *The Who Sells Out*.'

Why does Walter keep himself hidden at the back onstage?

'You've noticed that? The reasons are it takes the heat off me and I don't have to make my presence felt. As long as I can hear Jeff Porcaro's snare drum and hi-hat, I'm happy. I moved up there about ten gigs ago. I just want to hear the drums and it's all cosy up there. I have a seat, and it keeps me comfortable and happy!'

Jeff 'Skunk' Baxter

'Skunk' is in danger of becoming one of the biggest guitar heroes since the days of Jeff Beck, Eric Clapton and Peter Green. Certainly his English fans have taken him to heart: at all Dan's concerts there have been yells for Jeff and cries of 'Skunk!'

In fact, Jeff would rather drop the 'Skunk' bit. It came one night when he called on an old friend whilst under the influence of alcohol. As the friend took rather a long time to answer the bell, he decided to relieve himself against the door, just as the door opened, thus drawing forth the cry 'You skunk!'

Jeff has a zestful, enthusiastic guitar style that occasionally goes over the top of Steely Dan's otherwise disciplined standards but injects into the band a sense of fun and considerable excitement. Less tutored than the rest of the musicians, nevertheless he has had more actual live experience.

He has worked in a great variety of bands and is noted for his pedal-steel guitar playing, which has earned him a lot of country music work.

He first came to fame with the short-lived but highly respected Ultimate Spinach and has been doing a lot of touring with Linda Ronstadt. During his visit to Britain he has been thoroughly enjoying himself and is definitely responsible for the wilder off-stage scenes that accompany the band.

'It suits me fine that Don and Walter do all the writing,' says Jeff, through his moustache and spectacles. 'I thought it wouldn't until I heard their songs. I'm not a writer, I'm a technician. Donald tells me what he needs for a solo and I play it for him. Steely Dan for me is one of the finest bands I have played with, as far as both lyrical and musical content goes.

'Sometimes in the States the kids just shout for "Boogie!" So we just wait until they shut up and we can start to play. Boy, is that funny! I love that. We want the kids to have a good time, of course, and we're not into that Frank Zappa scene, the way Frank adopts a kind of missionary attitude towards the "kiddies". But we do like to think the people who come to our concerts are there to listen to the music and not just kids who come to hear the hits.

'It's true that we play more to ourselves than the audience sometimes, but we have a lot of fun. After the show, we scream at each other if we have made any mistakes. But I've never been in a band that has played so many different kinds of music before. I used to have to be in five bands at once to get this kind of experience.'

Denny Dias

Denny cuts an impressive stance on stage, with his massive, flowing black beard and broad shoulders dwarfing the guitar strapped around his waist. Denny, in common with most of the band, is a jazz enthusiast who prefers working in rock music for the excitement and opportunities it offers. He does not feel he is compromising his music either, and looks forward to a future when he will be able to present a wholly unique style.

Working in contrast to Jeff Baxter, nevertheless, Denny manages to strike up a firm musical partnership as a member of the 'guitar section'. He has thoroughly enjoyed his first trip to Britain and says, 'I love your country. I feel I have come to a civilised land. Just travelling around in a taxi, I have met so many great people. I'm not into museums or sightseeing – it's the people who interest me most.'

What had Denny been involved in before his work with Steely Dan? 'On a professional level, not much. I was going to school in

New York and playing guitar at the same time in small clubs. I felt guilty about neglecting my school studies and I was just really getting interested in my subjects when I had to make the decision. So I quit school in 1969 to be a full-time musician. I was studying biomedical computer science and I completed my first semester. But I couldn't bring myself to quit playing guitar.

'I had a rock band but it was difficult to get work, because I didn't want to play Top 40 stuff. We didn't have too much original material either. Our bass player decided to go back to school, so I put an ad in the *Village Voice* for a bass player and pianist. That's how I met Donald and Walter. When I heard their writing, well, I just stopped trying to write songs. We kicked out the other guys in the band, and you know, listening to Walter and Donald's songs was like hearing the Beatles with jazz chords. I was flabbergasted! If I hadn't met them, I'd still be back at school.

'When they went to California to work for ABC-Dunhill, I hung around and eventually got a call to join them in the new band – Steely Dan. Before the call, I was gradually losing faith and almost went back to school.'

Denny has a strongly jazz-influenced style and he says his tutor had been one of the finest jazz guitarists. 'Billy Bauer – he worked with Lennie Tristano when he was only sixteen years old. He's getting old now, but he can still play and he works mainly as a tutor. I play as if I were a jazz musician, except I'm working in a rock context with its feel and excitement. I never play licks off other rock guitarists, and I avoid bending strings or the use of vibrato.'

How did Denny find working with Jeff Baxter in a two-guitar line-up?

'There are no problems – except I'd like to play more. Jeff can play all the wide vibrato sounds and bend the strings, and he's really good. We only met up through the band, and we're on opposite ends of the stick, we're so different. I play the jazz, while Jeff is much more experienced as a rock player. It's fun to do the unison things as well – it's a challenge – and we have pretty nice parts.'

Jim Hodder

Jim's drumming has been aptly described as metronomic, and he is indeed a perfect foil to the more ambitious approach of his partner in the percussion section, Jeff Porcaro.

Jim is an original member, one of 'the five', and doesn't seem to mind too much the additional drummer. In fact, he says he finds it stimulating and their drum duet is one of the highlights of the group's act.

'I like having the two of us drumming. It doesn't always work in groups and you have to forget about your ego. With us, it sounds like one guy playing at times, but it makes for a better combination of sounds. From the time the band was put together, Donald wanted two drummers. I was against it at first, but what the hell, we had two guitarists and two keyboard players, so why not two drummers. And one of my favourite bands had two drummers – Frank Zappa and the Mothers. It can work like a locomotive, especially on tunes like "Do It Again". It gives us both time to relax in different parts and we can concentrate more on the next fill. And of course you can pick your nose or drop a stick and nobody notices! What we have to watch out for is Donald when he conducts those long endings. It's great material to play in this band, and we only clash occasionally, not so that anybody in the audience would notice.'

'That first LP we did was only rehearsed for a couple of weeks and I didn't even know the other guys. So it turned out remarkably well. Before Steely Dan I did a lot of session work around the Boston area and got screwed by managers – the usual thing.

'It seems everybody has to have a glitter image and I can't stand that. Nobody in the group can stand it! But the fact is, we have been accepted without glamour and fancy clothes. The whole glitter bit is stupid – it sucks. It's true we had two hit singles and on our second LP we didn't have any hits, so we had to be a little bit more commercial on the third one. Artistically, *Countdown* was our best LP, but for the sake of the survival of the group, we had to go more commercial on *Pretzel Logic*. But I think Donald and Walter are the two best songwriters since Paul McCartney and Paul Simon. You gotta have material. There are so many good players with no material. Us and the Doobie Brothers and the Eagles all started off around the same time, and I think good American bands are coming back.'

3

Review of *Katy Lied*

Jonh Ingham, *Let It Rock*,
June 1975

When I first received this album, it engendered dispassionate dislike, but the more I play it the more I become merely ambivalent.

Certainly there are some knockout songs, but the band's internal frictions have not benefitted the writing and recording of this platter and in the main the results are highly disappointing. In fact, it works best as muzak – when actually listening, I soon find myself reaching for a magazine or contemplating a smoke to alleviate the empty spaces.

Make that ambivalence admiration. There are sections, within some of the worst songs, that are gems, particularly the rhythm/percussion/piano body riding through the wimpy cocktail jazz-rock 'Your Gold Teeth II', or the bossa nova swirl of electric piano, marimbas, congas, incredibly subtle rhythm section and female 'oohs' of 'Everyone's Gone to the Movies', a song that is superficially dreadful, but for all its vacuous lyrics somehow works. But then the Dan have always paid close attention to producing a very clean, very ambient sound, seeming to take that West Coast passion for clinical, perfect productions and injecting life into what so often sounds merely sterile.

Apart from a lack of musical meat, there is a dearth of lyric content. Steely Dan's lyrics have never been gems of wisdom, especially when they get buried in that inside-joke university sphere Fagen and Becker love to draw from; but at their best, as in 'My Old School', the result is a refreshing shock, unlike anything before or since. Sadly, that state isn't achieved here. The lyrics are generally ordinary and, worse, they stand out in the mix, always intruding. It may be a cool rock aesthetic to have great music with lousy lyrics (though not vice versa), but only when they don't scream for attention. This is one inner sleeve that was better off blank.

In fact, there is only one song that is an unqualified success: 'Black Friday'. Riding in on a rocking rhythm driven by electric piano, a stinging guitar soon starts weaving lines around it while the vocals push along in a fine roar, harmonies adding further energy. At all times that guitar makes its presence felt – I'd love to know whether it's one of them or someone like Elliot Randall or Rick Derringer. (Very strange, the idea of using studio musicians in what sounds like a recreation of Monkees recording sessions.) Significantly, this is the track Capital Radio likes to push.

All in all, not the hot poop we've come to expect from Steely Dan.

4

Yes, it's Steely Dan Versus the Fifth Ice Age

Richard Cromelin, *New Musical Express*,
26 April 1975

Encino is a grisly, prefabricated hard-wood-and-metal sprawl, basking in the Beach Boys sun of the suburban San Fernando Valley. A seething mob of condominiums, gas stations, expansive shopping centres, tawdry lunch stands and slick sandwich shops. Glistening, seductive automobile showrooms. Tracts of houses – built before the apartment boom – lined up like a smart battalion. It's an arrogant, pathetic parody of itself.

The chaotic topography is dotted here and there off the main boulevard with broad green fields, the weary survivors of the farms and ranches that prospered here before the people came. In the lush hills to the south and west, there seems to be a scent of freedom, but down on the flats it's totally desolate and dispiriting.

This, to the body, soul, heart and mind of Steely Dan, *is* California, and they hate it.

'Gay '50s culture,' Walter Becker calls it. 'This neighbourhood – have you had a chance to peruse any of it? The Encino Spa, Vic Tanny's. Big shiny cars, condominiums.'

'It's about ten or fifteen years behind,' offers Donald Fagen.

'Well,' Becker suggests, 'they just got to the point where they liked it and they stayed there.'

'It doesn't change. The weather doesn't change.' Nor does Fagen's flat, arid monotone.

'Jacuzzi baths, I guess, are a big innovation . . . saunas.'

'They feel compelled to keep all the black people in one part of the town so you don't have to look at them.'

'Yoga lessons out in the rotunda.'

'We're going to have to relocate,' Fagen concludes.

'I hear there's a great studio in Tanganyika.'

'We follow the studios,' explains Fagen, 'like the guys in *The Endless Summer.*'

'Searching for the perfect noise reduction system.'

'The perfect noise-reduction system is our goal. I don't know, there's not much to say about California.'

———

Nonetheless, here they are, right in the midst of it, on this particular afternoon at the (you guessed it) condominium apartment of their producer, Gary Katz. (They only rent, Mrs. Katz insists, and are looking for something near the beach.)

Walter Becker has the round clean face of a malevolently impish 13-year-old smart-ass. He's sharp, quick and flippant to the point of brusqueness. He keeps looking at his watch.

Donald Fagen's chiselled face looks as if it has permanently clamped itself in that grim expression in order to support the weight of his eyebrows. He sits crouching like a gargoyle and glares straight ahead, as if he's about to pounce on something.

When he talks, he seems to swallow the words before they get out of his mouth, a perfect stylistic complement to his exceedingly droll pronouncements.

Becker and Fagen, rock's odd couple, the pair of disrespectful misfits who stuck by their unconventional guns until it paid off big.

They moved to California three years ago to become staff songwriters at ABC-Dunhill.

They came at the behest of Katz, who had preceded them from New York to be a producer. ('At that time,' Becker points out, 'ABC was in the market for a producer with a Fu Manchu moustache to produce underground records.')

As dismal as they make their life here sound, the kitschatropolis culture has seeped into and enriched Steely Dan's music (in songs like 'Show Biz Kids' and the unrecorded 'Megashine City'), emerging as one pole of the east–west odyssey which is at the core of the Steely Dan mythos.

Says Fagen: 'Our heart is still on Second Avenue, and that's what we like to write about. Our lyrics are basically experience combined with a little fantasy.'

'I think there's a lot of New York urban-area type imagery and settings and so on,' says Becker. 'Even the language in our songs is an imitation thereof.'

Fagen further elucidates the charm of New York: 'You can watch the weather, and there's a lot of people on the street doing funny things. You can walk.'

'Or run,' Becker advises.

'Or run, depending on who's chasing you, and it's just more exciting and dangerous.'

Becker, apparently forgetting 'My Old School' and 'Barrytown' for the moment, maintains that Steely Dan's music reflects little if any of their college days. But the mention of the beloved alma mater – Bard College in upstate New York – inspires Fagen to recall his first fateful encounter with his colleague.

'I was walking past this small building,' he says in his best *raconteur* manner, 'that they used for entertainment of the student body, who were very idle and bored most of the term. And I heard what I assumed was Howlin' Wolf playing in this particular building. I walked in, and there was Walter with this red Epiphone guitar.'

'Donald,' says Walter, 'was the dean of the pickup-band syndrome at Bard . . . At the beginning of every term someone would reopen the club and they'd need a band for two nights. There were about eight musicians on the whole campus, and most of those were poor . . .'

'Well,' Fagen clarifies, 'they were *rich*, but they were poor musicians.'

'Yes. They played poorly, although they spent handsomely. Most of our bands were made up of a collection of folk musicians, guys who hadn't mastered your basic Dave Van Ronk techniques. They had a limited exposure to the things that we were trying to emulate. We were jazz fans. We were writing tunes where some of the chords were not triads, and you couldn't use your capo that much.'

'Right,' says Fagen, 'and you had to be able to play in all eight keys, as they say. We had a jazz group. We had several versions of several rock groups.'

'It was all the same band and we just didn't bring in certain guys as it graded up towards imitation jazz.'

'I used to play the saxophone quite a bit,' says Fagen.

'Yes, I remember that. "The Star Spangled Banner", an avant-garde rendition . . . It was a shocking display.'

'It was a shocking display, but I really used to get my rocks off,' says Fagen, deadpan. 'And people would listen to it too.'

'They were *very* bored there,' says Becker, earning a hearty laugh. 'The drummers kept flipping out and leaving school – you know, it was hard to get what we wanted in those days, so it didn't come out in utter magnificence. It was very bizarre, the bands that we came up with. It was like the Kingsmen performing Frank Zappa material.'

———

Having cut their inimitable swathe through the inimitable music community, the team hit New York City to peddle their folio of songs.

'That's essentially what we did for the next three years,' says Becker, 'until somebody actually believed that we were songwriters.'

'Of course,' Fagen points out, 'a lot of people still don't believe that's true . . . We were very naive. We used to try to push these songs that were completely – no one wanted to hear them. The lyrics were completely unintelligible, except to us.'

'They were bizarre, depressing tunes,' adds Becker, 'and we had to play them for people who had record companies or publishing companies and stuff, and they got very depressed, and slightly hostile . . . They'd leave or make some kind of excuse and turn off the tape recorder, and they never wanted to see us again . . . All except for Gary Katz, and Gary . . . '

'No,' says Fagen, 'he ran out of the office the first time too.'

Katz, who's been sitting quietly in the background, pipes up. 'No, no, no. The first time was in the studio, and I didn't run . . . You were doing "Let George Do It" and "Brain Tap Shuffle". It was really strange to hear. The music was a little more bizarre than it is now. I was really intrigued, but it didn't hit me at all . . . They just kept playing it for me and said, "Listen, just keep listening." And one day I got it.'

———

Becker and Fagen joined forces with Katz to write some songs for – and to perform on an album (never released) by – a woman singer whom Fagen refers to as 'Gary's protégée'.

'She had three songs that she'd written in her whole life,' says Becker. 'One was about her mother, one was about her boyfriend, and the other was about the fall.'

Some of the Becker–Fagen titles from the period are 'The Roaring of the Lamb', 'Jones' and 'I Mean To Shine' (later recorded by Barbra Streisand), songs that contained glimmerings of the sound to come.

'There were,' says Becker, 'some proto-Steely Dan songs, and there were also what we conceived as good songs, nice pop songs for a female vocalist.'

'I think there were two songs that were more or less in the present style,' says Fagen, 'which sounded very strange by the way, with a very naive female vocalist singing them who hadn't the faintest idea what she was singing about.'

That was the last job (except sideman gigs, with such as Jay & the Americans) that they had before moving west. But first, destiny dealt them one more card in New York.

'"Bass and keyboard player with jazz chops",' says Walter

Becker, remembering Denny Dias's advert in the *Village Voice*. 'So we drove out to this house in Hicksville, Long Island, and Denny was there with his band . . . Denny had some songs that he had written, and they did all the Top 40 songs. They worked in clubs and stuff, which was something we'd never heard of. In fact, when we found out what the clubs were like and what it was supposed to be we refused to learn any of the songs and we never got any jobs. And everyone quit the band . . . That's how we met Denny, and he was the only one left in his band.'

'We used to chastise them and abuse them,' Fagen recalls wistfully, 'so they all quit. And so there was Denny and we'd ruined his band. So he had no place else to go.'

A couple of years later they gave him a call from Los Angeles. 'He was just waiting by the phone,' says Becker, 'and he hung up and drove straight out.'

Denny is now the only remaining member of Becker and Fagen's original Steely Dan.

———

Katz had recruited drummer Jim Hodder and guitarist Jeff Baxter from Boston, and there was a lead singer, David Palmer. They rehearsed after office hours in the ABC accounting department and when they had their ten songs they went in to record *Can't Buy A Thrill.*

'We knew,' says Fagen, 'if they got one song on the radio, if by chance one of them was played on the radio, we had a shot to do what we wanted to do.'

'It was that simple,' Katz agrees. 'If we could get someone that believed in the music and forced it down some radio stations, it would happen. And we were lucky. We found a guy who forced it down some radio stations and sat with them a long while until they did play it.'

But it hasn't been all bonbons and dumplings and No. 1 singles for Steely Dan. There was a period, following the success of 'Reelin' in the Years', when the threat of obscurity loomed dangerously near. The second album, *Countdown To Ecstasy*, proved a bit arcane for many of the original Dan fans, and the next single, 'Show Biz Kids', was, in Fagen's words, 'a brutal failure'. Few even know that they followed it with an edited 'My Old School', which saw even less action.

———

Becker and Fagen's contempt for record companies, disc jockeys, the media, most of the music that's popular these days – for the world, actually – was a bit more blatant fourteen months ago than it is today.

During the mixing of *Pretzel Logic*, they discussed their difficulties. 'It's all the record company,' Fagen was sneering. 'They felt that at that point in our career, when the album came out we should pick the single, for some reason that I couldn't understand. So naturally we would pick what we liked the best. Unfortunately, apparently, it was a little too bizarre for the single-buying public . . .

'These days,' he said of contemporary sounds, 'there ain't much that we hear. It's especially astounding to me that standards have been lowered to the point where it's hard to impress anyone with anything that's harmonically interesting or rhythmically interesting . . . We're basically all jazz fans and most of the records we listen to are jazz – the people who made them are dead or they were recorded so long ago that they've been forgotten. We're

definitely pretty cold at the moment. We've more or less abandoned hope of being one of the big, important rock'n'roll groups,
simply because our music is somehow a little too cheesy at times
and turns off the rock intelligentsia for the most part, and at other
times it's too bizarre to be appreciated by anybody. But we're hoping that we're going to make some sort of miracle sweep and just
sort of worm our way into the hearts of America.'

———

Which is, of course, exactly what they did, with the resounding
critical and commercial success of *Pretzel Logic* and 'Rikki' and
a smash US tour which garnered them further appreciation from
press and fan alike. In retrospect, Fagen's primary misgiving of
last year has proven false: 'I didn't think,' he said, 'most people
wanted to hear a Jew sing.'

But a couple of tribulations were to come in the midst of
prosperity.

A funny thing happened to *Katy Lied*, the fourth album, on its
way from the studio. 'The recording went very quickly,' explains
Fagen. 'The mixing went very quickly, and then we realised that
the mixes wouldn't play back because of a defect in one of the
pieces of equipment, which they were never exactly able to pin
down. But we fixed it, and it took a long time to fix it.'

'It was harsh,' adds Becker. 'It was bleak. If it weren't for that,
the album would have been out right around Christmas. But this
little thing came up and we realised we had to go back and do a
lot of the more painstaking things that you do to make a record
over again – such as mixing it.'

And then there was the matter of the departure of two original Steely Dan players, Hodder and Baxter. 'The only reason,'

Fagen says, 'that Jeffrey actually didn't play on the last album is he was on the road with the Doobie Brothers. And we missed him on the dates where we could have used him, so somebody else did it. I talked to him just the other day. The Doobie Brothers are doing very nicely. Going on a tour. He'll be in Oxford, Mississippi, before us.'

Baxter's move led to speculation that – what a shame – this must be the end of the line for the beloved Dan. Mention of their projected demise elicits incredulous smiles from Becker and Fagen, for the simple reason that Steely Dan is not structured as a conventional rock band.

'If you think of it more as a concept than a group of specific musicians,' says Fagen, 'there's no way it'll break up.'

'We have a situation,' Becker continues, 'where for a particular tour we select a band. We make up a band and then rehearse it and then go out and do it . . .

'You'll see two Steely Dan shows on different tours, it'll be different bands and a different kind of musical presentation. The nucleus of the band has always been the same.'

'We have a bunch of satellite performers,' adds Fagen, 'who more or less are interchangeable from time to time . . . Usually we pick musicians that we think will fit the particular song. Sometimes we'll just hear somebody on a record and hire them for the date, and if it works out it's all the better . . . You know, we grew up listening to jazz musicians, and they're always playing with different musicians, so I don't see why the same kind of thing can't happen here. It makes it much more interesting. I think the musicians like to play on our sessions and concerts, 'cause the material's a little more challenging than the fare they usually have to play. Like, I remember Rick Derringer. "Chain

Lightning" has all the aspects of a straight blues, except the chords constantly modulate, and he was sort of freaked out by that for about three or four seconds, and then realised he had to do something a little different from what he usually does.'

'On the other hand,' says Becker, 'there are people that don't like that.'

'Right. Every once in a while, we'll get somebody that'll come in and they won't know what's going on. We get somebody else.'

'They leave.'

Like a depressed executive confronted with 'Brain Tap Shuffle' maybe.

———

They say it's too early yet to discuss the next configuration of Steely Dan.

'We're always meeting new musicians,' says Fagen. 'There are certainly some that are well-qualified. Including Jeff.'

But before Becker and Fagen and their musical phalanx hit the civic halls and gymnasiums (gymnasia?) one more time, they're going to cut another album.

'The idea,' says Becker, 'is to get an ongoing recording process going and not have to be interrupted by a tour. 'Cause what usually happens is, just as you're finishing an album, you have some ideas on how you'd do it differently, things that you'd like to do while it's fresh in your mind, and it's always been for us that immediately on completion of the album we were pressured by various forces, internal and external, to go back on the road. As if we're going to make some money or something. The *Countdown to Ecstasy* album, we were actually doing gigs on weekends and recording during the week. And it was ridiculous, 'cause all the equipment would come back all mangled, and nothing would play in tune and everybody had the flu and so on.'

————

As for this next album: 'It's in its very early stages,' Becker says. 'It's really too soon to comment on the general character.'

'We have some warped songs already,' offers Fagen.

More warped than before, we wonder?

'The same general kind of warp.'

'It may be more warped than before,' says Becker. 'It's too soon to tell. The actual execution of the record has a lot to do with how warped it is. You can start out with a very warped song and if . . . '

'And if the vinyl itself is warped – '

'Then it'll be even more warped and you'll never get to hear it, 'cause your needle would just skip. Some dare call it vinyl.'

'Yes,' says Fagen, perking up a bit. 'We're going on a crusade to bring back records that don't go . . . ,' he extends his bony arms and shakes an imaginary, wafer-thin platter back and forth, mouthing the appropriate 'Whoop-whoop' sound effect.

'That's right,' says Becker. 'I remember when I bought my first copy of *Birth of the Cool* by Miles Davis and took the record out of the jacket and found that it weighed seven pounds. I knew this was a musical landmark . . . Fewer but thicker records.'

————

Now what about this 'concept' that is Steely Dan?

Becker and Fagen can't, or won't, define it:

'We've been working on it,' says Fagen, 'and as soon as we can articulate it properly, it'll appear on a record probably. See, all we can give is clues, 'cause we're too close to it. It's all on the record, you know. It's all there. There isn't much to say about it.'

'Even if we could answer the question,' says a smiling Becker, 'you know that we would lie. We would deliberately lead you off the scent.'

Fagen surrounds the matter a bit with a glimpse at the Steely Dan songwriting process: 'Because of the lack of input, experience, that's available to you in the United States of America, or the world in general these days, we more or less rely on pure imagination for song ideas. And we like to make them original, and we'll set up a framework, no matter how bizarre it may be, and proceed to write a song on that basis.

'I'll come up with an idea, and he'll come up with a scenario, and we'll decide what we think the song is about, and which part of the exposition of what's happening is in each verse, and get a title together, and no matter how strange the idea may be we just go along and hope that we can finish the song and that it actually emerges as something.

'When we go into the studio it's further refined by the musicians who are playing on it . . . Both of us in concert write the music and the words. You know, it's a lot of pacing around the living room. Whenever Walter has some free time he'll drop over, show me what he's got, I'll show him what I've got and kick it around a little bit. It's very informal.

'I'll tell you, there's a lot of stuff packed into the records musically . . . There's so much junk packed into each unit. We try to make it unboring, that's one of the main things we go for. If it's boring, that's the main indication that there's some failure.'

Fagen, who once described his (and by extension Steely Dan's) personality as 'venomous,' continues with some cryptic words on the *Katy Lied* material.

'Each song is seen from a different viewpoint. Some, I imagine, have an idealistic tone to them, while others are someone who's obviously suicidal. Obviously the narrator, if you will, is really in the deep stages of severe depression. And, of course, I probably was when I was performing them . . . Everybody's personality is just a symptom of the times. I always seem to see both sides of things simultaneously, for which reason I never seem to have an opinion about anything.'

———

One final stab at it, then, directed in Donald Fagen's direction: What kind of life do you like to live?

'I rarely step over the portals of my door to the outside world . . . I watch TV, I listen to old records and play the piano a lot. I think we insult people unintentionally – we keep getting invited to this and that. Like the Grammy Awards, I got a thing that said, "Wear beautiful clothes".' He suddenly becomes animated, in his own sullen way, for the first time, flashing a trace of the possessed, mad-professor demeanour he exhibits when he leads the band on stage. 'I don't *have* any beautiful clothes!'

'You have a nice sweater, though,' Katz reminds him.

'It said,' Fagen responds vehemently. '"*Wear beautiful . . .*" now *I* know what they wanted. They wanted me to come dressed like Cher!'

'You don't have anything like that,' Katz admits.

'I don't have anything like that! I don't have a little Hawaiian bra. I'd be petrified to go to something like that.'

'You do look beautiful, though,' says the ever-consoling Katz, 'in that sweater.'

Review of
The Royal Scam

Bud Scoppa, *Circus*,
24 August 1976

Donald Fagen and Walter Becker don't play by the rules. They won't tour, they won't talk to interviewers, they won't keep a band together – instead they prefer to ship out their best players to the Doobie Brothers and hire hand-picked freelance musicians for specific parts on specific tracks (they've been known to fly players from New York to Los Angeles just to lay down thirty-second solos).

Fagen and Becker write lyrics so cryptically personalised that they seem like riddles and, in an age in which most rock groups strive to synthesise raunch in the studio, Steely Dan make immaculately *clean* rock'n'roll records. Miraculously, this resolutely unorthodox approach works: in five attempts dating back to 1972, this 'band' (for want of a better term) has made five of the best records of the '70s. *The Royal Scam* sounds like the cream of the crop and one of the finest albums of the year.

There's more wit, imagination, and musical sophistication in the songs and structures of *The Royal Scam* than on any LP I've heard in ages. The playing of hired hands such as guitarists Elliott Randall and Larry Carlton, drummers Rick Marotta and Bernard Purdie, and keyboardist Paul Griffin is not only marvellously inventive but also perfectly integrated into the song settings. It seems almost criminal that individual parts aren't credited: the voice-box lead guitar in 'Haitian Divorce', which somehow unites a satiny, muted-cornet tone with a nastily jagged edge, and the furiously syncopated jazz piano in 'The Fez' – to cite salient examples – carry signatures so strong and individualised that they shouldn't remain anonymous.

There's nothing anonymous, however, about the songs, singing, and overall dynamics of *The Royal Scam*: Fagen and Becker have developed a style so singular that it's instantly recognisable. Fagen – who unaccountably spent the first three years of Steely Dan's existence trying to find the right lead vocalist for the group – has now apparently accepted the fact that if he wants it done right, he'll have to do it himself. He's surely one of the most inventive singers in pop, and who else but the writer of these tricky, tragicomic songs could sing them with the necessary understanding? Outside of Randy Newman, I can't imagine a writer-singer who could think up – let alone pull off – songs about prehistoric cave paintings ('Before the fall/When they wrote it on the wall/When there wasn't even any Hollywood'), a chemist-drug dealer with too much integrity for his own good ('Is there gas in the car?/I think the people down the hall/Know who you are') or homicidal jealousy ('Turn up the Eagles/The neighbours are listening').

Throughout the album's nine songs, the Fagen–Becker team is

in top form, but nowhere more so than in the disturbingly funny 'Haitian Divorce', where the writers work a Godard-like process comment into the middle of the narrative: 'At the grotto in the easy chair/Sits the Charlie with the lotion and the kinky hair . . . '

They're utterly calculated, perverse and – like the 'Show Biz Kids' they described a couple years back – 'don't give a fuck about anybody else'. But somehow these elitist oddballs continue to make remarkably human records – records I can't help falling in love with. Let 'em do it their way.

6

Art For Art's Sake

Michael Watts, *Melody Maker*,
19 June 1976

Donald Fagen and Walter Becker are living proof that intelligence is still regarded with suspicion in rock'n'roll. I confess it annoys me that they are more persistently categorised as 'oddballs' and 'smartasses' rather than considerable songwriters – which is what they are – because rock music and literary qualities are still held to be incompatible, even by those who write about rock. Or so it seems.

Yet I suppose that, ultimately, Fagen and Becker, progenitors of Steely Dan, have only themselves to blame for insisting upon erudition and references drawn from jazz, Latin and classical music, as well as pop, whilst concealing it all beneath shiny music that can demand very little beyond an acquiescent toe unless one wishes it. For the supreme irony of Steely Dan, for whom irony as a device is second nature, is the apparent equanimity with which they go about being most things to all men and everything to a few.

Probably, as they are children of the '60s (Fagen is 28, Becker 26), it was inevitable that they chose rock as their creative field but just as predictable, given their tastes and ambitions, that they would thereby appear conspicuous to those who did want more than to tap a toe. As Becker says himself, 'If we were novelists dealing with the subject matters of our songs . . . our thematic concerns would not stick out as much'.

Those concerns are the most wide-ranging within rock writing and have become the subjects for more interpretations than songs by any other artist since the Dylan of the period leading up to *John Wesley Harding*. Not usually very specific – the most recent album, *The Royal Scam*, is the least difficult of the five – they range from the typically black little tale of a compulsive loser ('Do It Again', the hit single from the first album, *Can't Buy a Thrill*) to the grandly worked title track of *The Royal Scam*, which in three verses encapsulates an epic story of Puerto Rican settlement in New York.

The extent of their ambitions for these songs is illustrated by Becker's statement that on 'The Royal Scam' they were trying to catch the inflection of the King James Bible (in fact, there's perhaps an echo of Psalm 107: 'They wandered in the wilderness in a solitary way' in the song's chorus line, 'And they wandered in from the city').

Nothing if not carefully constructed, their writing does not flow along with Dylan's stream of images; it relies upon nuance, upon literary style and the suggestion of atmosphere in a novelistic manner far removed from the traditional workings of the pop song.

In lyric terms, very few writers in rock – perhaps Randy Newman, Robbie Robertson, Joni Mitchell – are working as consciously towards the aesthetic experience. For a start, there is nothing in the whole of Becker and Fagen's output that is overtly autobiographical, which, because there's nothing except for the songs themselves to which the audience can relate, helps explain why Steely Dan seems so faceless.

Eng. Lit – in which Fagen graduated, incidentally – looms large in the Steely Dan canon. Of course, the name itself is an obscure term taken from William Burroughs' *Naked Lunch*. But their literary influences range from the American black humourists (Vonnegut, Terry Southern, Nathanael West) through to their (possibly) English counterpart, Evelyn Waugh, and on to such diverse writers as Beckett, Aldous Huxley, Voltaire, Nabokov, Borges and even Conrad. Only their big interest in science-fiction short stories, evident on another song from *Scam*, 'Sign In Stranger', seems familiar from conversations with other rock performers.

Hardly primitives, therefore, they are well able to talk of what they do in the context of art and the creative process, whether or not they acknowledge that it is art. But, in any case, they are saved from any pretentiousness by a very bloody sense of humour that's employed both in their songs and on a personal level. Their conversation can be as funny, dark and cynical as their writing and, again like the old Dylan, they often enjoy the technique of sending up whoever is in their company – particularly if it's an interviewer – out of impatience, for self-protection or just for personal entertainment.

This game of verbal ping-pong, in which the hapless person is batted about between the two of them, is generally initiated by Becker who, with his passion for word games, is sharp and perky, where Fagen is laconic and droll in a somewhat weary fashion. Withal, however, these are essentially serious men, whose ideas can be startling and invigorating.

During the following interview with them in London, where they were on a working holiday looking at studios, Fagen suddenly broke off at one point to make the observation that reggae music – or so he had just realised – was very much like German band music. This precipitated a rapid exchange of views between himself and Becker, who then went on to develop a theory of his own that the sound quality of English rock music was dictated by the humidity.

'That very full, mid-bass kind of sound,' he explained.

Finally, of course, it is music, their music, which justifies their lyric sheets, as it must do with all songwriters (and these are not 'rock poets'). Perfectionists who throw away an enormous amount of recording material, they have a fantastic ability to digest all kinds of popular music, no matter how dated, right down to the specifics of a style or a record – the Brazilian figure, for instance, that introduces 'Rikki Don't Lose That Number' or Becker's wah-wah reproduction of Bubber Miley's trumpet solo on 'East St Louis Toodle-Oo', the Ellington song.

On the second side alone of *Pretzel Logic* they move from a homage to Bird with 'Parker's Band' that includes a quote from 'Bongo Bop', to the odd pseudo-chamber work of 'Through With Buzz', to the almost straightahead rock'n'roll of the title track, and on to the Beatle-esque 'With A Gun'.

Their musical influences break down to essentially three categories. Firstly, there are the twentieth-century classical composers – probably from 1890 on – who would include Stravinsky, Debussy, Ravel and Hindemith; then in rock'n'roll the Beatles, Byrds, Stones, Chuck Berry, Johnny Rivers, Tony Orlando and Van Morrison (a very rough count). But mainly it's jazz: the Duke, Parker, and Miles Davis pre-eminently. Drawing upon this reservoir of source material, they produce music that is undoubtedly Steely Dan, but almost indefinably so because of the variety of techniques involved, although the jazz harmonics, the overdubbed ensemble singing and the many rhythmic twists are familiar trademarks.

Fagen's slight vibrato – on 'Bad Sneakers' he's not unlike Ray Davies – is always distinctive, yet the heart of their sound remains somehow elusive. It is so controlled. Steely Dan sound like the classiest MOR band in the world. This beautiful juxtaposition of be-bop devices and sinister lyrics with a Top 30 sound!

Fagen and Becker's coolly paradoxical style, with its intriguing tensions between lyric and music and between the appeal to the mind, the feet, and even the heart when they are realistically portraying sentiment, has its roots in Bard College, where the two met nine years ago.

Fagen was there from Passaic, New Jersey, Becker from New York. Situated in Annandale-on-Hudson, across the river from Woodstock in upper New York state, Bard is a progressive institution which encourages in its six hundred students a highly liberal outlook, and it's worth speculating that Steely Dan's unconventionality was nurtured here. It's often held, in fact, that their second album, *Countdown to Ecstasy*, has identifiable associations with Bard.

When the two left Bard – Becker was not a graduate – they tried to sell songs they'd begun working on during their period there, but with varying degrees of success. They did, indeed, cut a now very rare album for Spark Records, the official recording label of a large international publishing company: the album was a soundtrack for a schlock movie titled *You've Got to Walk It Like You Talk It (or You'll Lose That Beat)*. The film, which, according to Becker, was little better than an expensive home movie, played for only two weeks in Manhattan; the soundtrack is unlikely to be re-released, either, although Steely Dan producer Gary Katz – to the vehement denials of both Fagen and Becker – thinks there's some good stuff on it (notably a song with the typical Dan title of 'Dog Eat Dog').

They also scored a forgettable dance movie in which Becker's mother was involved, and for which they got paid £1,500. But their main activity was peddling songs around the Brill Building.

———

Around this time, in 1970, they met the guitarist Denny Dias, the only other surviving member of the original touring line-up of Steely Dan. They answered an ad in the New York *Village Voice* which said: 'Must have jazz chops. Call Dennis Dias, Hicksville, Long Island.'

They eventually joined Dias's band, which was called Demian after the Herman Hesse novel, and began rehearsing in Dias's basement. But their propensity for organising people seems to have ensured that Demian was short-lived. Fagen says they fired most of the band, whereupon Dias went into semi-retirement and they left to join Jay & the Americans.

Jay & the Americans' road drummer had been one of the musicians playing in the Dias basement, and the publishing company of Jay & the Americans had been the only office within the Brill Building to show them any real attention, so they went to play with them for about a year and a half, whilst at appropriate intervals striking up again the old Dias band.

'When we joined Jay & the Americans, we had access once more to a drummer who did not find us totally repugnant,' says Becker.

Neither were totally successful ventures, however.

With Jay and the Americans they were swept up in the oldies revivals of the early '70s, playing on extensive bills at Madison Square Garden with such as the Angels and the Shirelles, which offered great experience, but their real wish was for recognition as songwriters, not as bass and keyboard back-ups, and Jay Black's attempts to record their songs were all abortive. They did make a useful contact, however, at a studio session job, when they met guitarist Jeff 'Skunk' Baxter – and an even more important one in Gary Katz, a friend of Jay & the Americans.

Katz had been a partner for three years of Richard Perry in Cloud Nine Productions, which had been established with money given them by their respective parents. When that ran out he just hung out for two years, during which period he met the Dour Duo. But in November 1971 he got a producer's job at ABC-Dunhill Records in California, which he took on the proviso that Fagen and Becker be hired as staff writers. The two were hired sight unseen by ABC president Jay Lasker. 'I said to him,' recalls Katz, 'that if it didn't happen, I would quit.'

They maintain that it was always their intention to form a band, and the songwriting contract was terminated after six months as Katz pulled together Dias, Baxter, drummer Jim Hodder and other musicians for the first Steely Dan album.

They did, indeed, write a song for the Grass Roots in this period called 'Tell Me A Lie', but it was rejected. 'You could always tell we were laughing down our sleeves at the band,' Becker says. Streisand, it is also true, had cut another of their songs – actually, before ABC – called 'I Mean to Shine', but Becker claims that Richard Perry destroyed it. 'He changed the lyrics and the melody, and left out the bridge.'

Can't Buy A Thrill, which included the hit singles 'Reelin' In The Years' and 'Do It Again', was recorded in June 1972, and thus began in earnest Fagen and Becker's close working relationship with Gary Katz, whom they seem to value for his own perfectionist attitudes.

'Gary,' explains Fagen, 'is there to ensure that each album is a superb Gary Katz production.'

Katz: 'I think I get upset sooner than they do. They would be upset at the same things I am two days later.'

It is as a studio group, utilising a repertory company of session players, that Steely Dan have increasingly come to represent themselves. The last two albums have taken two years to appear, partly because of specific technical problems that tax the perfectionists in them, and there has been no touring in that period. Nor will there be – in Britain, at least – until next year, since there are contractual problems with ABC that necessitate the delivery of two albums by January 1977. 'Caesar wants a record every three months, it turns out,' Becker says, 'so we have to render unto him before we can render unto the concert-goer.'

However, they have never been very happy performing, anyway. They claim that in the early days of Steely Dan they were 'coerced' into extensive performances with ill-prepared bands, although they were satisfied with the line-up that played here in 1974. Even that trip, though, was marred by Fagen's problem with his throat, for which he says he was wrongly treated by a Harley Street doctor and had to seek medical help in California. Fagen still lives in California – more precisely in Malibu and within hailing distance of Becker – but it does look as if the next album will be cut somewhere in Europe.

This interview was recorded one recent afternoon in London at the Montcalm Hotel, where both they and the Rolling Stones were staying. I was amused that they had conveyed the message, through ABC, that the conversation had to be conducted 'on a certain intellectual level', for Fagen was once to exclaim, 'This is really serious! Jesus! It's only rock'n'roll.' Perhaps the Stones next door were at the back of his mind.

Gary Katz, a drawn, bony man, sat mostly in silence throughout, while Fagen slumped down in an armchair behind his shades and delivered his replies unsmilingly in an adenoidal New Jersey accent. Becker perched himself on the edge of his chair, from which he could better twinkle in his inimitably sardonic fashion.

I had been informed by the press office that they'd been woken up one morning at 4 a.m. by Keith Richards playing *Katy Lied*.

'Apocryphal,' Fagen replied shortly. Their answers generally, I found, were just as succinct and scholastically phrased . . .

———

You say in 'My Old School' that you'll never go back to Annandale, which is a specific reference to Bard College. What can you tell me about Bard?

Walter Becker: It was one of your basic beatnik colleges they have in America. There's a couple of them strategically situated throughout the country. Everybody there, just about, was a beatnik, except for the people who were in the religion department.

Donald Fagen: They're progressive schools. You don't get as much foundation material as I would have liked to have gotten, actually. They emphasise creative aspects of learning rather than basics, so it turns out that if you want to get some kind of formal education you have to do a lot of reading on your own. The system is basically a failure.

WB: In the winter they sent you off for a coupla months to go out into the world and achieve some kind of meaningful relationship with humanity at large, which was a general license to take a coupla months off and go to San Francisco and sleep on the floor under your Jimi Hendrix poster. It was within commuting distance of New York City, too.

DF (who has been grunting approval to Becker's reply): There are a few others. There's one called Goddard, there's one called Antioch, and one called Reed College. There's Brandeis in Boston, too, isn't there?

WB: The difference being that in Brandeis they would take a somewhat eccentric youth with bizarre ideation as long as he had a 96.3 grade point, whereas at Bard they would take anyone that had *potential* [he beams the word].

DF: And four thousand dollars a year.

WB: Which, of course, neither one of us had.

DF: But we were subsidised . . .

WB: . . . by our respective states to attend this institution.

DF: We were the only poor kids there, really.

WB: It took me a long time to realise that too – why everyone else had cigarettes and Porsches.

Bard does seem to have had an effect upon you. There are certainly references on the second album, *Countdown to Ecstasy*.

WB: Well, it didn't have that much effect upon me, since I obtained virtually no education there.

But experiences at Bard were reflected in your writing?

DF: I don't think so much of Bard as experiences of the late '60s which were common to a lot of young swains in America. I don't think it had so much to do with that particular college as it did with the mood of the country at the time. Bard College is not so much different from living in Manhattan, except that you couldn't get a good meal, 'cause everyone who went there was basically from the Manhattan area.

But that line 'El Supremo from the room at the top of the stairs' does relate to Bard, doesn't it?

Both: No.

WB: I can't see why you would think that it did.

I understood it from Wayne Robins (an American rock writer), who went to the same college.

DF: Because Wayne Robins went to the same school as we did, I think he imagines some heavy association with the college, and tends to associate a lot of our lyrics with experiences that would be common to his.

WB: At the time we went to Bard College, the going thing was, everyone would say, 'See that dormitory over there? That's where Bob Dylan wrote blah, blah, blah,' or, 'See that pump handle there? That's the one that the vandals took.'

And it wasn't so?

DF: Well, Bob Dylan did hang out there – it was near Woodstock – and he did have some intercourse with that college –

WB: And its faculty.

DF: And the pun is intended. But, as far as the association with his lyrics, I wouldn't know.

So the references have all been overstated?

Both: Yeah, yeah.

And 'My Old School' is not about a drug bust at Bard?

WB [eating a grape]: Not that I know of, no [pause]. Which is not to say that there was never a drug bust at Bard College. Which is not to say that I was not rounded up at that drug bust. Which is not to say that I was never even attending the school at that time. And which is not to say that the school didn't have the decency to bail me out.

DF: Which is not to say that the judge didn't run a snowplough into a river, which I think was poetic justice if I ever heard it.

WB: That's right. Which is not to say that G. Gordon Liddy was the arresting officer.

DF: He was the assistant district attorney of Dutchess County, NY, at the time.

WB: The Wild Bill Hickock of the judiciary.

DF: And believe me, he wanted to be re-elected.

WB: He was 'the man in the trench coat,' as a matter of fact. He was an extremely corny cop. He thought he was a detective, Dick Tracy or something.

DF: In fact, we had an attorney in common. In other words, my attorney at the time I was busted by G. Gordon Liddy was later G. Gordon Liddy's attorney when he was busted for his nefarious acts in government.

WB: Which gives you some idea of how justice works in America.

It meant a lot of money?

WB: Yes, that's right [meaningful look]. That was it. I had some idiot communist lawyer that my girlfriend's uncle knew from the roaring thirties, and of course he took me up there for a court appearance and the judge didn't even show up; he was out farming.

DF: It was one of those very small-time communities. Everyone is a sheriff's deputy – the guy who runs the general store, and so forth.

WB: Come the spring, you know, and a young man's fancy turns to raiding Bard College.

DF: If they just catch you in your underwear, they'll say they have you *in flagrante delicto*.

Would you say that the subsequent move from the East Coast to California meant anything to your writing? Perhaps a tension created between the intellectual demands of the East Coast and the sunny nature of California?

WB: I would say changes in *musical climate*, and the fact that we had an actual mechanism for presenting our songs after we moved to the West Coast, which we didn't have when we were on the East Coast – in other words, the band – was more a violent change in what we were doing.

DF: If you never cross the threshold of your own domicile, it doesn't really matter where you live, now does it?

And that's the way you live?

DF: I would say, generally, yes, except for a trip occasionally. But in New York we had some lyric sheets and someone's office with a piano in it, which was the only outlet for our songs, and on the West Coast we have multi-million-dollar recording studios. And if you know you're going to get something on a record, you generally tend to write better.

WB: Especially if you write it for yourself, because back in New York as often as not we were writing it with another singer in mind, or just with hopes that somebody would record it, please God.

DF: Neither of us considered performing the songs ourselves vocally till our first record, when we finally ran out of time in which to find a suitable singer.

So that meant changing the way you wrote?

DF: Well, I hadda narrow the range down a little bit on the melodies.

WB: There were certain things that Donald prefers not to do that we had written into songs before which we didn't do any more, certain words that Donald doesn't like to sing – such as 'kinetic' and 'tonic.'

I threw at you the relationship between east and west coasts to see if it might partly explain the fact that, superficially, the music is very pop and attractive, and yet underlying that there are all these interesting themes.

WB: I'd like to help you out with that theory, but, as I recall, when we were located on the East Coast it was that way too. We've always written *outré* lyrics and pop structures.

DF: It's got more mature, I think, but that's about the only change. It's simply a matter of logistics. The record company is there. We got offered a job there as staff writers. And we'd had no luck in New York. So that's where we ended up.

I'd like to get onto a discussion of your albums. This latest one is perhaps more accessible than the previous album, *Katy Lied*.

DF: Well, we did bring in some musicians we hadn't used before, particularly some New York musicians, which I think changed the sound and made it a more live, rhythmic sound.

WB: It's got kind of a stomping mood to it compared with *Katy Lied*.

Which initially seemed cooler and cerebral. I had to play it a dozen times before it really started to grow upon me.

WB: That may be why I've never liked it, because I haven't played it that many times.

DF: 'Course, I tried to play it a few times, but the quality of the disc that ABC puts out, you play it six or seven times and then you can't hear it at all.
WB: Well, those are re-treads. Those are all Hamilton, Joe Frank & Reynolds albums, and the music is just encoded on top. That's the toughest part of making albums for us – having to make all the songs the same length as on the Hamilton, Joe Frank & Reynolds albums so the grooves will come out the same place.

Do you see a specific mood for each album?

DF: You know, I don't listen to them after we've made them. In a restaurant the other night, some guys from the record company played it while we were eating, some old record of ours, and it sounds like some other group to me, really, in a lotta ways.

WB: We do try to put together a programme of songs that somehow hangs together.

DF: But mostly that's things like tempo.

WB: Yeah, not in terms of themes, really.

DF: In other words, we don't wanna have too many songs with a very moderate tempo on one album; we like to break up the musical flow. But lyrically we feel we write the songs and the album will take care of itself. We sequence for sound rather than for narrative potential; we sequence for how it affects the ear, rather than cerebrally.

Gary Katz [entering the conversation]: There's no concept. Never.

DF: Chance is very important to an artist, you know. Dostoyevsky wrote in instalments for magazines, and I'm sure he wasn't aware of the entire flow until it was all together.

You know, if there is a lyrical unity to each album it's simply because most of the songs on each album are written in a certain time period, and naturally a certain phase of our personalities would be prominent while the songs were written, and that would give it a lyrical unity, certainly.

There's not usually more than two or three songs that were written long before we start recording them.

———

Let me ask you about individual songs, beginning with those on *The Royal Scam*.

DF: We don't have to answer anything, but take a stab at it.

'Kid Charlemagne', for instance – could that be about a Leary or a Manson? Am I in the right direction?

DF: You're on the right track. I think it would probably be about a person who's less of a celebrity than those people.

Did you have a definite person in mind?

WB: Well, there is a particular individual, whom we naturally can't name . . .

DF [straight-faced]: For legal purposes.

WB: . . . who hovered over the creation of the song like a sword of Damocles, like Hamlet's father. Basically, it's a chef.

A chef?

WB: Cooks.

GK: Master cooks.

WB: Chemists.

'Sign in Stranger' – that's almost like a school for gangsters?

DF: That's true. Of course, it does take place on another planet. We sort of borrowed the Sin City/Pleasure Planet idea that's in a lotta science-fiction novels, and made a song out of it. But, indeed, you're right.

Turning to the last album, *Katy Lied* – is that a praying mantis on the cover?

WB: It's a katydid. They may not have them here, or they may not call them that, but it's a little bug that looks like a grasshopper, except that it has larger translucent wings. It makes a sound that is onomatopoeically rendered as 'katydid'.

How about the phrase 'Lady Bayside'?

WB: Aah! In Queens, New York, there is a community called Bayside, where I culled numerous members for my first rock'n'roll band, and Bayside had a particular character to the community, which ranged from politically, rabidly conservative to absolute congenital mind-damage among its younger citizens. So the young women growing up in this community had a particular kind of character.

DF: It would be kind of like saying 'Lady Knightsbridge'.

WB: It may not mean anything to anyone but me, but it sounded good.

Is 'The Royal Scam' about Puerto Ricans trying to settle in New York?

DF: Because the interpretation is so accurate I wouldn't even want to comment any further.

WB: In other words, you already know more than is good for you.

DF: To tell you the truth, we tend to refrain from discussing specifics as far as lyrics go, because it is a matter of subjective interpretation, and there are some things that are better that man does not know. You are on the right track, and whatever you make of it will suffice. Really.

You leave yourself open to the interpretation of playing guessing games with your audience.

WB: Well, hopefully the idea is that there won't be any guessing games. You see, you have a fairly precise picture in your mind of what is in that song, I can see, but when we write the songs we hope that a listener hearing that song who does not translate St John into San Juan would still be able to enjoy the song without being too worried about what it means. In other words, it should work for somebody who doesn't get nearly that far.

Yes, but it would work for him if he understood it, wouldn't it?

WB: Well, maybe so, but I would hope it will work for him even if he considers it a complete fairy tale.

On some songs you are quite specific. 'Don't Take Me Alive' is a very specific song. I don't think people would have any problems understanding that.

WB: I shouldn't think so.

So why do you intend some songs to be very mystifying?

WB: Well, it's not that it came out to be mystifying. We did decide to write that song in a kind of . . .

DF: Allegorical.

WB: We were trying to imitate the inflection of a King James Bible just a bit, so that made it vague necessarily.

DF: It's kind of like the Trinity, you know. We think we'd probably destroy the spell if we laid it on the line, you know what I mean? There's a certain mystique that that song depends upon for it to be effective.

WB: We're not topical songwriters. We're trying always not to write the same lyric, but to write lyrics that have to do with something interesting; and so, when we get an idea on the lines of that one, we don't want it to sound like a Phil Ochs song [pause] – may he rest in peace.

We don't want its political or social overtones to be so specific that someone who hasn't lived in New York would have no use for the song.

But one of the great virtues of your writing is that it's not autobiographical – or, at least, overtly.

WB: That's another thing.

And neither is it hog-tied to a particular mood of the times, as is the case with so many rock writers.

DF: That's true. I guess one of the great cornerstones of what rock'n'roll is supposed to be is that it's somehow supposed to reflect now – the time we're living in – and not reflect back. And, in fact, there is very little reflection in rock'n'roll.

WB: It's generally the cry of an anguished teenage soul. And we're not doing that too much anymore [short laugh].

DF: As far as specifics like that, our audience will have to trust our sincerity, just trust us in not just laying down some bullshit. When they think they don't understand something it's certainly not a random lyric.

It's been suggested that your writing is after the image of your own world, in the sense that you create a private world and your themes and lyrics relate more to that than the actual world outside it. Do you take the point?

DF: Well, I think it's more a way of viewing the actual world through our eyes. I think probably in our earlier works we were fantasising more than we do now. I think now we're synthesising what we see.

WB: Nevertheless, it may be right in saying that the world crystallised through our eyes bears very little resemblance to anyone else's world, even though we think we're recording it as we see it. We may be so bent that it's unrecognisable. I would like to think so. That would certainly make it more interesting.

———

You could say that you were preserving the analogy with William Burroughs, inasmuch as very many of his references are extremely private.

WB: Yes, almost embarrassingly private, and I don't think we as a rule have veered as far into personal psychomimetic fantasy as he has. But I suppose you could say that. And – did you write the article that suggested we recorded 'East St. Louis Toodle-Oo' because it was mentioned in a chapter in Burroughs? That isn't so. I mean, you're right – 'East St. Louis Toodle-Oo' is mentioned in the book –

DF: That was brought to our attention after the fact.

WB: But the actual genesis of that piece is to do with the fact that – aside from it being a very attractive theme from one of our favourite composers – when wah-wah pedal started to come into vogue for guitar, that was a very fun piece to play on the wah-wah guitar. Immediately the simile between wah-wah guitar and Bubber Miley's wah-wah trumpet playing came to mind. That's more how that came about.

DF: Yeah, and without having a missionary attitude we still thought it would be interesting for the audience to realise that that kind of expression is not a new thing, and that in 1926 a trumpet player was doing with his lip what it takes a rather complicated set of electronics to do on an electric guitar. Walter had been putzing around on the guitar with that song for years.

WB: I was fortunate enough to have a wah-wah pedal, and that was one of my big numbers, so we decided the time had come to do that.

Staying on Burroughs, do you take the relationship with him – if we can go so far as to call it a relationship – do you take it far enough to write, at least partially, in a cut-up style?

WB: No [slightly hesitant]. We don't write in a cut-up technique, as I understand he does. I don't think he does anymore either.

DF: We sometimes will juxtapose styles of writing in one song, but that's about as far as it goes, really. Because we have a fairly broad popular musical experience, there will be the kind of harmony associated with bebop and various kinds of jazz right next to a section that has more common rock'n'roll harmony. 'Green Earrings', for example, has a very contemporary vamp which leads into a cycle of fast progression, and another section which is actually from another era.

WB: 'The Fez' is a disco song which suddenly has a lot of chords. And disco songs, as we understand them, one of the most characteristic things about them is that they're lacking in harmonic movement . . . all of which has really nothing to do with William Burroughs.

DF: There's a very superficial relationship between what we do and what William Burroughs does, except for perhaps the late '50s bohemian spirit.

What would you say were your main themes as writers?

WB: Well, of course, we have all the usual ones. Unrequited love, destructive love, er . . .

DF: Self-destruction.

WB: The erotic.

DF: Violence . . . Oh, we can write about anything. In fact, we were recently thinking of writing something about the Congress of Vienna, which is actually part of the reason I visited the Museum at Monaco, to get a little atmosphere. We thought of the Congress of Vienna because it was a turning point in European affairs and we see certain parallels between that and what's going on now. But that's yet to come. We haven't quite crystallised it yet, but we're thinking about it.

WB: It will work out. If you can do that kind of thing without making it pretentious, that's the secret, because then you're dealing with really interesting and unusual subject matter and still making it into a pop song that doesn't sound like a, er . . . Frank Zappa epic, or a Kinks musical comedy number.

DF: You see, we use that more as a starting-point to write a song which may, when it's finished, not suggest to anyone what we had in mind. The song that we wrote about the Beer Hall Putsch, for instance, no one ever had to think about the Beer Hall Putsch to think about that song. That's our method of writing a song: to have something in mind that may not actually be in the song.

———

How does the marriage of lyric and music come together?

WB: Often there will be a fragment of music and lyrics we have that is very open-ended and could suggest a lotta things, and then we'll decide what would be the most interesting to write the song about with that piece in it. Or a piece of music, for example, will suggest that its lyric be concerned with a certain type of affair; either a little short story, or a more free-form type of imagery.

DF: We always start with a fragment that will suggest the whole of the song. The way we write the fragment is the way any so-called artist will write a fragment, and I don't think you can explain that, unless you want to get into discussing the philosophy of art or expression.

WB: Oh, please, let's not!

So how do the two of you assemble your writing? How does the contribution of each break down?

DF: The fact is, I can't finish a song and Walter can't start one. The way we go about composition is dependent upon both of our limitations, really.

You've never actually written songs independently of each other?

WB: Oh, there were maybe a few, years ago. But I think in the last coupla years they've all been total collaborations.

DF: You see, we were some of the few people in the New York area that used to listen to the same obscure radio programmes and read the same obscure novels. It just seemed to work out that way.

How are you different as writers?

WB: I'm less concerned with tying everything up. I like swatches of colours, images that don't necessarily make so much sense. But, of course, Fagen makes me tell him how it makes sense when we write it. He's gotta make it all come together, and that's good. And Donald has a more organised mind than I do.

DF: It's just that, if there's something in a first draft that sounds like it shouldn't be there and doesn't lend unity to the song, I will argue endlessly to exclude it or replace it.

WB: It works out pretty well, actually. When I consider how difficult the collaboration actually is, I'm amazed that we're as single-minded between the two of us.

DF: We rarely have any disagreements about any part of a song. The only thing, in fact, is the way Walter sometimes perceives. If I have some kind of – usually – vamp, Walter will perceive it to be in another key than I do. Sometimes we have problems in song structure. But that also leads to some rather interesting constructions.

WB: In other words, what Donald sometimes thinks of as a one-chord I will think of as a five-chord, and what Donald thinks of as a strong beat in a bar I will think of as a weak beat.

DF: In other words, sometimes he's thinking of the song *backwards* as far as I'm concerned.

Do you have a working routine?

DF: I wish we did, I wish we did! I am able to get up at a certain time and proceed to write. I spring awake in a great burst of guilt and commence to come up with whatever I come up with. And then, after several foolish calls to Walter, in which I make *a fool* of myself [here, amidst some laughter, he flourishes a mock-French accent], finally he comes over and we finish what I've begun.

There's a feeling that underneath all your themes there's a pervasive tone of cynicism.

WB: That's an accusation with which we are not unfamiliar.

DF: Well, we like to keep a certain distance from the protagonist.

Might not your music, therefore, be generally symptomatic of the times?

WB: In terms of cynicism? Oh, I dunno. I don't think these are particularly cynical times. You just wait to see what's coming up! I'm inclined to think that things are going to become far more pessimistic. Of course, pessimism and cynicism are not the same thing at all. Cynicism, I contend, is the wailing of someone who believes that things are, or should be, or could be, much, much better than they are.

Would you say pessimism is a more accurate description for what you do?

WB: No, I wouldn't say that. I suppose we are cynical by comparison to the people who are sincere, but musically I wouldn't have it any other way.

A song like 'Charlie Freak' is unusually tender when set beside most of your writing.

WB: Well, I think so, and hopefully those little glimmers of tenderness are all the more effective in the context they are in rather than a constant syrup being poured over our audience.

DF: In other words, without putting emotional limitations on what you're doing, tenderness is just sentiment rather than a true glimmer of affirmation, or whatever you wanna call it.

WB: They always accuse Vladimir Nabokov – however he chooses to pronounce his silly Russian name – of having such a cold aspect as an artist, whereas it seems to me he can be the most touching, poignant and beautiful writer that I know of. Many people are put off because they think he's cold, icy and vicious, but I've never felt that way, and I don't feel that way about what we do either. But I can see how they read that perception.

DF: I should tell you, though – sometimes, when we play an album back to sequence the songs, sometimes I get the feeling that we *are* hitting a little hard, that it's too *down*. But it's getting back to what I was saying before: there's so much distance from what is actually happening to the protagonist of each song, to use a literary word. In other words, when I sing a song I just take the role of narrator; I'm sort of acting out a part. It's really quite impersonal, although the music in me, and the words themselves, can be very personal – like 'Don't Take Me Alive', 'Kid Charlemagne'.

WB: I think we probably are conspicuous in our thematic concerns in rock'n'roll. But if we were novelists dealing with the subject matters of our songs it would not stick out as much, because in the literary field what we are writing about are more the traditional concerns than in rock'n'roll .

No other rock band I can think of has so positively this Eng. Lit. side to it.

WB [chuckling]: That's kinda true. I hope it's not obtrusive. I guess it is, but I hope it's not.

DF: Bob Dylan had it covered a long time ago.

WB: Yeah, but he had the 'dead end kid' angle.

DF: But he did work in a literary way.

WB: Well, he copped a lotta things. He read a lotta French poetry.

DF: In fact, I think a lot of his singing style comes from that very popular way of reading poetry in the '60s. The cadences, the breaths after pronouns, and things like that.

The irony is that you are so literary-aware, and do make music very much for yourselves, and yet you have had three top five singles in the States and the albums all go gold.

WB: We're very lucky in that, I'm inclined to think.

DF: Well, I hope we have more, because I figure sooner or later they're going to take the ball away from us if they're not making money, although the album sales seem to subsidise us, even if we don't have a hit single off an album. We never get questioned about budget. But we've always been very attracted to commercial, popular music as well as jazz, and it is the mainstay of the kind of structured writing we do. I think the albums are very entertaining, you know. I think they're much more entertaining than most other rock groups' albums. That's a very simplistic way of putting it, but I really think they are.

But how far do you think you can take your literary concerns without losing your audience?

WB: It's an interesting question, and it remains to be seen. I do notice that reading seems to be going out of style. Younger people that I meet, even people just a few years younger than me, are much more distant from any kind of literary traditions than we are, so maybe it'll all be new to them.

DF [disgruntled]: Hell, we'll go into television! We'll sneak through somehow. You know what the key is? It's the music. You see, you're only talking lyrically. But if you look at it just on a superficial level, if the music is contemporary and smart and interesting and entertaining, you can't put people off that much. Especially if you put forth these themes with a little humour. I mean, we're not gonna get any blacker. It's gonna get funnier if anything, right? It is 1976.

WB: Keep 'em laughing, that's what we say.

So how different are the songs you write now from those you wrote as staff composers at ABC?

WB: Oh, we were merely posing as staff writers at ABC. We were impersonating staff writers at ABC. We were actually preparing to launch our fine, fine, superfine career that now exists.

How optimistic were you two of succeeding?

GK: Oh, they weren't at all.

DF: We needed the money.

WB: No, I've always assumed it was only a matter of time before we got the recognition we deserved.

GK: You're kidding!

WB: No, I always had that secret belief.

DF: We were always confident we'd get to record.

GK: But you never thought it would be popular.

DF: No, we never thought it would be very popular. And, in fact, it isn't all that popular.

GK: Yes, it is. *Very* popular. You'd be wrong to assume otherwise.

Fagen [reflectively]: I wish it was more popular sometimes.

How popular?

DF: *Very* popular.

As popular as the Stones?

DF: Yeah.

WB: I'm glad it's the way it is.

GK: Me too.

DF: I don't think I'd like the recognition on the street, that kind of thing – I don't care for that. But I'd like a broader audience. I mean, I wouldn't do anything to compromise the music; I just wish more people liked that kind of music.

GK: I think that will come in time. It has with every album we've done.

You've never sat down to write something you think will be a hit?

DF: No, not really. We can't, believe me. When we were attempting to be staff writers, God knows we tried. But it always comes out weird.

GK: The most you can say about that is that in the studio, after something is mostly complete, somebody might say, 'If we had a harmony it might make it a little more accessible.' That's the most.

DF: No, that's 'cause I don't wanna hear myself singing along with no support! [A slight, embarrassed laugh.] I don't like my voice.

Which presumably was why David Palmer was brought in to sing on the first album?

DF: Well, the idea was to save me the trouble of actually having to sing all these songs. I was hoping that he would turn out, but I felt that his interpretation wasn't quite what we wanted, and he wasn't happy, either, with the kind of things he was doing.

———

Then, for the next album, you got Royce Jones, who sounded rather like him.

DF: Well, we need people to sing high-register harmony parts.

And that's still a problem for you?

DF: Well, sometimes I can do them, and sometimes I can't. It depends on the range. So we've used various singers. Tim Schmit from Poco did some work for us, and Clydie King and some studio singers in Los Angeles, and Royce Jones, Mike McDonald . . . I couldn't possibly tell you the importance of individual contributions from musicians to our music. We use the very finest musicians we can find and we have a very good relationship with them. I think it's a more intimate relationship than other producers who use session people. But it's very difficult music compared to most pop music. We throw a thing away if it just has a little flaw, if it doesn't feel quite right, or the drummer was a little off that day. We can't accept it.

WB: It's done in a certain way. There's very little written for the drummer – accents only. Chord voicings are written for piano. The guitar player is prepared by spoken word from the composers. And the bass players that we use are always people that we know and don't need to have a written part – I haven't played very much bass lately on Steely Dan albums; I play a little guitar and a little bass. It's a quintet or a sextet that lays down the track, and everything else is overdubbed. Vocals are all overdubbed.

———

You use a lot of jazz people. Phil Woods, Plas Johnson, Victor Feldman.

DF: It's our background. Jazz is what we've always listened to. It's been the mainstay of our listening. It's from New York radio in the '50s and '60s.

There are also undoubted Latin influences in your records.

DF: Both of us heard a lot of Latin music in New York. The old jazz stations, in order to survive, played a lot of Latin jazz in the late '50s and '60s – Mongo Santamaria, Tito Puente, and things like that. So we heard a lotta that music.

I think Duke Ellington's whole exotic jungle trip contributed a lot to our tropicality numbers. It's certainly no attempt at real Latin music – it's more like Duke Ellington in that it's an idealised, exotic atmosphere – Cotton Club jungle music, you know. Showtime, Ricky Ricardo stuff. More *I Love Lucy* than Bob Marley.

Why do you find you need so many guitarists? There are five on *The Royal Scam*.

WB: Just to keep it interesting. We're constantly trying to expand the number of musicians that we think will fit into what we're doing. It's more fun for us to have different musicians.

How does Denny Dias like that?

DF: Denny is an extremely tractable human being.

I presume Jeff Baxter was not.

WB: He was less tractable by a good margin, although he was an exceptionally good sport about what we were doing, always, and extremely co-operative with us.

I also presume his problem was you weren't touring.

WB: That was one problem. Another problem had to do with money, in that being a member of Steely Dan was tantamount to a kind of enforced poverty at that time. And there were musical things.

DF: It was always a compromise.

Do you tend to be martinets, then?

WB: I wouldn't put it that way. Good grief! Perhaps you would care to rephrase the question. I know you can do better.

GK: It's their show.

WB: What we try to do is nudge very, very competent musicians into doing something extraordinary, even for them.

DF: A musician will come in and see some of the changes we've got, and he'll go, 'Mmm. This is some sort of music here!'

Are you thinking of recording here?

DF: We're looking at some recording studios here. We may.

Is it just because you want a change of scenery?

DF: That's just about it, yeah, really.

WB: Well, actually, our main motivation in coming was that we might pick up some inspiration or stimulate some provocative vision or experiences or feelings.

You won't find much in dear old, apathetic London.

WB: Well, even that's something. For us that's grist for our mill.

DF: Apathy – we can get a lot of mileage outta that.

WB: Yes, we can take that and make it into a silk purse.

Becker and Fagen in Malibu, Los Angeles, 1980.

Michael Ochs Archives/Stringer/Getty Images

THREE: Glamour Professionals

'We both liked recording studios. As much as anything else, it was just the coolest place to be on a hot afternoon.'

Walter Becker, 1995

1

Review of *Aja*

Richard C. Walls, *Creem,*
January 1978

S teely Dan, in case you don't already know, isn't a group in the conventional sense (although it began that way) but rather the umbrella name that the duo of Donald Fagen and Walter Becker give to whatever group of musicians happens to be playing their compositions at any given time.

There are seven cuts on this record and seven different line-ups – and although a lot of this involves different combinations of a basic pool of studio musicians, they do manage to use six different drummers (Bernard Purdie appears twice). The reason for pointing this out is to be able to marvel at the coherence of the record: it's a remarkable continuity of conception and execution – an indication not only of Fagen and Becker's control over their music, regardless of their physical presence (Becker doesn't even appear on two cuts, and Fagen's synthesiser contributions are minimal although he does sing lead throughout), but also of the assertiveness of its originality. Steely Dan isn't a group; it's a concept.

The concept, as of *Aja*, is cynicism tempered by romanticism, dark without being brooding, resulting in an engrossing midnight album. The famous enigmatic Steely Dan lyrics are not much in evidence here, although it's not all directness and clarity either. There's a healthy appreciation of the oblique phrase to describe the elusive emotion, but insular references are kept few and unobtrusive. The only lyric that can really be regarded as obscure as far as intent is concerned is the title track, whose main appeal is musical anyway. An eight-minute track with a jazzy start/stop rhythm and subtle Latin and oriental motifs running through the melody, it's highlighted by a too brief full-bodied tenor solo by Wayne Shorter (more reminiscent of his Art Blakey days than his wispy Miles days) and Steve Gadd's imaginative and energetic drumming.

Another musical highlight is provided by yet another jazz-man, Victor Feldman, perhaps best known for his sympathetic ballad playing on Miles' classic *Seven Steps To Heaven* album. Here, on 'I Got The News', a reasonably straightforward love-and-lust song, he gets in some angular, Monkish licks that enhance an otherwise monotonous rhythm backup. But despite all these jazz references, this definitely ain't no jazz album. Nor is it (God forbid) a fusion/crossover album. I'd prefer to leave the labelling to someone else.

Despite the varied groups of musicians, the record's continuity comes from Fagen/Becker's insistence on writing songs with long melodic lines and almost sombre harmonies (even on the up-tempo cuts). Fagen's singing is appropriately dramatic without pushing it too hard, i.e. he's not a very good singer but he sings it well. The lyrics have a way of covering themselves, of protecting themselves from the vulnerable emotions they arise from.

'Black Cow' is, on the surface, a song of rejection, but it doesn't take too much scratching to see the feelings of compassion that inform it. 'Deacon Blues' is a romantic loner's song, but when the singer reaches the point of self-pity that lurks behind the loner's image – 'I cried when I wrote this song' – he immediately regains his distance from the listener with the next line – 'Sue me if I play too long'.

If you're willing to invest some feeling with your listening, you'll discover a richness of emotion here, both musically and lyrically, that makes this one of the most satisfying records of the year. And even if you'd prefer to listen casually, there are enough hooks here (as opposed to *The Royal Scam*) to keep you coming back for more.

2

Retrospective review of
Aja

Daryl Easlea, bbc.co.uk,
2011

———

If ever a record knew its worth, it was *Aja*, the sixth album by
Steely Dan. Released in late 1977 when half the world seemed
to be down the disco and the other half were pogo-ing, here came
an album that oozed detached sophistication, using every trick
that keyboard player and vocalist Donald Fagen and guitarist
Walter Becker had mastered over their first decade together.

Following on from 1976's *The Royal Scam*, any notion of Steely
Dan being 'a band' had gone, with a huge stream of well over
forty highly skilled session musicians creating textures to support Becker and Fagen's musical vision. As a result, you get a
masterclass in laidback solos and awkward time signatures, all
beneath a highly polished surface.

At the time of the album's release, Fagen said, 'We write the
same way a writer of fiction would write. We're basically assuming the role of a character, and for that reason it may not sound

personal.' Becker added that 'this is not the Lovin' Spoonful. It's not real good-time music'. It's true – these seven tracks are like miniature works of fiction, paying no mind to length or rock convention.

Aja was (is) a very influential work. In Scotland, Ricky Ross heard the song 'Deacon Blues' and named his band after it, while 'Peg' is widely known because of De La Soul's sampling of it for 'Eye Know'. The jaunty 'Josie' and the sublime title-track are further stand-outs on a record that barely breaks its bossa nova beat. It is impossible to hear this record without thinking about LA sunshine, even though Fagen's lyrics were often nostalgic, ironic and bitter; hardly surprising for a group that named itself after a – ahem – marital aid from William Burroughs' *Naked Lunch*.

To complete the feeling that you were holding an old jazz album in your hands, the original pressings came in a gatefold sleeve with a note from ABC Records' president Steve Diener and the mock reverential critique by 'Michael Phalen': 'In this writer's opinion, *Aja* signals the onset of a new maturity and a kind of solid professionalism that is the hallmark of an artist that has arrived.' Phalen was, of course, Becker and Fagen.

To emphasise its importance, in 2011 *Aja* was deemed by the Library of Congress to be 'culturally, historically or aesthetically important' and added to the United States National Recording Registry. But with or without such an accolade, *Aja* remains a remarkable piece of work.

<u>3</u>

Steely Dan Dare to give Sylvie Simmons a more-open-than-usual interview

Sylvie Simmons, *Sounds*,
22 October 1977

It's not every day that Steely Dan bare their souls to the public. But amid the palm trees and coke bottles at the Bel Air hotel, all was revealed – if not all, at least a lot for Steely Dan.

Warning: at times this interview degenerates into the Becker and Fagen Laugh-In, a crazy double-act, in which Walter B. (bass, vocals, long hair) and Donald F. (keyboards, vocals, Brooklyn drawl, shades) play off each other with the sole purpose of pushing unstable journalists over the edge.

Beach boys Becker and Fagen left their Malibu home for nearby Bel Air to promote their latest offering, *Aja* – follow-up to last year's *The Royal Scam* and their sixth album since the birth of the Dan in '72.

This one is not, despite the rumours they've spread to the

contrary, a double album in the States (sense of humour, remember?). It just looks like one. They needed a gatefold cover to fit all those sleeve notes on. Journalist Michael Phalen's terrifying tale of an interview rife with insults and threats and a CIA-like confiscation of the tape, a warning to would-be interviewers, balanced with some real-nice-guys-type praise from the president of ABC records; can they be talking about the same people?

Part I: Aja, an oriental name of no significance, probably Korean

Did you start out with any particular idea or concept in mind?

Donald Fagen: We do it song by song. We don't really plan the shape of an album, except perhaps subliminally. First, in this album we ended up with too many medium or slow-tempo songs, so we went in and cut a couple of up-tempo ones. 'Peg' was the last cut. We had a song slated for it, 'Here in the Western World', that had originally been cut for *The Royal Scam* album. It was laying around and we liked it a lot, but it didn't fit on *Scam* and we thought we had too many songs in that tempo on this album, so it's still sitting around. We'll get it out sooner or later.

Are you influenced, or put under any pressure, by what your fans expect of you?

DF: No, not really. We really aim to please ourselves, you know.

Walter Becker: Plus, we have no way of knowing what the audience expects of us.

DF: I think we put pressure on ourselves. I think we've topped ourselves with every succeeding album in quality.

WB: Good for you! I never know for sure. I have a good feeling about this one, but it's too hard to tell when you've been working on it for as long as we have. I mean, you can't listen to it objectively any more without dissecting it in your mind in a funny kind of way, because you know how it was put together. But I'm really proud of it. Now I can forget about it and start the next one.

DF: I usually think the one we just did is better than the last one. Must be something to do with our mood rings, I guess. When we were writing this our mood rings were green.

Any particular favourite?

WB: The title song I like. It was an interesting cut. We'd gotten this drummer we didn't know but had heard a lot about, named Steve Gadd – he was flown in from New York. We had a chart for the tune and it was like eight pages long – three music stands in front of every musician. What's on the charts is very specific for some of the players – like the keyboards – but very open for others. Like, there's nothing written for the bass player except the chord symbols, the guitar player basically works on his own concept, and particularly the drummer – he really had to outdo himself on that one.

No track immediately offers itself as a single. Are you releasing one?

WB: I'm sure we will, but I don't know which tune it will be. When we write the songs and prepare the album, we really don't concern ourselves with that, because we're not a good judge collectively of what's going to strike the public's ear in that way. And a lot of our things are too long – there's all kinds of restrictions in radio here, it can't be more than two minutes long or something.

DF: It's a very unlikely choice for American radio because of the length of the cut.

WB: They're still a very puritanical society as far as the media goes. I think it's loosening up a bit, but not on Top 40 radio. You're allowed to have simulated orgasms on record . . .

WB: Yes, as long as you do it quietly.

Part II: The way we were and the way we are now

You started out as pop song writers, didn't you? [After two years as back-up musicians for '60s pop-harmony group Jay & the Americans, Gary Katz, their producer, found them a cosy niche at ABC as staff songwriters. One of their pop songs, titled 'I Mean To Shine', was recorded by no less than Barbra Streisand.]

WB: Well, not really. We tried to be, but we weren't. When we came out to ABC we were hired as staff writers; we would be writing songs for their artist roster. We knew very well that what we were going to do was end up with our own band, recording our own songs, as no one else particularly wanted to record our songs. Then and now. So we just kind of played at that for a while, then once we had the band assembled we said, 'Hey, we're ready to record,' and that's it.

We had what is now a studio at ABC, which was then under construction, making more offices for accountants or something. Anyway, there were these empty offices, and they were nailing up stuff during the day. We had all our amplifiers in one of these rooms. After six we went over there with the band and rehearsed for a couple of hours. That's where we got our first album together. [Original members Jeff Baxter, Dave Palmer and Jim Hodder have long since passed on. The only old Dan remaining is guitarist Denny Dias. Otherwise it's session men – the best.]

How did you come across the musicians on *Aja*?

WB: We hear them on records . . .

DF: We meet them at parties . . .

WB: Yeah, and we ask other musicians about them, and go out and buy more records, and hear about them that way. Then we just call them up and hire them and see what happens. Sometimes we run into cases where we thought we had the perfect musicians for a particular thing, but then nothing happens and we all go home early. Usually something happens because we check out as much as we can – what kind of musicians they are, what they're capable of and best at.

They're quite happy to adapt to your concept?

WB: It seems to happen by itself because of the nature of the songs, and because of the kind of freedom they have at the sessions. In other words, there are certain things – certain harmonics and certain motifs in our music – they do have to pay attention to. And I guess that's what takes care of the continuity in the sound. But they also have a certain freedom. There are always sessions where they can play a little more than they do at most of the other things, and do what they do best, rather than being too confined. We never ask anybody to consciously adapt to our style. In fact, a lot of musicians come here, and I don't think they have any idea of what our style is – don't know or care.

Will you ever get a permanent band together?

DF: We use a lot of the same players anyway. On the last three albums – like, Victor Feldman's been on all three, Chuck Rainey's always at the sessions, and Larry Carlton. We actually have a band with a few substitutions.

Part III: In which the Dan are content to sit in Malibu and live off their royalties

Rumour has it that you'll be touring the States before long. [Steely Dan haven't toured since '74. Their only visit to Europe was a year earlier]

WB: Not that I know of! We had intended to tour, but the album release was delayed, so we put it off. Now we've no plans to tour.

DF: Making these records pretty well takes up our time. Once we've finished one, we start the next. That's the reason we haven't been touring.

WB: Touring is an expensive hobby.

DF: We spend money on a tour. We have an expensive set-up. We don't like playing big halls – the sound is bad. So we have four thousand people coming in, and it's not enough money to meet the expenses of putting on a show.

WB: And we spend a longer time preparing our albums, I guess, than other people do.

DF: Stevie Wonder spent two years on his record.

WB: But we found from past efforts that being on the road wasn't enhancing what we were doing in the studio. So we decided that we'd do either one thing or the other.

Do you go see other bands?

WB: Very rarely. In concert halls here you get a lousy sound, parking costs a buck and stuff like that. No.

Part IV: Lyrics, language problems, black humour and the American Dream

Your lyrics have sometimes been called impersonal.

WB: We don't feel the urgent need to bare our souls that Ted Nugent probably does, or Kiss or Queen or Black Death or the Bees' Knees or . . . [collapses in laughter]

DF: We write the same way a writer of fiction would write. We're basically assuming the role of a character, and for that reason it may not sound personal. But I try to assume the role and make it believable – not to the extent of doing dialects . . .

WB: . . . I've heard you do dialects . . .

DF: I say his words, try to express some of his emotions, some of his problems, hang-ups – primarily the hang-ups.

WB: This is not the Lovin' Spoonful. It's not real good-time music. Anyway, we think those are happy thoughts.

DF: It's a part of life, so why not enjoy it?

WB: Also, we feel that these give us the more fertile ground that we've been trampling on for the last five years. It's hard to keep trying to write songs about something you haven't written about before – you keep coming back to the same themes. There's some truth in the fact that happy situations tend to be more or less static and not that interesting to hear about.

DF: When you read a novel in which there are no rough spots for the characters to get over, if everybody did the hustle from the first page to the last, it wouldn't be much of a novel. It wouldn't enlighten you in any way.

Do you look on your lyrics as enlightening?

WB: Not in a Buddhist sense.

DF: But they do shed light on certain situations. I think a lot of people in Britain know about Haitian divorces now that probably didn't before.

WB: Of course, you can't get a Haitian divorce anymore. You used to be able to go to Haiti and get a divorce real fast. They give you this document in French with ribbons and plumes and everything, and it's recognised by the American government. In a way, that's enlightening. It's a situation people probably thought we made up. There are probably people out there who think we made up the name Haiti. We've been accused of everything else.

DF: There are people who think we made up the word 'Aja'.

But your lyrics are nothing if not obscure.

WB: To us it's a perfectly straightforward story. On the other hand, if anyone finds the lyrics obscure, there's always the music. So, even if you don't know anything about Haitian divorces –

DF: You can always look in the *Steely Dan Listener's Companion*.

WB: We feel that we use basically the English language. In the United Kingdom, I don't know if people know what the word 'scam' means. There was some question as to whether the word 'pretzel' makes sense to English people. There were a lot of reviewers asking us what a pretzel was.

DF: So it's basically just a language problem.

WB: We hadn't anticipated either of those things. So it may appear to people in the United Kingdom that we are writing very much in code.

They're pretty cynical, though, and bitterly realistic.

WB: A lot of what you'd call bitter or cynical, we'd call funny.

DF: We think these are very funny songs that we're writing. And when we're writing them, we really do have a grand old time yukking it up about the lyrics.

WB: We may have a slightly blacker sense of humour than your average person. I'm always surprised that divorces and things aren't funnier than they are. The American Dream? That's very funny too.

What about your home, California?

WB: I think that's very funny – it's probably the funniest of the fifty states that I know of.

DF: We're not as negative as the Eagles. They're totally down on California.

WB: When we first came out here it was pretty different from New York, and it does give you a creative vacuum in which to work. It gave us some new characters and new ideas, and it gave us a laboratory-type sterile atmosphere to work in. Because if you walk down the street here in California, you'll be the only person doing it. Nobody gets out of their cars here. It's a different kind of society.

Part V: Time to light another cigarette, get some fresh game and discourse on books, films and fans

WB: We're pretty bookish guys.

DF: In our profession, we're as bookish as I've met. But I think that's more a reflection on what everyone else is doing than what we're doing. I think people should be asking themselves why they're so goddam illiterate.

What do you read?

WB: I like instruction booklets a lot, science-fiction and re-cipes. My favourite author in the English language is Vladimir Nabokov. Of course, he just recently died. So I feel that now he's dead, he won't be writing anymore, so I have nothing new to look forward to until they start publishing whatever they can find in his apartment.

DF: I read novels, history, anything that's lying around. The only things I don't read much are self-help manuals or poetry.

What would you say is the effect of your lyrics on the audience?

WB: We hear from a few psychotic fans, threatening and malign-ing us or alternatively renting huge football stadiums to perform in and telling us after the fact or writing to us in strange languages . . .

DF: If a person's on the edge, you know, we could probably throw him off.

WB: We're just trying to cheer people up, Also, we're thinking about writing a movie.

How near to a reality is that?

WB: Very far. It's just . . .

DF: Just a gleam in Irving Azoff's eyes.

WB: It's the potential ringing of cash registers in our manager's mind. Irving's been encouraging us. He keeps telling us, 'Hey, if you guys can write these songs you can write movies, it's the same thing. You just fill out a couple of hundred pages with the same story on it.'

Part VI: Heroes and villains; featuring a change of record company and Irving Azoff's strange disease

Another quote. Mike McDonald [keyboards on *Katy Lied*, back-up vocals on *Aja*] said you'd like to have been Duke Ellington and Charlie Parker.

WB: I'd rather be Charlie Parker than anything.

DF: Everyone would like to be possessed of genius.

WB: Those are a couple of our heroes. Do you mind being Duke if I'm Charlie?

DF: No, I'll be Duke Ellington.

WB: We have other heroes, other jazz musicians, but those are two particularly outstanding examples.

DF: Like Root Boy Slim [sings 'Put a quarter in the juke, boogie till you puke']. He's the sound of the '70s. When Root Boy goes [sings 'Awl-riite'] that's the sort of thing that can really get us going.

Why are you changing record companies? [Steely Dan have one more album to do with ABC before moving to Warners]

WB: When we realised our contract was going to be up, we shopped around.

DF: We were just going to sign up with ABC, but they didn't want us – enough.

WB: They weren't putting up the same amount that Warner Brothers was. And they have this nice building at Burbank, Warners . . .

DF: Knotty pine . . .

WB: Very ethnic. This move will mark a new development in the band's career, because from that point on, instead of that ABC label in the centre of the records, there's going to be a WB label with palm trees . . .

DF: . . . coconuts, everything.

WB: Actually, the reason we signed with them was because of Bugs Bunny and Daffy Duck being Warner Brothers characters. We try to catch the Bugs Bunny show in the afternoons when we can. Of course, you can't see it every day, so that influenced our decision a lot.

Any other reason?

WB: Irving Azoff, our manager, wants us to come out and socialise, mix with the other guys from the other bands a lot more now.

DF: We were supposed to go to the Eagles' wedding.

WB: No, that wasn't the Eagles' wedding; it was Jimmy Buffett's wedding . . .

DF: . . . or birthday party.

WB: We couldn't make it. I was in San Francisco and the wedding was in Colorado. Irving got some kind of amoeba disease which we tried to keep secret. The water supply in Colorado is a little tainted. We want people to know that so they won't go there and ski.

Part VII: The Future

WB: We've already started writing our next album, and of course we'll be working on the theme song for Irving Azoff's forthcoming movie. That's about all – Donald's going to learn how to drive his new Jaguar.

DF: We're buying up options on science-fiction stories to be made into movies, going down to Washington DC to see Root Boy a lot.

WB: We're going to branch out and start to merchandise the Steely Dan name . . .

DF: . . . Steely Dan breakfast meats . . .

WB: . . . Kewpie dolls and things like that. Anything we can put the Steely Dan name on and sell for some of the coin of the realm. That way we can become real capitalists. That's the only thing left for us.

DF: Except for politics, and that's so boring.

WB: Anyway, Irving's going to run for governor of California next year. So I guess we're just going to keep on doing the same thing we've been doing all along. Whatever that is.

4

Retrospective review
of *Gaucho*

Ian MacDonald, *Uncut*,
March 2002

───────────

rassness is contagious. Fortunately, so is intelligence – which
is why listening to Steely Dan is good for you, whereas grind-
ing your ears on, say, the Butthole Surfers mostly isn't.

However, aside from an early flurry of good reviews, *Gaucho*
(1980), the Dan's seventh album, has never been critically rated
and figures relatively low in fan priorities, only *Katy Lied* (1975)
being less admired. The fourteen or so months spent recording
the album were something of an endurance test, the music being
squeezed out in the face of endless problems. After *Gaucho*,
Walter Becker and Donald Fagen drifted apart and no new Steely
Dan music was recorded for twenty years. Over time, the verdict
on *Gaucho* has been coloured by this – unjustly, since apart from
being the pair's biggest-selling album after *Aja* (1977), it's one of
their wittiest works and, while low-keyed and dryly detached, is
by no means as cold as it's often been painted.

In fact, detachment, good and bad, is the album's main theme. *Gaucho* shows the first world as a decadent drive-in peopled by stud-eyed users, preposterous losers and those for whom cocaine is God's way of telling them their wallets are too plump – this vision being a manifest offence against the poverty of the third world (Mexico and all points south of the border), which can drive undetached souls mad with loathing. One distances oneself from this with irony or one succumbs to it. The deeper irony is that Becker and Fagen weren't quite as distanced as they would ideally have liked. The success of their previous album, *Aja* (five million units shifted in two years), allowed them, for the first time, to indulge. In earlier years, studio costs had eaten up their profits. Fagen would fantasise affluence by hopping into the limos of financially successful fellow artists and riding round the block. Before *Aja*, he was considering becoming an English teacher if things didn't look up. When they did, it was hard not to spend a little, then a little more, on the Cuervo gold and fine Colombian.

Cocaine was key to the mechanised drive of the disco beat that Fagen and Becker wished to emulate, partly as an emblem of the cultural deterioration they so enjoyed chronicling and partly because, when done creatively (as, for example, by Dr Buzzard's Original Savannah Band, a New York dance outfit Fagen liked), the rhythmic precision of the discoid effect catered to the duo's need for perfection. Using one of the first programmable drum machines, the Linn 9000, together with a computerised drum sequencer called WENDEL, they set about building their tracks from the drums up, sometimes replacing each synthetic beat with a real one played by a live drummer, a process that took hours. Instruments would be added, often to be later erased or edited. Months could be spent working on the same track.

While Becker and Fagen were notorious perfectionists, minutely attentive to the tiniest blemishes, Fagen was probably the more neurotic, his drive to eliminate anomalies and square off every awry detail leading to legendary feats of fussiness and the nickname 'Mother'. While recording 'Home At Last' on *Aja*, he reportedly spent four days punching in the words 'Well, the' (as in 'Well, the danger on the rocks is surely past'). During mixing on *Gaucho* at Village Recorders in LA, Fagen encountered his ideal: one of Neve's earliest automated desks, which allowed incremental tweaking of infinitesimal details. After the 250th mix of 'Babylon Sisters', the maintenance crew awarded him a 'platinum' floppy disk, hand-painted with silver nail polish. When engineer Elliot Scheiner reached mix 274, Fagen decided an acceptable compromise had been reached and took it home to New York. A week later, everyone was back in the studio to fix the second bass note in the second bar, which Mother had noticed was too soft.

Steely Dan's quest for perfection – which encompassed throwing out four or five half-finished tracks that weren't deemed up to scratch (known titles: 'I Can't Write Home About You', 'Kulee Baba', 'Heartbreak Souvenir') – is justified by the result, in which every bar repays close attention and every instrument has its own lustre. (Done in 1984, MCA's original CD transfer was presented in relatively dull, low-level sound. The 2001 update, the last instalment of the remaster programme commenced in 1998, brightens and amplifies the sound, recovering the sharpness of the original LP.)

Such high standards, however, come at the cost of studio time and nervous tension. When, in December 1979, an assistant engineer accidentally recorded calibration tones over most of what had been shaping up as the album's best track, 'The Second Arrangement', Becker and Fagen were thunderstruck. After a half-hearted shot at re-recording it, they sanctified it as the most perfect track they'd ever attempted and glumly fell back on a number left over from *Aja* called 'Were You Blind That Day?', rewriting it as 'Third World Man' and importing it more or less complete with Larry Carlton's guitar solo.

'Third World Man' turned out to be a silver lining, surviving into Steely Dan's 1993–4 touring set, but worse was to come. In January 1980, Becker's girlfriend died of a drug overdose. Already remote and unreliable due to his heroin habit, he withdrew even further before being removed from the picture when, in April, he was knocked down by a New York cab, incurring fractures to his right leg. Fagen took over the mixing tiller and further months dragged by, made worse by a background of contractual disputes with ABC Records.

Despite this, gloom never descended on these sessions, thanks to the team's confidence in the quality of the music. With demonstration pieces such as 'Babylon Sisters' and the highly complex and sophisticated title track aboard, not to mention soon-to-be-cherished Dan characters such as Jive Miguel and Hoops McCann, there was no need to fret. The album even contained an unlikely Top 10 single in 'Hey Nineteen', scheduled to resound surreally in US supermarkets during 1981 ('the Cuervo gold, the fine Colombian . . . '). Indeed, *Gaucho*, while downbeat, is never depressive and sometimes almost merry.

From verse to verse, deadpan laughter is rarely absent, though it can take a dry ear to appreciate it. Though anyone can smile at lines like 'Brut and charisma/Poured from the shadow where he stood' and 'I loved you more than I can tell/But now it's stomping time', it requires a specialist to guffaw at 'Love's not a game for three', let alone every other syllable of the title track. Suffice to say, if you don't find 80 per cent of *Gaucho* hilarious, you shouldn't vex yourself with *The Larry Sanders Show*. The only departure from the ruling mood of hood-eyed mockery is the album's sombre finale, 'Third World Man', which, with its melancholy story of demented youthful idealism gone psychotic, reaches a depth of tragedy rarely achieved in rock.

In 'Third World Man', the only uncynical soul in the cheerless world of *Gaucho* goes crazy. Steely Dan always cruised little more than a block away from nihilism and, on this album, the corrosive irony is deeply encrusted. Two songs are about hookers, two more the doings of coke dealers, and a fifth depicts the denouement of a seedy marital dispute. Even the sublime enlightenment of 'Time Out Of Mind' turns out to be chemical. What redeems it all is the humour and artistry. Lyrics exude class as well as underclass, while the music, whatever its guise or disguise, is immaculate.

Steely Dan's funniest album is also their most urbane. A gem in the trashcan of Californian entropy, a ray of coherent light amid LA's louche neon, a chuckling oxygen-nozzle dropped through the smog of modern nothingness, *Gaucho* sort of loves us – give or take a sin or ten. Which is about as much good news as we deserve.

Disaster and Triumph in the Custerdome

Robert Palmer, *Rolling Stone*,
5 February 1981

'**Y**ou got to shake it, baby, you got to shake it, baby, you got to shake i-i-it.' The disembodied phrase, sung by six backup vocalists and stripped of its instrumental arrangement, pulsed through a pair of home-size speakers in a Manhattan recording studio.

Donald Fagen, the half of Steely Dan who plays keyboards and sings, stood squarely between the speakers, squinting intently and inhaling a cigarette in spasmodic gulps. He was wearing a black pullover, Calvin Klein jeans and Adidas tennis shoes, and he was not smiling. Neither was producer Gary Katz. Roger Nichols, Steely Dan's chief engineer, sat next to Katz at the console with a day's growth of beard. 'Hey,' he said, breaking the silence that ensued as the last 'shake i-i-it' died away. 'We could sort of make it *sound* like the fade starts there and then start the real fade a little later.'

Fagen stubbed out his cigarette and turned to face Katz and Nichols. 'You mean start a *subliminal* fade the first time through?' he asked, his voice laced with the sarcasm that Steely Dan fans have learned to love. 'Why not a *symbolic* fade?'

Katz stared into the ashtray. 'The tigers are symbolic until page 53,' he said wearily. 'Then the *lions* are symbolic and the tigers are real.'

'What about the cows?' Nichols wanted to know. 'We airlift 'em to the top of the World Trade Center, photograph 'em and call the album . . . '

' . . . *High Steaks*,' Fagen and Katz groaned. Nobody laughed, but the malaise seemed to have passed. Katz was on his feet. 'OK,' he said, 'fade thirty-five.' It was their thirty-fifth try at mixing the voices and instruments in the fifty-second fade-out at the end of 'Babylon Sisters', a song slated for *Gaucho*, the first Steely Dan album in three years.

An hour later, after about thirty more tries, the fade seemed to please everyone. 'All right, Donald,' said Katz, 'it's the perfect mix. *Now* what do you want to agonise over?'

Fagen knit his brow. 'Let's do an alternate ending without the girls,' he said. 'You know, like Francis Coppola.' Before long, they were back where they'd been, listening to the vocalists' track by itself. Fagen directed Nichols and two assistants to add minuscule helpings of echo and delay to the voices and, when they had the exact amount he wanted, he asked if they could abruptly cut out the echo after each 'i-i-it'. Nichols and Katz manned the mixing board and began punching out the last milliseconds of echo each time the phrase came to an end. 'I like that the best, I think,' Fagen said, sounding less than convinced.

'Are you happy, Donald?' Katz asked.

Fagen looked glumly at the clock; they'd been working on fifty seconds of music for four hours. 'This,' he deadpanned, 'is the happiest night of my life.'

It was the summer of 1980, and Steely Dan were not happy. *Aja*, their last album and first multi-platinum seller, had been out since the fall of 1977 and, just when they'd finally overcome a series of unexpected delays and were almost ready to mix their next LP, disaster struck. Walter Becker, the guitar-and-bass-playing half of Steely Dan, was walking back to his apartment on New York's Upper West Side late one night when an automobile came careening down the street toward him. He pushed the woman he was with out of the way but the car hit him, breaking his leg in several places and causing other injuries.

Later, relaxing on a bed in Fagen's apartment (they live in the same luxury building), Becker would joke about the incident: 'That car and me, we were attempting to occupy the same space at the same time. We were definitely in violation of certain fundamental laws of physics; we were quantum criminals.'

After the accident, Fagen, Katz and Nichols carried on with the incredibly meticulous process of making a Steely Dan album and nobody was in a joking mood. Becker gamely practised his guitar for hours at a time, but the pain was intense and there were complications, including fever and secondary infections. Fagen and Becker had been a team – as musicians, songwriters, bandleaders and finally as rock's most popular and notorious non-band – since the mid-'60s. Without Becker or, for that matter, without Fagen, there'd be no Steely Dan.

———

Before crossing paths at artsy Bard College in upstate New York, Fagen and Becker were budding instrumentalists and song-writers. Fagen, thirty-one, who was born in Passaic, New Jersey, and grew up near Princeton, heard jazz at an early age; his mother had been a big-band vocalist and would play records by the likes of Tommy Dorsey, Helen O'Connell and Sylvia Syms. By the time he was eleven, he was listening to Symphony Sid's jazz radio show; a turning point came when he found a record he'd heard Sid play, pianist Red Garland's *Jazz Junction*. 'I went down to E. J. Korvette's [US department store],' he says, 'and there it was, right in this bin, along with a lot of albums with unfamiliar names. I bought it and ever since then I've tried to imitate his style in the privacy of my own home.' Fagen took 'three or four' piano lessons, and later spent a summer at the Berklee College of Music in Boston. 'But I never had the patience to become a professional musician,' he insists. 'There are great gaps in my musical know-ledge; I'm mostly self-taught.'

Becker, thirty, grew up in Queens and also tuned into jazz at a young age, via late-night radio shows and albums by the Dave Brubeck quartet. Both future Steelies had been excited by early rock'n'roll: 'I liked Chuck Berry's records,' Fagen says, 'because of the lyrics and that sort of nasty, strident sound. But after I started listening to jazz, I developed a strong prejudice against rock'n'roll, which I didn't lose until 1966 when I heard some of the English bands.'

With Becker it was much the same. 'I bought rock'n'roll records first,' he says, 'but after I got *the word*, I gave away all my little records with the big holes; I put away childish things.'

Fagen and Becker were, in fact, jazz snobs but, by 1965, when they struck up an acquaintance, rock'n'roll was beginning to interest them again. In fact, Fagen was leading a rock'n'roll band – of sorts. 'He had a three-man guitar section,' Becker recalls, 'one guy who played badly and offensively, one guy who played very crudely and one guy who just wore the guitar in an interesting way.'

At the time, Donald was attempting to incorporate jazz ideas into his music, with considerable resistance from his band. Then he heard Walter play guitar 'with a little amplifier turned up all the way, bending notes and getting sustain. He'd been listening to all these Howlin' Wolf and B.B. King records. Well, I'd never really heard anything like that.' Before long, the two were inseparable. They led several college bands, including a jazz trio and various rock units, one of which included drummer Chevy Chase. After Walter quit school ('My services were no longer required') and Fagen graduated, they settled in New York and began haunting the Brill Building, hoping to sell their songs to the music publishers who rented offices there.

The songs, some of which made it onto the first Steely Dan album several years later, were not exactly Brill Building material. The harmonies were circuitous, dense and jazzy and the words were difficult if not utterly impenetrable. The duo scored isolated successes, most notably placing their 'I Mean to Shine' on a Barbra Streisand album, but for more than a year they eked out a living as backup musicians for Jay & the Americans. During this period they met Gary Katz, a struggling independent producer who actually liked their music.

One day, Katz called from Los Angeles, where he'd gone to work as an A&R man at ABC Records. 'He said he'd got us a job as staff songwriters and we should come at once,' Fagen remembers. 'We went. We found places to live in Encino, this oasis of nothing in the middle of a desert, and every morning we'd hitch a ride to West Hollywood where we had an office and a piano. ABC was involved in commercial AM singles; they had the Grass Roots, Tommy Roe, stuff like that. But they wanted to get into the "underground" and sell albums too, so they'd hired Gary, who could certainly pass any criterion for being underground at that time. He neglected to tell them that, with underground music, you don't need staff writers. It was obvious we weren't gonna make it doing that, so with Gary's help we put together a group and started rehearsing in the ABC building.'

Can't Buy A Thrill, the first Steely Dan album, was released in 1972. It was different: jazz harmony, rhythms that drew on soul and Latin prototypes and intensely lyrical guitar solos. To ABC's surprise, the album yielded two AM hits, 'Do It Again' and 'Reelin' In The Years'.

'ABC got us a manager and sent us out on the road,' says Fagen. 'At first it was really a nightmare. After the record took off, we were able to add more people and, once we'd done two or three records, the gigs got better. I mean, we weren't opening for the James Gang and Uriah Heep any more – we were opening for Elton John. By the time we closed down shop in 1974, we were headlining.'

At that juncture, the five-man Dan (guitarists Jeff Baxter and Denny Dias, drummer Jim Hodder, Becker on bass, Fagen on lead vocals and keyboards) had added several backup singers (including future Doobie Brother Michael McDonald), a percussionist and a second drummer, Jeff Porcaro, now a Los Angeles studio mainstay. 'Bodhisattva', the B-side of Steely Dan's current hit single 'Hey Nineteen', was recorded by this final configuration at the Dan's next-to-the-last gig. Although it's a tight, energetic performance and Fagen admits that 'the band was presentable', Steely Dan's intensely self-critical perfectionism was already much in evidence. 'I would see shows I thought were just incredible,' remembers Katz, 'some of the best rock'n'roll shows I ever saw. Then I'd go backstage and Donald and Walter would be sitting with their heads in their hands, complaining about how rotten they'd been.'

After they toured to support their third album, *Pretzel Logic* (their second LP, *Countdown To Ecstasy*, featured extended soloing and is named by many Dan fans as their favourite), Becker and Fagen decided that enough was enough. 'We took the band apart in a decisive fashion,' says Becker, 'so that it could not be put back together and we could not be sent out on the road. What were they gonna send, me and Donald with banjos?' Adds Fagen: 'It was 1974, and the mystique of rock was starting to fade, certainly as a cultural item. The concert scene seemed sleazy to us and we weren't satisfied with the way the band was clicking. It was taking a tremendous psychic and physical toll on us. Basically, we couldn't hack it; we just didn't want to live that way anymore.' Becker concludes: 'It takes a certain disposition to really enjoy what that life has to offer. And the less said about what it has to offer, the better.'

———

On *Pretzel Logic*, Steely Dan had already been augmented by a large number of session musicians. With 1975's *Katy Lied*, the group officially became Fagen, Becker and a veritable army of studio professionals. But the team that had shaped the music since the beginning – Fagen, Becker, Katz and Nichols – remained intact, and so did Walter and Donald's personal vision. Though they were living in LA, they wrote about New York's Lower East Side ('Daddy Don't Live in That New York City No More'), dope deals in South Florida (the unforgettable 'Doctor Wu', with a perfect one-take solo from jazz saxophonist Phil Woods) and, on 1976's *The Royal Scam*, aging acid chemists, gun-waving psychos and the plight of Puerto Rican immigrants in New York ghettos.

The songs were getting longer and more complex, with harmonies so convoluted even studio pros had trouble with them. The lyrics were getting more ambitious. 'Aja' tackled the west's double-edged fascination with the east; 'Home At Last' was a distillation of a key episode from Homer's *Odyssey*. Yet each album sold better than its predecessor, and *Aja* made Steely Dan one of America's most popular rock acts.

Along the way, they also acquired a reputation as rock's most obsessive nit-pickers. It was said that they'd throw out a track if one note was out of place and, while that's probably an exaggeration, Fagen and Becker admit to being 'fussy'. They're particularly hard on guitar players, especially when trying to get one of the exquisite solos that grace their albums. Last fall, I spent several hours watching Fagen work on guitar parts for 'My Rival' with Rick Derringer – one of their favourite hired guns since contributing the ringing slide solo to 'Show Biz Kids' on *Countdown To Ecstasy*. Though he has a reputation as a barnstorming hard-rocker, Derringer is a well-rounded musician who executes difficult chord progressions with ease. Yet his evening with 'My Rival' was arduous.

When I arrived at Sound Works in midtown Manhattan, Derringer was sitting behind the console next to Fagen, looking over a chart and cradling a guitar. 'A little too much treble,' Fagen and Katz agreed. Before long, everyone liked the sound, and they began working on some punctuating figures that might recur throughout the song. 'Do something here like this,' Fagen suggested, humming a figure. Derringer picked it up and executed it flawlessly. 'But it shouldn't come in there,' Donald decided. 'It should come in in a funny place.' Derringer tried a tricky syncopation and Fagen suggested an even trickier one. 'OK,' he said when Rick had mastered that, 'now play it up an octave, and kinda like this.' He clenched and unclenched his fist to demonstrate the play of rhythmic tension and relaxation he wanted. 'And don't use so many of the high strings when you're playing that fall-off.'

After working on the song's eight-bar introduction for more than an hour, Fagen concluded, 'OK, the phrases are all in the right place.'

Katz disagreed. 'The last one,' he said, 'is desperately late.'

'Well,' said Fagen, 'they're all right *stylistically.*'

'Christ,' said Derringer, who'd been bearing up like a trouper. 'You guys are just a buncha punks, that's all.' After a few more adjustments, they started recording, and eventually Derringer's punctuations met with everyone's approval.

Then it was time to move on to the solo – more guitar playing by committee. After they worked on it for an hour, I began to feel restless. In the studio lobby, I encountered Rick's wife, Liz. 'Poor Rick,' I said, 'they're really putting him through it.'

'That's OK,' she said. 'He loves playing for them.'

When *Gaucho* was finally released, I was surprised to find that while Derringer's punctuations could still be heard on 'My Rival', the solo was by Steve Khan. 'The parts Rick did were voted "Yes",' said Fagen, 'the solo was voted "No".'

There were brighter moments, like the night Fagen and Katz pitched a baseball back and forth across the studio. On another occasion, Fagen complained that he couldn't listen properly after hours of going over the fine points of a mix, and he wandered into the studio to play the piano. He ran through some credible modern jazz, including several standards and a difficult Thelonious Monk tune. His technique wasn't spectacular, but he enlivened the music with creative chord voicings and rhythmic suspensions.

Katz listened for a while and then sat down to talk. 'I would like to think the next album won't take this long,' he said. 'Donald and I depend on Walter to do some things that we've had to do and that slowed us down. There were other factors that delayed us. An engineer accidentally erased a completed track. That was one of the most serious emotional setbacks we've had in the studio. At the time, it was my favourite tune on the album. We started it again from scratch, building up the rhythm arrangement, the guitars, the voices and, when that didn't pan out, we had to start another tune from scratch.' The new number turned out to be 'Third World Man', perhaps *Gaucho*'s most striking piece of music.

There were other setbacks, too. The death of a close friend earlier in the year had devastated Becker, and *Gaucho* had gotten off to a slow start. 'We took some time off after *Aja* came out,' says Fagen, 'and then we tried putting a touring band together, as per a contractual agreement. We had several rehearsals, and I noticed I had lost my enthusiasm for reproducing what we had already created on records; it seemed artificial. Besides, we'd asked the musicians how much money they wanted and given it to them, but they didn't all ask for the same amount. When they found out some were getting more than others, there was a socialist revolt. We didn't feel like being perceived as capitalists, so we called the whole thing off. That took time. And then we went back into the studio before we had a selection of songs that met with our standards, and with some misconceived ideas.'

As *Gaucho* neared completion, Steely Dan manager Irving Azoff attempted to find out how many records the Dan had sold before ABC was absorbed into the MCA conglomerate. According to his accounting, ABC owed Fagen and Becker several million dollars in royalties, and MCA was asked to pay. MCA claimed that the royalties were not its responsibility but, after some legal wrangling, paid part of them. The label also said that since the Dan had owed ABC one more album, *Gaucho* was rightfully MCA's. A judge declared that the album did indeed belong to MCA but that the Dan were then free to move to Warner Bros., their label of choice. With that settled, *Gaucho* reached the stores in a matter of days. It was immediately added to virtually every FM rock playlist in the country and bulleted into the Top 20, rapidly surpassing *Aja*'s performance.

With *Gaucho* launched, Fagen and Becker were ready to talk under less-pressured circumstances and I met them one night at Fagen's apartment. Becker, who was stretched out on the bed, was still having difficulty moving and didn't stir throughout our three-hour conversation. Although friends had worried several months earlier that he was in an emotional tailspin, Becker seemed to be in excellent spirits. I'd been wondering about the Custerdome, which is where most of the action takes place in the song 'Gaucho' and, when I asked what it was, Walter chortled.

'It's, ah, it's one of the largest buildings in the world,' he said, indicating with his self-righteous tone and arched eyebrows that I was an imbecile for having to ask. 'You know, an extravagant structure with a rotating restaurant on top.' His act was so convincing that I fell for it.

'Where is it?' I asked.

'It exists only in our collective imagination,' said Fagen. 'In the Steely Dan lexicon, it serves as an archetype of a building that houses great corporations . . . '

' . . . And yet becomes a recreational centre for the business-men's bounce set, the, uh, butter-and-egg set,' added Becker.

'Named after *General* Custer, of course,' I managed to say, laughing uncontrollably.

'Of course,' said Becker, 'and catering to its clientele's varie-gated whims.'

'A hint of disaster is subtly present,' Fagen noted. 'It's definitely headed for *Towering Inferno* status.'

'There is that Irwin Allen aspect,' Becker concluded. 'It's the Little Big Horn of architectural marvels.'

When Becker and Fagen write a song, they often indulge in similar dialogues, stimulating each other's fantasies and seeing where ideas will lead. 'I usually come up with the harmonic framework and basic structure,' Fagen said, 'and then Walter comes over and we take it from there. Also, a lot of the songs are a sort of testimonial for saving things. I have cassettes left over from college that contain ideas, little snatches of things. They sometimes become useful in other contexts if you keep them around long enough. For example, the chorus in "Glamour Profession" – I can't even remember when we wrote that.'

What about those complex and unexpected harmonic modu-lations, which are as challenging as the '30s' and '40s' pop classics on which many jazzmen base their improvisations? 'Just a way of making rock'n'roll but trying to keep it interesting,' said Becker.

'It's trying to do something you haven't done before that's hard to do and worth having done when you're finished. I think a lot of people in the audience are unaware that anything unusual is happening harmonically and so much the better, because there are people who are offended by that sort of thing, who think it's Ed Sullivan pop, Broadway show music. For the benefit of that portion of the audience, we try to make these things work so that they don't stick out.'

In 'Hey Nineteen', the protagonist is a fellow roughly Fagen and Becker's age who tries to pick up a nineteen-year-old in a rock'n'roll club and has trouble communicating with her, especially when he begins to lecture on the merits of soul music, a genre she's too young to remember. The music may be cleverly convoluted, but the lyric hits home with a directness that's surprising, considering Steely Dan's reputation for distanced cynicism and verbal hide-and-seek. Could Becker and Fagen be mellowing? 'We could be losing our sense of fantasy as we age,' Fagen suggested. 'Or confusing it with our sense of reality,' Becker countered, 'along with the rest of the world. But mellowing? I would hope not. I think we've maintained a healthy level of misanthropy.'

'I think that song's self-explanatory, if not strictly autobiographical,' said Fagen. 'I figured a lot of people could identify with it.'

Were they both soul fans during the '60s? 'Yeah, of course,' said Becker. 'And we're fiercely proud of our cultural heritage. In fact, we're a soul band. Just look at the guys who play with us – Bernard Purdie, Chuck Rainey, Paul Griffin. We even used to sing duets like Sam and Dave.'

'We're one of the best black bands going these days,' Fagen wisecracked. 'Aside from the Bee Gees. Despite what our individual and collective sensibilities are, our music still comes down to being some kind of R&B music.'

Becker concurred: 'It's got electric guitars, a real good backbeat; it's clear to me that it's, you know, rock'n'roll. What else could it be?'

Not everyone agrees with this assessment. Critics have taken Becker and Fagen to task for being overly slick, and for using facile studio musicians instead of gritty, spontaneous players. 'Hey Nineteen' is a rarity among recent Dan tunes in that the most prominent instruments are manned by Becker (lead guitar, bass) and Fagen (electric piano, synthesiser), and it has a more distinctive sound than any other tune on *Gaucho*. Why use so many session men?

'We've got it all,' said Fagen, 'except the fingers. Both of us have terrific feel. I think we get a lot of points for style, but technique and execution are weak; there tend to be a lot of mistakes and inconsistencies. If we can't find a studio musician who's comfortable with a particular feel, *then* we'll haul out our instruments.'

Katz thinks that Becker and Fagen drastically undervalue their own musicianship. 'I'm always trying to get them to play more on the records,' he says. 'I don't think I'll ever stop asking them to tour again. That comes purely from being a fan; I want to go see them. There were shows toward the end of their touring career that were absolutely magical. I still hope that one day, not too far away, it'll happen again. On the other hand, Donald has said to me, "It's easy for you to say we should work. You don't have to go out there and make a fool of yourself." And he's right.'

Gary Katz is a patient man, but he's probably going to have to wait a long time to see Steely Dan onstage again. Fagen and

Becker guard their privacy as obsessively as they perfect their music. They seem content to inhabit a Custerdome of their own devising, where they listen to jazz records (mostly from the '50s; the post-1960 avant-garde is one of their pet peeves), play for their own amusement and turn their rapid-fire rap sessions into quirky pop masterpieces. And with their music enjoying extraordinary critical and commercial success, who's to say they're wrong?

Donald Fagen in London, 1991.

Martyn Goodacre/Getty Images

FOUR: New Frontiersmen

'In Steely Dan, we were very arrogant kids. And when life starts to kick you around, you have to swallow your pride.'

Donald Fagen, 1993

1

Review of Donald Fagen's
The Nightfly

Charles Shaar Murray, *New Musical Express,*
23 October 1982

Ahem, where were we? Steely Dan go out on the worst album of their entire career, Walter Becker gets involved in one of those stupidly seamy Hollywood drug scandals that are the infallible identifying mark of the terminal arsehole, and Donald Fagen bides his time and eventually comes up with *The Nightfly*, an album which doesn't so much dilute the arctic smart-assery of the Dan as warm it up, loosen it up and present it in a new context: as the chosen style of a naïve, half-smart young man with fantasies of sophistication.

Fagen prefaces the album with a note to the effect that 'the songs on this album represent certain fantasies that might have been entertained by a young man growing up in the remote suburbs of a north-eastern city during the late '50s and early '60s, i.e. one of my general height, weight and build.' In other words,

Fagen can use his patented approach while mocking it and simultaneously revealing its true nature as a device.

You could almost say he has brought himself nearer to the listener in this flashback album by re-distancing himself from his distanced approach. I mean, you could say that, but I'd rather you didn't.

The music is, of course, synthesised swing served up in a rather less-unconscious-than-usual mentholated LA style. Even the album's oldie, Dion's 'Ruby Baby', gets a disturbingly cool, splintery treatment: a '50s vision of what the swinging nightclub music of the '80s would sound like. People like Larry Carlton, Jeff Porcaro, the Brecker Brothers, Chuck Rainey, Valerie Simpson and the VERY GREAT Marcus Miller (whose bass playing on Miles Davis' *Fat Time* has made him my hero for life) are along for the ride, and the end result is like something Stevie Wonder might have concocted if he were white, Jewish, sighted and in the throes of an acute attack of nostalgia for the Kennedy years.

Fagen spends a lot of *The Nightfly* playing the eagerness and optimism of his younger self for either poignancy or laughs and he kicks the album off by achieving both on 'I. G. Y. (International Geophysical Year)': 'Standing tough under stars and stripes/We can tell/the dream's in sight . . . '

His singing is light and carefree; he actually sounds younger than he did on the Dan's albums. 'New Frontier' catches the atmosphere of the excited young suburbanite trying hard to fake some boho cool and places it squarely in time: 'I hear you're mad about Brubeck/I like your eyes, I like him too . . . '

However, the two best moments come in the middle of the second side, where – in the title track – Fagen becomes the sophisticated all-night DJ he used to listen to ('an independent station/WJAZ/with jazz and conversation') and then jets off to the Caribbean for a calypsonic account of political intrigue among the synthesised steel drums that would almost sound like Creole if the musicians didn't seem to be wearing disgusting clothes and not sweating. 'The Goodbye Look' (named after a Ross McDonald novel which has absolutely nothing to do with Caribbean politics) is the most Dan-like performance on the album, and Fagen's wit suddenly regrows its fangs. 'Now the Americans are gone except for two/the embassy's been hard to reach,' sings Fagen through his teeth as the fake pans chime around him.

The Nightfly is – as I would say – a mandatory purchase for all old farts with a few Steely Dan albums stashed away at the back of the pile, and a fine introduction to Donald Fagen (single personality . . . STAR) for anyone unencumbered by any preconceptions about his past. Anybody who responds to genuine wit and craftsmanship and who is interested in a non-rocking look at the Kennedy era could do worse than investigate.

Substituting warmth for spite has not dulled Fagen's acuity one iota and he's still almost too cool. More you could ask for?

2

Donald Fagen Revisits an Era of Innocence

Fred Schruers, *Musician*,
January 1983

___

'Lack of irony,' says Donald Fagen with a wry grin, 'is not exactly my speciality.' It's an odd apology – more like a boast – from the man who shared status with his Steely Dan partner, Walter Becker, as a mandarin of pop irony.

But he's simply trying to explain that when he wrote his current hit song, 'I. G. Y.', he was doing his best to squeeze the lyrics dry of any irony. In fact, his entire solo record, *The Nightfly*, is a tale told by a young innocent who tolerates his days in a suburban high school but lives for his late-night rendezvous with the jazz music and the fantasies of tropical or oriental romance that his favourite hipster DJ purveys.

The record sounds much like the intellectual swing-time tracks that made Steely Dan famous and profitable. So why is he a solo now? 'After fourteen years, we both decided we needed a break. And about the same time, I was getting this idea to do an album that would be more personal than a lot of the stuff we were doing together.' Fagen doesn't mention Becker's recent personal torments – the death of girlfriend Karen Stanley and a subsequent lawsuit from her mother, settled out of court – but he's careful to point out that neither partner held a patent on the Steely Dan sound.

'If and when Walter does something, I think it will still have that same sound, to some extent. He grew up in Forest Hills, me in New Jersey, but he had basically the same kind of childhood musical experience and sensibility, listening to jazz. So I imagine the general sound would be very similar. I just sort of started writing my record after we finished *Gaucho* and decided to call at least a temporary halt to the collaboration. Since it's my first album, I thought it should be at least vaguely autobiographical. But I think a lot of the themes have precedents, like "Deacon Blues", on Steely Dan albums.'

The fantasy landscape *The Nightfly*'s high-school hero inhabits is 'a mythical blues country', but the world he's escaping from is quite like the one Fagen knew as a 1965 graduate of South Brunswick (NJ) High, 'a really idealistic period of the '60s, when the cold war was on, but technology (e.g., the International Geophysical Year, or I. G. Y.) and nuclear weapons were going to straighten everything out.'

So it went in the I. G. Y., in the fallout shelter where denizens of the LP's 'New Frontier' hold a party to lust after Tuesday Weld lookalikes and listen to Dave Brubeck. This is the voice of the man-child who will soon learn irony and might end up with a Haitian divorce. But meanwhile, he could stay up late and listen to 'the alternative – this hipster talking over the air in the middle of the night, sort of a cultural lifeline to Manhattan or to that blues country outside this rather arid atmosphere of the suburbs. Black music and culture was so much more compelling because it was completely outside my experience. I used to listen to Symphony Sid at the time and a lot of great jazz shows on WRVR. And I'd hear Gene Shepherd, this monologist who was a hipster type who'd talk for forty-five minutes every night. He had a vaguely subversive way of looking at America. And there were the movies that would conjure up the exotic potential for something different than the suburbs.'

Thus the Chinese 'squeeze' of the 'Green Flower Street'; the Mexican holiday with 'Maxine'; 'The Goodbye Look' one gets from the sunglassed colonel in some 'Graham Greene-ish' banana republic; the 'Walk Between Raindrops' on the Florida coast. Somehow these fantasies are engendered in our young man with his ear by the magical radio. 'Steven Spielberg makes movies about the suburbs and seems comfortable with them, but I detested the suburbs I lived in. He has his fantasies, I had mine – I think Thelonious Monk was the alien in my bedroom, rather than a little guy from outer space.'

So for young Fagen it was Monk and Miles Davis. 'I was a jazz snob, wore black turtlenecks – the only problem was you become sort of a social pariah. I didn't have many friends.' A call to central Jersey reveals that things maybe weren't all that bad. His high school yearbook blurb calls him a jazz 'enthusiast', an 'individualist', 'the thinker'. Music teacher 'Chub' Chatten remembers a shy young man who paced the gridiron with the marching band, solemnly tooting a baritone horn. His mother had been a singer with trad jazz bands, so the very young Fagen was steeped in Sinatra and Sylvia Syms. ('She quit due to stage fright,' says Fagen. 'I have a bit of that myself.') He had an early taste for Chuck Berry, too, but put that aside and ignored rock and blues until his arrival at Bard College. Walter Becker arrived at the small liberal arts school a year after Fagen, who one day heard the B.B. King disciple playing. 'I heard this guy practising guitar. There was actually a college music club and he was rehearsing. I was immediately attracted to his guitar style, which was similar to some of the black blues players. I went in and introduced myself, and that's how we got together.'

The pair started composing together 'very shortly after that. I don't know if we really had a plan. We wanted to get a band together. Our main problem was finding singers, 'cause I had never sung before. Walter had done a few gigs, before he got to college, at the Night Owl in the Village, so I was sort of hoping he would sing, but neither of us wanted to do it.'

They wrote songs and gigged occasionally while studying theory, harmony and composition. After college, Fagen, a largely self-taught keyboard player, took a year at Boston's Berklee School of Music. The duo ended up backing Jay & the Americans 'in one of their later phases – playing community gardens in Queens, that kind of scene'. Fagen liked playing 'behind a wall of backup singers. I wish we had a recording of some of those gigs. It was fun. We'd change chords to the songs, wonder if he was gonna make that long note on "Cara Mia" . . . '

Their friend Gary Katz was working in-house at ABC Records in Los Angeles, and played a demo to company head Jay Lasker. They moved out to LA as 'staff writers' for a roster that included the Grass Roots, but 'we were so bizarre we had a little trouble getting covers done of our material. The only people who actually ever recorded our tunes were John Kay, the old Steppenwolf guy, and Barbra Streisand.'

By now they'd hooked up with vocalist Dave Palmer and gui-tarist Denny Dias and with 'Reelin' In The Years', bizarre began to work just fine. The hits kept coming; in retrospect, says Fagen, it's hard to say who wrote what. 'We developed the sound together, it's very hard to say who did what. Generally, I would develop the original structure and then Walter would fool around with it and then we'd collaborate on the lyrics. Walter was very good on the recording side, he had a definite idea of what he wanted sonically and I learned a lot from him.'

The Fagen singing style, which could be so plaintively effective on songs like 'Doctor Wu', is undimmed on *The Nightfly*. It par-takes of his favourite singers – Marvin Gaye and Mose Allison among them – but has its own, elastic precision. 'Dave Palmer was a good singer for us early on, but he didn't really have the attitude to put the songs over. So I started doing it myself, much to my chagrin. It seems to have worked out.'

Indeed it has. Through a succession of stellar sidemen, Fagen's voice was the distillation of the Steely Dan sound and attitude. As he sits talking in a Warner Bros conference room, old band-mates Michael McDonald and Jeff Baxter stare at him from a carelessly stashed Doobie Bros cardboard stand-up poster. When, he's asked, was the last time Steely Dan were heard on stage? 'It was 1974, Santa Monica Civic Auditorium. The flip side of "Hey Nineteen" has a live version of "Bodhisattva" if you want to hear what the band sounded like.'

Part of the problem in recording with an ad hoc studio band, says Fagen, is 'getting the players to sound like a unit, with its own specific sound'. In making *The Nightfly*, Fagen used a Yamaha acoustic piano, Rhodes electric piano and Prophet and Oberheim synthesisers. 'I play when I feel I can handle it. I have a nice style, but I tend to be a little shaky on the technical side.' Nonetheless Fagen's LP is definitely space-age. 'For "I. G. Y." we started out with a rhythm machine to get the feel, then used a sequenced synthesiser for the backbeats, then I put down a bass line for reference using the piano, then Greg Phillinganes came in to put the basic thing down using the Rhodes. At that point we had the basic track.'

While Fagen's solo effort has a musical resemblance to Steely Dan, the words are not so wilfully arcane. 'We've been charged with obscurism a lot. I think it's probably true to some extent. Steely Dan's songs treat subjects that ordinarily aren't treated in that kind of format. If you listen to the albums, they become a little more lucid in being able to treat a sophisticated subject in a certain space.'

The Nightfly, Fagen says, is a definite throwback to some of his pre-Steelies influences. 'The title cut uses a lot of images from blues. That hair formula gets its name from Charley Patton, the old Delta blues guitarist, and Mount Belzoni gets its name from another old Mississippi blues lyric – "When the trial's in Belzoni/ No need to scream and cry". It's music I associate with a time of innocence, and in a way I can say "Goodbye" to that now. That Leiber-Stoller song "Ruby Baby" is a rearrangement of the old Drifters version. I liked the innocence of the lyrics. We needed party noises for it and, since our studio was right next to Studio 54, we surreptitiously suspended a mike from the ceiling of the club during one of Steve Rubell's "business parties". But it sounded more like a stadium crowd, so we threw a party in the studio. A lot of people got very drunk, and we got our party noises.'

It's somehow not so far from partying in the fallout shelter. There are no more 'hipster presidents' like JFK (Fagen calls his

and Lee Harvey Oswald's televised shootings 'a hell of a weekend') and innocence is hard to come by. Still, Fagen seems
determined to spend part of his time lost in blues country; beyond
plans to work on a movie soundtrack or two – Robbie Robertson's
asked him for a 'jazzy ballad' to go on the soundtrack of Martin
Scorsese's *King of Comedy* – his programme is loose. 'I'd like to
keep it open, without too much career planning – keep my ama-
teur status, you know?'

3

Walter Becker:
Breaking the Silence

Mark Leviton, *BAM*,
December 1985

O ne of the most difficult-to-understand phenomena in a musician's life is silence, the silence that comes occasionally when
a talented performer or songwriter simply stops working after
years or decades of dedication to The Muse.

Walter Becker, as co-leader and co-songwriter with Donald
Fagen in Steely Dan, has more than his share of sterling moments
to look back on. Few popular musicians have achieved fame from
the kind of idiosyncratic recordings Steely Dan issued, and fewer
still ever manage to combine left-field lyrics with a glossy, professional sound that's the envy of the industry.

Since Steely Dan's last LP *Gaucho* in 1980, Becker has remained
completely silent, while Donald Fagen has issued only one solo
album and co-produced one original cast album. But recently
Becker finally emerged with a one-off production job on China
Crisis' album *Flaunt The Imperfection*. He then flew into Los

Angeles from his home in Hawaii to do a little more nosing around in search of production work, just putting one toe back into the water of the music business he's had nothing to do with for five years.

'The last few years were a period of readjustment for me,' he says. 'I had to change certain things about the way I was living and get into a whole different groove. And that meant living in Hawaii and having no ambition to do anything in the business. I stopped practising scales on my instruments, hardly picked up a bass or played the piano and felt no pull to write songs either. Then about a year ago I started missing those leather couches, those little knobs and faders on the control panels . . . I thought producing would be a way of getting back into it without living in LA. When I was in Steely Dan, I'd get up at 4 p.m. take a shower, go to the studio and work all night, and that was all my life. For a long time, rock'n'roll was *all* I wanted to do. By switching to family life more, I lost the interest in music that used to be so central.

'I figured with production I could make my little contribution and then get out. So I dramatically announced the availability of my services to some people at Warners, which is my record label – even though Steely Dan never got around to recording anything for them. I looked over the roster and came up with China Crisis. I thought their first American album was pretty good.'

The album at moments (especially on 'Black Man Ray') sounds as if Becker had a hand in songwriting, although he's credited only with production, arrangement and a bit of synthesiser. 'As it turned out, some of the songs weren't finished when I first met them and they were counting on the producer in the process of recording to contribute certain things. Their other albums were not tremendously textured, they had a few ideas with a kind of fill-in "wash". Gary Daly and Eddie Lundon are self-taught musicians, so their parts tend to be very essential, but past that point they are not virtuosos. They used a lot of legato things, sustains. It turned out to be a good marriage as we got underway, since I was always into arrangements. In Steely Dan, with Donald and Gary Katz co-producing with me, everything took a tremendous amount of time, of boredom and repetition. The basic tracks would run by a million times. The tedium was incredible. And in doing China Crisis I tried to find alternatives to building up thick pads, of always doing that one more take to get something perfect. The guys took the title from a TV show they'd seen that sort of jokingly suggested, "If you don't have it, flaunt it."

'You see, I had to learn that in England they do a few takes and that's it. Nobody records like Steely Dan. I started to see the value of limitations in time and money. Flaws that would bother me, they wouldn't even hear. They'd tell me "flaunt the imperfection". As you can hear from Donald's solo record, there were a number of solutions to problems we developed together in Steely Dan and that's why you can hear that sound in his work alone. We had years of technique-development together. With China Crisis, a number of those things were just inappropriate, so I tried to develop different ways of dealing with problems.

'The hardest problem we had in Steely Dan was making machines not sound like machines. Now everybody uses drum machines without disguising them. Steely Dan used to get attacked for not being a "real group", because Donald and I would hire whomever we wanted to play, but today nobody much cares about that. Now you can elaborate and develop musical ideas quickly, making demos with machines. But I find that unless you are really proficient with machines, you can't afford the labour-saving devices because you're spending so much time setting them up to work right. And then you pass it in front of a tape once and it's over. What I've come back to thinking about is capturing live performance and getting away from the mechanical stuff. If you listen to "Show Biz Kids", say, you can hear how we used tape loops, and Donald especially is still enthusiastic about combining loops with machines in interesting ways.

'But in Steely Dan we could have any band we wanted and we began to arrange parts for specific players, which is a very old-line jazz kind of thing that Ellington, Basie, Monk could all do. The songs we wrote therefore grew up at least partly as *recorded* experiences. Our songs were always a little idiosyncratic and it did conspire against things like cover versions being done. People used to do one occasionally and get all the chord changes wrong. Critics used to say that the session musicians we employed weren't really creative, just robots, but if you work with the guys you know that's ridiculous. Somebody like Elliott Randall is very volatile, never plays the same thing twice. Consumers would have to hear all sixty takes before they'd realise that we could only pick one to make the record and they were all different! It's strange, but even when you record all the parts separately and each line of the vocal might be recorded on different days, the listener creates the link for you. You can almost feel the band getting excited together, even though in reality most of them never saw each other in the studio.'

Steely Dan went about things the 'wrong way' quite a bit. For instance, they almost never gave interviews and, after a brief time of touring early in their careers, were never seen live again. 'If I did want to start a solo career now,' says Becker, 'I could stay in Hawaii and send these things called videos out to tour for me.

But since I have no financial need to write songs or record and Hawaii is such a nice place to do nothing – it breeds lack of ambition, I think – I just don't have the desire. In Steely Dan, we were never really hiding from people, we just didn't act like pop stars are supposed to act. There were always magazine stories with the most outrageous statements, because no one really understood us. And I have to admit that Gary Katz, Donald and myself are all pretty odd people in certain ways. Our working relationship was very special, and we still keep in touch.'

So for the moment, Becker is only a little closer to reclaiming his rightful place in the limelight. After years of being labelled a perfectionist, he's content to leave the intensity of constant creation to others. 'I'll tell you what I find interesting about production,' he concludes. 'Someone once said it takes two people to paint a picture: one to paint and one to shoot the guy so at some point the painting will be finished. Otherwise he'd go on painting forever. That just about sums up the producer's role on rock records and it's something I'm comfortable with right now. I'm not really asking for more.'

<u>4</u>

Donald Fagen:
Reeling In The Years

Rob Steen, the *Independent*,
21 November 1991

Not before time, the man who did it again is doing it again. But, after nine years of soundtrack credits and precious little else, muffled is the only way to convey the re-emergence of Donald Fagen, a.k.a. Lester the Nightfly from WJNZ, the co-founder of the group Steely Dan, the Catcher in the Wry.

For one thing, the record that Fagen has broken his silence to promote, *Live at the Beacon* – by the sublime Rock And Soul Revue band he assembled last February (members including Michael McDonald and Boz Scaggs) – does not so much as bear his name, merely an etching of someone who might be him. For another, he has a stinking cold and has just completed a madcap dash through the Manhattan traffic after oversleeping. His condition has the additional side effect of embellishing that adenoidal, sarcastic whine – the one Nick Kent of the *New Musical Express* once referred to as 'that unique cartoon of a voice'.

For a writer who has expressed himself almost exclusively in the third person, Fagen is decidedly less detached than expected. It may be tucked away somewhere, but the infamous sneer is undetectable. The virtual silence since 1982's autobiographical album *The Nightfly* is over, usurped by a zestful warmth unimaginable in someone who until last winter had not performed live in sixteen years, let alone the man who, with help from his friend Walter Becker, had defined cynical pop while David Byrne was still in his art-school nappies.

These perceived changes have much to do with Fagen's recovery from what was evidently a painful and protracted dose of existential angst. Now that he's forty-three, a sly, fiendish grin supplies the sole clue to a legacy of scathing social dissections matched only by the songs of Randy Newman. Happily ensconced with his girlfriend and her teenage children in an apartment on New York's East Side, muse intact, the eagerness to communicate is transparent. Heavens, on his upcoming solo album he and Becker are almost as one again.

The long sabbatical suggests otherwise, but Fagen did once contend that it was possible to compose in a vacuum. Does he retain that conviction? 'No,' is the instantaneous reply, one cloaked with disbelief that he should ever have said such a thing. 'I see now that I was writing from memory, which is not really a vacuum. I think you can write from memory, but that only lasts until your memories run out. That's probably why I didn't write much in the 1980s: I needed to assemble a new bunch of memories. After *The Nightfly,* I had a kind of a writer's block. It took me a while to get over it and I did a lot of self-analysis. Mind you, the 1980s were also very boring.'

From 1972 to 1980, the fluctuating array of stellar session

musicians orchestrated by Fagen and Becker produced an acutely original, immaculately manicured body of work that dared to weld jazz to pop and evolved into something best described as 'bepop'. So effortlessly did they transcend the age barrier that the septuagenarian scientist James Lovelock recently chose Steely Dan's 'Haitian Divorce' as his first selection on *Desert Island Discs*.

'If you don't understand the words, you can always tap your foot,' advised one review of *Can't Buy A Thrill*, Steely Dan's debut. Yet tales of bodacious cowboys and big black cows were intrinsic to the whole, lending a touch of humanity to music so cool it nearly froze. That said, the messages were often obtuse. Fagen once claimed that 'no one will ever get to the bottom of "Chain Lightning"', one of three self-penned contributions to *Live At The Beacon*, and originally recorded for 1975's *Katy Lied*. 'I think the lyrics were, er, a little less lucid early on,' he concedes. 'That song was about a couple of guys going to a fascist rally – we had the Berchtesgaden [sic – Fagen may be referring to the Nazis' annual Nuremberg rallies] in mind – and then remembering it forty years later. We almost inserted a spoken part before the last verse saying "Forty years later". That might have made it clearer.'

Was working alone difficult? 'Sure, I missed the spark we gave each other,' Fagen confesses. 'But Walter and I needed a vacation from each other. After a couple of years, we'd both changed a lot.' Becker's luck certainly needed to: after breaking both legs in a car crash, he was later sued by a woman who held him responsible for the drug-induced death of her teenage daughter. Currently residing in Hawaii, he has recently produced records for Rickie Lee Jones, China Crisis and various artists from the Windham Hill 'new age' stable.

Now, though, he's back with Fagen. 'I asked Walter to co-produce my new album and he came to stay for a couple of months. We worked together every day, just as we used to. I would usually initiate the tune in those days, then show it to Walter and we'd do the rest together. It's not exactly like that now because it's my record, but we have some other projects that we're working on. Steely Dan was part of its time, but we'll come up with something.'

At least one collaboration – drawn from a wad of songs the pair wrote during a brief reunion in 1985 – will surface on a collection that Fagen, rarely a strict observer of deadlines, anticipates releasing next autumn. In the meantime, new converts are being offered the dubiously-titled *Steely Dan Gold (Extended Edition)*, containing only three tracks that do not figure on any of the three previous compilations. The forthcoming four-CD box set had better be more imaginative.

Fagen is nonetheless grateful for some interest from a new generation. 'It's great to know our albums still sell to college kids – the luxury of working only when I'm really inspired is made possible by that. But I'm not sure what exactly it is about those records – I know the early ones irritate me – aside from a certain amount of technical excellence. If we were ahead of our time, it was simply because we grew up with a certain natural ironic stance which later became the norm in society.'

Insiders attest that Becker and Fagen were merciless perfectionists who even scripted solos note-for-note. 'We didn't usually chart them in their entirety,' Fagen insists gently, visibly embarrassed by the implications. 'A cat would come in and just blow. If he had trouble with the chords or stylistically, we'd coach him along. Maybe every few bars we'd punch something in, or take a lot of different tracks and combine them. These things are exaggerated – it may have happened once or twice. On the song "Aja", Wayne Shorter, as I recall, did two or three takes. The first was kind of a rehearsal, then he wrote down the changes because they were tough and hard to remember, so he wrote out the scales and did two more takes, which we later combined. If Larry Carlton found a guitar part complicated, he'd play a bit and then we'd come up with a couple of suggestions. It seemed like we were doing a lot of takes, but we were recording on tape.'

What, then, of the alleged three remixes that supposedly delayed *Aja's* release by nine months? Fagen pleads innocence: 'I can remember doing two or three versions of "Babylon Sisters" for *Gaucho*, but we remixed very quickly. Coupla weeks, tops. I wish I could push out albums quickly just to keep my career afloat, but I don't know how. The only way I know is to let time pass and the record make itself. I have a happier domestic situation now, I'm happier within myself. I've resolved a lot of personal problems. I also let myself screw up more now. I just needed time to change.'

But in dispensing with his demons, might Fagen have shed some steel? 'I certainly hope not.' Cue another throaty cackle, followed closely by a mock gesture of offence: 'Do you mean, did *I* lose my *edge*? Well, I'm certainly not going to put out those Paul McCartney-type records full of cutesy love songs, that's for sure.'

5

Review of Fagen's
Kamakiriad

Geoffrey Himes, the *Washington Post*,
March 1993

D onald Fagen's first album in eleven years, *Kamakiriad*, can be judged from two different perspectives. On the one hand, it marries tartly ironic lyrics with lush jazz harmonies in ways well beyond the reach of today's ambitious pop-rock composers from Sting and Billy Joel to Mark Knopfler and Brenda Russell. On the other hand, *Kamakiriad* has neither the substance nor the impact of Fagen's best work with Steely Dan.

In other words, anyone who's missed Fagen's lusciously scored tales of alienation will enjoy his new solo album much as they enjoyed lesser Steely Dan outings like *Gaucho* or *Can't Buy A Thrill*, but won't get the high-voltage thrills of *Aja, The Royal Scam* and *Katy Lied*.

Fagen wrote all eight songs on *Kamakiriad* (one with Libby Titus and another with Walter Becker) and handled all the lead vocals and most of the keyboards. In many ways, though, it's a

Steely Dan album, for Fagen's partner in that band, Becker, not only produced but also played the bass and lead guitar parts. It sure sounds like a Steely Dan album with Fagen's film noir narrator's voice singing over the syncopated R&B rhythms, the catchy pop-rock melodies and the expansive jazz harmonies fleshed out by impeccably precise horn and guitar parts.

The lyrics describe a sci-fi near-future much like that of *Blade Runner*, where dazzling Japanese technology is triumphant, but lust, violence and disenfranchisement are as common as ever. Fagen sings of cruising across the 'Trans-Island Skyway' in his steam-powered Kamakiri bubble-car and encountering one heartbreak after another. The songs cruise along as smoothly as an anti-gravity car, but they never seem to shift into the higher gear of forceful passion that marked the best Steely Dan tunes.

6

Donald Fagen: The Man Who Came in From the Cool

Barney Hoskyns, *Arena*,
Spring 1993

Sabbaticals have become essential career moves in today's music business: any self-respecting rock legend will tell you as much. Put out an album a year and you blow all credibility; wait five (or ten, preferably) and the world will be salivating.

Even so, few legends have taken quite as much time out as Donald Fagen, erstwhile frontman with the indisputably legendary Steely Dan. Over a decade has now elapsed since Fagen released his masterful solo album *The Nightfly*, and in that time there's been scant word from the man: a short-lived column for *Premiere*; the soundtrack to the lame *Bright Lights, Big City*; a low-key reunion with his old partner Walter Becker on flame-haired Rosie Vela's *Zazu*. But nothing substantial until his appearance as ringmaster at the circus that was 1991's New York Rock and Soul Revue, an all-star live affair on which the likes of Boz Scaggs and old Dan hand Michael McDonald applied their chops to a batch of Fagen's favourite R&B/soul chestnuts. So what in God's name has Donald Fagen *done* for ten years?

'Well, the '80s weren't very inspiring, for a start,' says the un-assuming-looking character who sits opposite me in lopsided wire-frame glasses and a pair of shoes that definitely do *not* become a legend. It's as if I'm meeting the man Donald Fagen could so easily become: a forty-something Jewish academic on some upstate liberal arts campus, not the singing half of the most brilliant rock duo of the '70s.

'More to the point,' Fagen continues, 'I'd used up all I knew on *The Nightfly* and I had to live another ten years to write a new album. Basically, I was just trying to get a life, having been a workaholic ever since I was in college. I'd never been able to fig-ure out what to do with myself when I wasn't writing or recording and it was time to learn. You know ... getting into relation-ships ... getting out of relationships. I even, uh, practised the piano a little.'

He manages a faint smile and sinks into the black leather sofa in his publicist's office. Outside, high above Broadway on an early March afternoon, snowflakes whirl ineffectually through the sky, failing to settle on the window ledge as on the blustery streets below.

This 'new album', for those of you who've given up keeping tabs on the activities of Messrs Becker and Fagen, is the intri-guingly titled *Kamakiriad*, on Warner Bros – a company that wisely agreed to let Fagen take his time when they signed him back in 1981. ('I told them there was no way I could be sure of meeting any particular deadlines,' he says.)

Produced by Becker and recorded over a period of two and a half years in New York and Hawaii, it's an extraordinary 'comeback' for two principal reasons: first, because it's set in the future, towards the end of the millennium, thereby dashing the hopes of anyone counting on some retro-*nuevo* reprise of *The Nightfly*; second, because almost every one of its eight tracks boasts the kind of kick-ass funk grooves that were only ever implicit in the music of Steely Dan. Rhythm one expected of Donald Fagen; a virtual *dance* album comes as something of a shock.

'It's a little more aggressive than anything I've done before,' concedes the man behind the wire frames. 'Dance music to me is still the soul of the '60s and the funk of the '70s, and that's kind of what I wanted to capture on the record – funk based on six-teenth rather than eighth notes, everything from Sly to Earth, Wind & Fire. I was writing the album at the time when we were putting the Rock and Soul Revue together, and that whole ex-perience had a major impact on the songs.'

The marriage of Fagen and Becker's nouveau '90s funk with Fagen's inspired sci-fi imagery – the Kamakiri of the title, for instance, is a steam-driven car with its very own hydroponic vegetable garden! – makes for some curious listening. Take 'Springtime', a close encounter between early Marvin Gaye and recent William Gibson in some twilight zone timewarp. Or 'Tomorrow's Girls', a song whose glorious pop chorus marks it out as a potential hit single of the order of Fagen's classic 'I. G. Y.' – the B-52s meet *The Stepford Wives*, anyone?

In the album's brief sleeve note, Fagen explains that *Kamakiriad* is the story of a journey in which 'each song is a charming detour or dangerous adventure along the way'. Slumped on the sofa opposite me, he adds that his peripatetic hero is 'kind of a fuck-up, but with excellent intentions'.

'As in all the grand old myths, he only really discovers his destination as he continues along,' Fagen adds. 'The journey can be taken on different levels, of course: the literal level of the action, and then a deeper, more psychological level.' He further contends that *Kamakiriad* 'completes some inherent trilogy, with *The Nightfly* being the past, the Steely Dan records being about the present as it unfolded and this album being about the future.'

Whether any of that will make the record less bemusing to the world at large is hard to predict: I fear Fagen may lose hardcore Dan fans without gaining a substantial number of new ones. (I also have reservations about Walter Becker's production: perhaps it's the hand of Dan/*Nightfly* producer Gary Katz that's the major missing ingredient here.) For the sake of sabbatical-taking iconoclasts the world over, I hope I'm wrong.

———

Whatever one's feelings about Fagen's new groove – and an initial disappointment may be inevitable after the pristine perfection of *The Nightfly* – it's hard to begrudge the man his new spirit of celebration. (There's a deliciously desolate jazz ballad that dates back to the *Nightfly* era – 'On The Dunes' – but the remainder of the songs are all upbeat.) It would seem that, for Fagen, 'getting a life' has partly entailed the thawing-out of everything that was so coldly aloof about Steely Dan, a process which began with the Rock and Soul Revue and now continues with the kinetic workouts of 'Countermoon' and 'Trans-Island Skyway'.

Certainly the Revue was hardly something that Steely Dan – those malcontented New York misfits let loose in Hollywood Babylon – would have had much truck with. But Steely Dan never had much truck with anyone but themselves.

'In Steely Dan we were very arrogant kids,' says Fagen. 'And when life starts to kick you around, you have to swallow your pride. See, there was a real family feeling about the Rock and Soul Revue that I'd never experienced before, and certainly not in Steely Dan. In a way, people from my generation have had to create new families, since their own families have so often failed to satisfy the needs that a family historically provided.'

Donald Fagen, a dysfunctional family man? Never thought I'd live to see the day. So is he repudiating the blistering cynicism, the merciless irony, of the great Becker/Fagen songs?

'No, because it wasn't like we were promoting or endorsing that cynical attitude. We were just reflecting the zeitgeist, talking about the way the world seemed to us in the '70s. But by the end, when we were making *Gaucho*, I think both Walter and I were down and depressed, and both of us really had to make changes.'

In Becker's case, the changes included the termination of a hazardous drug habit and the adoption of an idyllic Hawaiian lifestyle that, in Fagen's words, 'is very amusing to me, and to him as well'. In Fagen's case, the changes have simply been about coming in from the cold.

———

That Fagen has begun to *join in* is evident from his appearance several hours after our interview at a sub-Rock and Soul Revue hoedown at the Lone Star Roadhouse on West 52nd Street. This 'New York Night', like the Revue itself, is the brainchild of Fagen's companion Libby Titus, who I suspect has had to push her reclusive paramour into having the kind of sloppy, informal fun for which all these all-star Lone Star jams are renowned.

'The whole thing started when Libby asked if I'd do a jazz evening with Mac Rebennack [Dr John],' says Fagen. 'I then helped put together a show celebrating the songs of Bert Berns and Jerry Ragovoy, using all the great New York musicians who'd played on their records, like Paul Griffin and Jerry Jermott. The evenings got so popular that we ended up at the Beacon Theatre.'

The trouble is, the moment Fagen walks on, unannounced, to take his place alongside such luminaries as Al Kooper and Elliott Randall (the almost-legendary axeman who soloed on 'Reelin' In The Years'), he looks distinctly out of place. In straining to get down with these dishevelled old lags, he only accentuates the distance between himself and rock'n'roll in general. For the fact is that Fagen is not a joiner-in, even if Libby Titus has managed to convince him that he is or that it's somehow good for him. Nor are his makeshift renditions of 'Green Earrings', 'FM' and 'Josie' far short of torturous, since Fagen is barely able to stay in tune on any of them.

Only when Chuck Jackson, that now-forgotten legend of the uptown New York soul which Fagen so adores, strides on to sing Leiber and Stoller's wacky 1963 beat concerto 'I Keep Forgettin'' (covered by David Bowie on *Tonight*) does our hero's face momentarily light up.

As I watch him, I'm asking myself whether this is supposed to be some sort of therapy for the man who called a halt to all live performances after the ill-tempered *Pretzel Logic* tour nearly twenty years ago. And I'm wondering if, after all, the point of Donald Fagen doesn't lie precisely in his detachment, his distance from such beery gatherings as this 'New York Night'. Yes, Steely Dan were cold, soulless, fetishists of the studio and 'funked-up muzak'. But next to all the phoney passion and bravado of most rock music, that in itself was bracing. In the wake of the Great Grunge Overkill, moreover, we have much to learn from the classicism and strategy of vintage Becker and Fagen. I'm far from convinced that whooping it up with clapped-out Al Kooper and co. – or exhuming soporific '70s' jazz-funk on *Kamakiriad*'s 'Florida Room', come to that – is really the answer for Fagen himself. At the Lone Star Roadhouse, he doesn't look too convinced either. Perhaps that's why he failed to mention the show during our interview.

'From somewhere deep inside you,' Fagen sings on 'Teahouse On The Tracks', the album's spirited finale, 'some frozen stuff begins to crack . . . ' Me, I'll miss the frozen stuff of Steely Dan's glory days: the grim comedy and clinical precision that sheared away all the bullshit of rock'n'roll. I just hope Donald Fagen doesn't thaw out completely.

7

The Dream Ticket

Nick Coleman, *Time Out*,
September 1993

A. J. Liebling, the great *New Yorker* columnist, used to describe the walk to Madison Square Garden with epicurean keenness, as if New York in flood to its boxing mecca were a flux of wine and food and bodily functions, in which small but exquisite truths about life might be nosed. Going to the Garden was a meal in itself then, in the '50s, when the Garden was still the Garden (it's moved), and when Marciano slugged heavyweights into the cutlery box, by which symbolic act people learned to know their place.

Tonight, however, New York in flood is a thing without special flavour. There's an even press of bodies not shoving against the crash doors of the new-ish Garden, comprising nervously amiable, white, 30-pluses dressed to patio-party and maybe shout a bit – we got our shorts, we got our Nikes, we got our Steely Dan T-shirts – the lot of us acting bleary-cheerful but not wanting to trouble our neighbours with anything, like, *too* picaresque, man. Check this. There's a spod in front with a bucket of popcorn so voluminous he's happy to shower the escalator brushes every time he rams a fistful between his mandibles, which is happening every two or three seconds. Dangerously exuberant, this. Irresponsible, even. But then in the land of the bland, the man with bad table manners is King Kong.

Still, fifteen thousand of the suckers cleaned out all the tickets within forty minutes of box office opening time, which might not be a record but is a much sharper reaction than Prince gets these days. Fifteen thousand in forty minutes. However you look at them, these are decent figures on the first concert in nineteen years by a band who never much liked playing concerts and were never really a band into the bargain. Donald Fagen has had his successes since the duo 'disbanded' at the end of the '70s – *The Nightfly* and *Kamakiriad*, which was *Nightfly 2* in lots of ways – but hip nostalgia will always succeed like disease. So what's scary about Danitis is that no one really, but *really*, can say how many of the suckers swarming all over the Garden tonight are here for the Steely Dan *thing*, and how many are here because they liked Steely Dan with a frankfurter in the '70s. Looking around, it's hard to tell. The Dan reformed because it seemed like a good fun thing to do after Walter produced *Kamakiriad* 'n' all. This lot are here, at the very least, because a frankfurter can be a wonderful thing.

Walter Becker and Donald Fagen make one of the great entrances, in that it's almost certain that no one in the Garden tonight can have seen an entry like this in their adult life; certainly not in the last decade and a half, during which time the conventional rock entrance has become so enslaved to the choreography of bombast that most large gigs are now dedicated in their entirety to the single effect of getting their star on and off the stage. (One day, indeed, rock concerts will run backwards, starting with the encores, so that the show can climax with the artist's entrance.) What happens is this. The band do a little overture on the themes of 'Bad Sneakers' and 'Aja', and Becker and Fagen walk on. And that's it.

What then follows is the sound of fifteen thousand people holding a rabbity debate amongst themselves on what the hell it is Becker looks like. A lab assistant. A computer journalist. A Shake n' Vac salesman. A projectionist in a porn cinema. 'A science nerd,' is how Donald loyally described him earlier this year and, when Donald introduces Walter in his black jeans, black shirt, purple tie, scrotty beard and slightly full bottom, the little fella shuffles to the microphone and says, 'I guess I get a cheer, huh? Thank you. Marvellous.' We then listen to him sing one of two songs, called 'Book Of Liars', from his own forthcoming solo album. This sounds like a very beautiful song – groove underscores lilted melody, sung in the woodgrained, hangdog, country-romantic style of pre-*Nighthawks* Tom Waits – but we'll need to study the words to be sure. There was one line with 'electrons' in it.

Meanwhile, Fagen has returned to his Fender Rhodes, where he jerks from side to side as he plays, with his head back, shades like two boreholes, mouth ajar. One does wonder whether his impersonation of a Jewish-geek Ray Charles on downers is self-conscious or not, and one makes a note to ask him should the opportunity arise. ('Go Walter,' Fagen drones flatly through his nose at the beginning of Walter's solo in 'Hey Nineteen', not unlike Dustin Hoffman encouraging a vegetable, thereby intensifying the confusion.)

What you get, then, for your twenty-year wait and frantic

plastic-flashing in the first forty minutes after the markets open, is two and a half hours of tricky detail.

Steely Dan were indeed a barbecue hits band of the '70s. But they were also a twisty subplot in the history of man's cruelty to man, all educated and eaten up with longing to be hip; a subplot involving terrible sarcasm, brilliant musicianship, a sordid anxiety about being white and suburban, a writing style so coldly acute you *knew* they must hate themselves and a Leiber 'n' Stoller-esque attachment to the simple pleasures of the pop tune.

This is a group that used to write the sleeve notes to their own albums in the style of a dimwit rock journalist. (Walter, indeed, took the trouble to introduce Donald as 'Tristan Fabriani', the self-same dimwit.) And who frazzled so comprehensively in the glare of their own brilliance that whatever chance they had of inadvertently becoming happy rock stars was Charlie Parker'd every night by a shared metabolite: Steely Dan were outsiders in everything. The only thing they were in love with was the eloquence of their contempt for the world they came from.

So, yes, two and a half hours of all that, including material from the whole canon, solo and collective – though not, oddly, from *Pretzel Logic* – is a fine thing. They tackled the songs as if they were new, re-stroking arrangements for added poke (only 'Reelin' in the Years' copped a total re-bore), driving a band of extreme funkiness with unversed, chopping arm motions, as if one or the both of them were indeed Thelonious Monk at the wheel of a car.

A brief chat later, in a hotel room, which Becker and Fagen occupy uneasily: yes, well, *maybe* they'll come to Europe 'if things go well'. No, they don't fantasise about being black, though Walter occasionally wishes Donald were black when he wants a cab. And certainly, Becker and Fagen are working from the same basic set of assumptions they always did, though their lives have changed and they do now at last consider themselves adults.

And how do Steely Dan reckon they're perceived by the amorphous, flavour-free fifteen thousand flower of adulthood who pressed so gently at the crash-doors of the Garden last night?

Becker: 'Oh, we're perceived as crusty old fucks.'

Fagen, overlapping: 'It's not for us to say. It depends if it's a fan or whether it's someone who just remembers "Rikki Don't Lose That Number" when they were making out in the back of a car in 1973. It depends.'

And what are Steely Dan's expectations of their audience?

Fagen: 'I'd expect them to be attentive, well-dressed, cheerful, thrifty, clean-bred and reverent. By which I mean, naturally, that they be open to what we're doing. I don't wanna participate in a nostalgia-fest.'

The couple in front of me at the Garden were in frankfurter heaven. They whooped with recognition at the beginning of every song and then talked about something else until the next one came along. They were both confident they were going to have sex later.

8

Review of Becker's
11 Tracks Of Whack

Geoffrey Himes, the *Washington Post*,
December 1994

As the team called Steely Dan, Donald Fagen and Walter Becker wrote, produced and performed some of the smartest, most seductive rock'n'roll of the '70s. Fagen's two subsequent solo albums sounded just like Steely Dan releases and fans were left to wonder exactly what Becker had contributed to the partnership. When Steely Dan took to the road last year, Becker's guitar solos were so modest and his few vocal spots so thin and shaky that doubts about his talent only grew.

In that context, Becker's first solo album, *11 Tracks Of Whack*, qualifies as a major surprise. It too sounds like a Steely Dan release, with the same sort of literate, elliptical lyrics and jazzy chord changes. The vocals are underwhelming, but given repeated takes in the studio they're much better than his live performances and serve the songs adequately. The songs, all but one written by Becker alone, are powerful and bleak portraits of characters who have slid from a wild, glamorous youth to a bitter, damaged middle age.

'Lucky Henry', a racetrack jockey, becomes a homeless drifter; Johnny Boy, a hang-glider daredevil, falls out of the sky and leaves his family searching for his car keys; one college-town partier becomes a 'Junkie Girl'; while another, in 'Cringemaker', becomes 'the wife from hell'; an old college pal becomes 'This Moody Bastard'; a good-time Romeo becomes a bitter drunk without his 'Girlfriend'. These cynical but sharply drawn vignettes suggest Becker's contributions to Steely Dan were his lyric detail and anti-romantic sensibility, two qualities missing from Fagen's sketchy, sunny *Kamakiriad* last year.

Becker and Fagen produced *11 Tracks of Whack* at Becker's home studio in Hawaii. If the minimalist results lack the usual Steely Dan lushness, the arrangements are marked by meticulously planned and sparklingly executed jazz-rock parts, often played by Becker himself on guitar. Even as he unflinchingly describes his characters' fall from grace, Becker implies a lingering fondness for them, often in the seductive melodies that accompany every song.

Becker and Fagen collecting one of the three Grammies for *Two Against Nature* in Los Angeles, February 2001.

Kirk McKoy/Getty Images

FIVE: Heavy Rollers

'I don't think I'll ever stop asking them to tour again . . . '

Gary Katz, 1981

1

Stand-Up Rock'n'Roll: The Return of Steely Dan

Andy Gill, *MOJO*, October 1995

O nce upon a time they were the odd couple in rock. They wrote songs that featured knuckle-knotting chords and brain-twisting lyrics. They welded jazz and rock into an alloy so smooth and shiny it was impossible to tell where the one ended and the other began. They gave up on live performance a decade before it became commonplace. They sneered at the world from a position of bohemian priority so rarefied it was hard to tell exactly where it was situated. They routinely ran rings around interviews. They haven't changed.

Separately, Donald Fagen and Walter Becker can be charming, witty, imaginative, accommodating, the most fulsome of interviewees. But put them in a room together and something else takes over: the synergy that brought forth Steely Dan still operates its acid magic on the duo. Ask them a question – any question – and they'll bat it around for a few moments, testing it for comic potential, before volleying it back over the net, largely unanswered. Faced with the prospect of an in-depth interview to promote their new album, *Alive In America*, they immediately put up the psychic barriers.

Walter Becker: We've been doing these interviews now all week. Because it's a live album with all these old songs on it, interviewers have used that as a pretext to ask questions about things that happened years and years ago. So we've rehashed things that we barely remember now to a point where we're becoming increasingly alienated from anything that could be said to resemble the truth.

Donald Fagen: So you've come on the scene at the perfect moment.

Stylised lies is exactly what I'm after.

DF: We call them 'Styles' for short.

WB: I think the important thing is to try and stay in the present and not have any painful sorties into the distant past. If you find yourself wanting to ask something about the Brill Building or questions like, 'Why did you decide to go out on the road again after nineteen years?', stuff like that, I think we've heard that one a few times too many, haven't we?

DF: See, you don't even have to ask any questions!

Well, I think that's the first four pages of my questions gone.

WB: There've been journalists in here all week that have already gotten better answers to these questions than we could possibly give you, due to repetition. Maybe Gail [the PR] could hook you up with one of those guys, and you could just download what they got?

On the other hand, your answers would be more finely honed now, where before they would have been rough drafts . . .

WB: Thus putting the lie to the concept that you can't polish a turd!

You've got a new, or newish, live album coming out . . .

DF: That's 'newish' in the sense of distinguishing 'Jew' from 'Jewish', is it?

WB: This is beginning to remind me of the joke where the guy from Oklahoma goes up to a New York cabbie and says, 'Excuse me, could you tell me how I can get to Times Square, or should I just go fuck myself?'

Indeed. Has anyone ever suggested you might be difficult to interview?

WB: Yeah, that has been suggested and, as I say, it has to do with overload. Y'know: the horror, the horror!

DF: The guys who came round Monday thought we were, like, sweethearts. But the last couple of days, no.

WB: Also, we had to film our EPK [Electronic Press Kit] over two days.

Oh. And what kind of stuff was in that?

WB: Shit. Utter shit. It was kind of like another rehash of the same questions . . .

DF: . . . that we hired someone ourselves to ask!

WB: They'd ask us these things, then we'd decide maybe we should do it indoors, and they'd ask us again, then we actually went to the Brill Building – 'So, here we are, at the Brill Building . . . '

DF: At one point the director wanted us to read some stuff as we were walking down some stairs and he said, 'Say this as though it's stuff the record company is making you say, and try to say it with a mocking tone.' Assuming that everything we'd said previous to that wasn't in a mocking tone.

Have you ever thought you might be in the wrong business?

WB: Yes, through most of the '80s.

Rock music is at least partly about communication, after all . . .

WB: Not in our case it's not.

DF: Actually, our new album is going to be called *Stand-Up Rock'n'Roll*.

————

So here we are at the Brill Building, it's the late '60s and these two sullen, nondescript youths, fresh out of college, are hustling their songs around the various music publishers in the building. One has wire-rimmed spectacles, shoulder-length blond hair and looks a bit like River Phoenix. The other is thin to the point of emaciation.

They troop into an office. The thin one sits at the office piano and opens an exercise book of songs. Together, they sing one for the man behind the desk. It's about androids discovering they're alive, a bit like in that Philip K. Dick book. They sing another.

It's about Charlie Parker and is full of odd, show-offy changes. A third, a putdown of some place called Barry Town, makes good use of the spiteful undertone in the thin one's voice, but is too nasty. A fourth appears to be about a dildo – it even mentions that Japanese one from the William Burroughs book. The man behind the desk sits there, nonplussed. What are these two kids thinking of? No one wants to hear songs like this. Do they?

They troop out of the office, up the stairs and into another office.

'This was before cassettes, so we would just play and sing,' explains Fagen. 'We met a lot of people in the Brill Building. We met Jerry Leiber, which was great, because he was an idol of ours, and there were still some other great songwriters there, like Jeff Barry. We knew about the scene and we were into the craft of the thing. We wanted to become great songwriters. It was almost over then, but at 1650 Broadway there were still some things happening. The Lovin' Spoonful. Buddah Records had an office there, and there was a lot of one-shot soul stuff coming out of there.'

'I don't think we were trying to imitate any of the top songwriters,' says Becker, 'except, in a roundabout way, the very arty songs Burt Bacharach had written for Dionne Warwick. Those were an immense source of inspiration for us, but we weren't trying to copy them: his pieces had these formal, Stravinsky-esque angularities that were reminiscent of twentieth-century classical music. We were impressed by how far out he was able to get and still make it sound sort of like pop music. At one point our demo was played for Leiber and Stoller, who had an office upstairs. Jerry Leiber's comment was that it reminded him of some German art songs brought into the contemporary style. We subsequently learned that it was better to have our songs pass as pop songs and then have whatever else we wanted in them afterwards.'

Fagen, a jazz fan from Passaic, New Jersey, had already put in a good few years developing an anti-social personality when he met Becker at Bard College. Influenced by the hipster humour of stand-ups and monologuists like Lenny Bruce and Gene Shepherd, and by Paul Krassner's magazine *The Realist*, Fagen hated the New Jersey suburbia, and would take off to Manhattan on the weekends to see the likes of Monk, Rollins, Miles and Mingus at Greenwich Village clubs like the Village Vanguard. When he was bought his first piano at the age of twelve, his main influence was Red Garland, from Miles Davis's great quintet.

At Bard, Fagen studied literature, graduating in 1969 with a thesis on Hermann Hesse, but spent much of his time running a band which went under various names – the Leather Canary, the Don Fagen Jazz Trio, the Bad Rock Group – according to the gig. He ran into Becker, two years his junior, playing loud blues guitar in a college rehearsal room. Becker, it transpired, had learnt his blues licks from a young neighbourhood kid, Randy Wolf, who later found fame as Randy California, prodigal guitarist with Spirit.

'Randy's uncle in LA owned a folk and blues club called the Ash Grove,' he explains, 'so Randy had learned to play blues stuff from these old guys who had played his uncle's club. He also knew Taj Mahal and had learned all these techniques. The first time we played, I had just gotten this electric guitar, but hadn't figured out shit about how to make it sound like these guys. Randy took the guitar, plugged it in, turned the amp all the way up, and started bending the strings and using a bottleneck and all this stuff. It just sounded exactly like a B.B. King record, and I learned how to do that from him. I was always attracted to that style of playing. Jazz guitar is tame by comparison.'

Discovering a shared affection for the improvising skills of Paul Desmond, Dave Brubeck's sax player, Becker and Fagen became firm collegiate chums, and were soon writing songs stuffed with jazz allusions and black humour. Becker having flunked out of college after three terms, the duo relocated to New York after Fagen graduated, determined to make it as song-writers. By this time, the Tin Pan Alley era was, as Fagen says, all but over, swamped by a tide of hippie bands who wrote their own material, rendering the specialist songwriter sector redundant. But the Brill Building was still the songwriting mecca for smart-pop disciples like Becker and Fagen.

'There was a lot of scurrying around,' recalls Fagen. 'A lot of the business took place right out on Broadway outside and in the City Squire hotel next door, and there were all these weird characters in the Brill Building itself. During the late '60s, the Brill Building had been converted so that the offices now had all these shag rugs on the walls, this sort of cheesy drug-era stuff – everyone had gumball machines. It was very amusing.'

'We knew we were only pretending to be something that belonged there,' says Becker, 'because the kind of songs we were writing didn't fit in anywhere; there was no artist out there looking for this particular kind of song, put it that way!'

WB: We live in the past, y'know . . . the Brill Building, Beverly Boulevard. Don and I like to sit around and rehash, talk about the good old days. Like the Golden Boys.

DF: We were there when they invented digital recording, y'know.

WB: In fact, Donald was actually in the studio the night that Debbie Reynolds recorded 'Aba Daba Honeymoon'. That's a little-known fact!

And a little-known song.

WB: You had to be there . . .

Barbra Streisand recorded one of your songs, didn't she?

DF: The first song we ever had recorded – 'I Mean to Shine'. Not a good song, but at least she recorded it.

What kind of royalties did you see from it?

WB: The royalties from that song were actually signed over to our previous manager, to escape from his clutches.

Which manager?

WB: One of the previous managers.

You had several?

WB: Well, the tradition is to have a succession of previous managers. Like suitors at a gang-bang, y'know?

———

'I remember one day,' says Fagen, 'we were at the Brill Building and there was a big convention going on, so there was hardly anyone left in the building except for this one production company called JATA, which it turned out stood for Jay & the Americans. We knocked on the door and there was someone there – in fact, it was one of the Americans! – and we did our usual rap: 'Hi, my name is Donald Fagen, this is my partner Walter Becker, we have this song . . . ' And we went through a few of our numbers, and they started paying us fifty dollars per song and tried to help us out.'

Kenny Vance, the man from JATA, became one of the duo's first managerial suitors, and promptly had them record some rough demos of their songs which subsequently appeared under a variety of titles like 'Berry Town' (sic) and 'Sun Mountain'. They also recorded a soundtrack for a low-budget movie a friend of his was making, called *You've Got to Walk It Like You Talk It Or You'll Lose That Beat* – the album of which, likewise, also magically appeared, prominently bearing their names, once Steely Dan became a bankable prospect.

Becker remains philosophical about the situation. 'It's embarrassing, but if people are that interested in it, I guess it's OK,' he says. 'My son got hold of it, and he liked it better than any of the Steely Dan records! "Dad, I love that song 'Android Warehouse!'" I thought, Holy shit, what does he think this is?' Despite this welter of activity, though, the duo were making little headway in the songwriting business and welcomed the offer of a paying gig as pianist and bass-player for Jay & the Americans, despite the anachronistic nature of their music.

'It was fun,' says Fagen. 'We toured the East Coast, and we'd go to Florida in the winter time and do a lot of those oldies shows in Madison Square Garden where they'd have, like, forty acts. We toured for a while opening for the Four Seasons, who were really a good band. It was a great job for us – we were straight out of college, and we got paid in cash!'

In typically droll fashion, they adopted the stage-names Tristan Fabriani and Gus Mahler, though Jay Black had a rather more acid handle for the smartass duo, dubbing them the 'Manson and Starkweather of rock'.

'That was Jay's little joke,' recalls Becker. 'We got involved with Jay & the Americans via one of the more forward-looking members of the group, who had actually noticed that the '60s had happened: Jay never did – for Jay it was still *The Blackboard Jungle*.

'Some of Jay's friends were the same guys from *Goodfellas* – they were not all fictional characters. I think what his life was like – he was married to the niece of one of the guys, which I think was a survival move: he was levering himself up into a position where he could be forgiven some debts. We would see them once in a while around the office. Some guys would come in and say, "Hey Jay! Whyn't you get these guys to take a fuckin' haircut?" Or they'd come backstage after show and say, "Hey, Jay, your voice sounded beautiful, but that drum, that fuckin' drum's givin' me a headache! Can you tell 'em to turn down that fuckin' drum?"'

DF: See, now you can't help talking about this stuff, it's like you're in a groove . . .

WB: I know. I'm programmed. It's like *The Manchurian Candidate*. In fact, I'm thinking of going over to Elsa Lanchester's [sic – she didn't appear in the movie and he may mean Angela Lansbury here] house after the interview!

DF: How about a game of Solitaire to pass the time?

WB: Good idea! I'm thinking of catching the senator's speech later, down at the press club. Wanna come with me? You can carry some of my stuff. See, I've identified with my captors now – I'm thinking of going into journalism.

———

Meanwhile, Becker and Fagen had met some rather more sympathetic musical spirits by answering a *Village Voice* ad for a bassist and keyboard player with jazz chops. 'No assholes need apply,' warned the ad. Denny Dias, who had placed it, was immediately impressed by the pair's abilities and particularly by the fact that they already had a whole stack of original material. Demian, Dias's band, was just trying to broaden its set beyond the Top 40 covers and R&B numbers that were the staples of the day and this new source of songs, he could tell, was of high quality. 'They were sophisticated,' he says, 'something more than your typical pop song; they were musically interesting.'

Before long, Becker and Fagen had effectively taken over the group, replacing the drummer with one of their own acquaintance, John Discepolo, and steering the set in their own direction. Kenny Vance recorded a batch of demos with this line-up, including Becker's ingenious setting of 'The Mock Turtle Song' from Lewis Carroll's *Alice Through the Looking-Glass* and a striking, six-minute number sung by Fagen in a weary, Dylan-esque drawl, called 'Brooklyn (Owes The Charmer Under Me)'. These too would obtain a belated release (as *Walter Becker/Donald Fagen: The Early Years*), but proved just as ineffectual as their earlier demos in arousing record company interest.

Help was at hand, however, in the form of Kenny Vance's chum Gary Kannon, an independent producer who had previously worked with Richard Perry and Bobby Darin, and was building a name for himself in the music business. He introduced them to some musicians he'd met in Boston – drummer Jim Hodder, from a band called the Bead Game (named, as was Dias's band, after a Hermann Hesse novel), and session guitarist Jeff 'Skunk' Baxter, from the late and largely unlamented Ultimate

Spinach. More importantly, he also persuaded Richard Perry that a Becker and Fagen song, 'I Mean To Shine', was just right for a Barbra Streisand album that Perry was recording (*Barbra Joan Streisand*), thus acquiring the duo their first proper song sale.

Shortly after, Kannon was offered an A&R job at ABC Records in Los Angeles, where he dropped his pseudonym and reverted to his real name of Katz. One of the first things he did upon taking up his new position was to persuade his employers that they really needed to hire these cool songwriters he knew back in New York. It was the smartest move he ever made, though for a while it seemed as though it may have been a mistake. Becker and Fagen were offered a position as staff songwriters at $125 a week, this being an advance against any song royalties they might earn. They didn't need asking twice.

'For cynical, wise-ass kids from New York like us, going to Los Angeles was an endless source of amusement,' says Becker. 'I'm sure you're familiar with the characterisation of sunny, air-headed optimism in glitzy LA and dense, rye-bread, cynical, intellectual New Yorkers. I had never been there before in my life when I moved there – lock, stock, and barrel – and we didn't know how to drive or anything! Gary Katz had an apartment in Encino and we just went there, then picked out our apartments from this newly-finished block and started taking driving lessons. Until we'd learned, Gary had to drive us back and forth to ABC.

'It was our first real job in the music business, for a real record company, so there was the shock of that too: the bullshit factor soared another thousand per cent. The reason ABC had signed Gary and us was they'd decided they wanted to make more, quote, "underground" records: they only had bubblegummy hits – and the Impulse! jazz label. One of the first few days we were in

LA, Gary took us to an A&R meeting in some hotel and we drove over to Laurel Canyon, which we'd heard about from all these Frank Zappa records, and went into this room where Roger Nichols had set up this PA for a playback.

'There were all these record executives there: at the head of the table was Jay Lasker, president of this company, in this Hawaiian shirt, and the other guys with their hokey records, then Ed Michel puts on this Alice Coltrane record – their first quad recording! – and Ed's got the speakers in the corners of the room, and he turns it up real loud, and it's Alice Coltrane's harp, and Rashied Ali playing no discernible beat of any kind and finger-cymbals and all the other space-jazz conventions of the day, and just to watch these guys try and groove along with this was great!

'By the time we got there, the great days of Impulse! were over, John Coltrane was dead and they didn't do much else from that point on, but of course they had made all those neat records in the '60s. They had their little mastering studio next to the recording studio, and we'd see the masters for *A Love Supreme* hanging around out in the hall. I thought: these guys aren't taking care of this stuff – I should take it home to my house! But I never did . . . '

What did being staff writers entail?

DF: We were supposed to write pop songs for the other artists on the label, which included at that time Three Dog Night, the Grass Roots and John Kay and Denny Doherty from the Mamas & the Papas. John Kay actually recorded a song of ours, but other than that we were complete failures.

Which one was that?

WB: It was a song called 'Giles Of The River' [sniggers].

DF: That's the reaction the artists tended to have too. As Gore Vidal once said, 'Shit has its own integrity.' We didn't have that kind of integrity, though.

What was it about your songs that made them different?

DF: They had some of the irony that became the lingua franca of the '80s, to some degree.

That's not a very American thing, is it?

WB: Well, my friend from high school, his mom had that Flanders and Swann record, and my father had a few English friends, y'know?

DF: Yeah, and we used to listen to those Brecht/Weill songs . . .

WB: So we were kind of suave and continental, at least on the intellectual level, if not on the haberdashery level.

DF: At least compared to, say, Freddy Fender.

WB: On the haberdashery level or the intellectual level?

DF: I'm not sure. He may have it over us on the haberdashery level!

WB: Even Freddy Fender had us aced! Also, we were interested in the black humour tradition in literature, which was highly charged with this sensibility.

DF: We were both fans of William Burroughs . . .

WB: . . . Nathanael West . . .

DF: . . . Bruce Jay Friedman, Philip Roth, Vladimir Nabokov . . .

WB: . . . Kurt Vonnegut, Terry Southern, Thomas Pynchon . . .

DF: They were very big in New York at the time.

Fairly big in England, too.

DF: Well, you guys invented irony, so . . .

WB: When you've lost the empire, what are you gonna say? They got a great empire, they see it slipping away – here comes your irony!

DF: We can sense that happening here too. The end of the American empire. We can see it coming.

———

Gary Katz managed to get a few Becker and Fagen compositions placed on albums he was working on – notably Thomas Jefferson Kaye's *First Grade* – and he put a little session work their way, but it was obvious to all that, as songwriters, their material was too eccentric and personal to fit most other artists' styles.

'We realised, even before we were doing it, that we would have to do these songs ourselves,' says Becker. 'We could see that nobody was going to come along and pick up on them because they were too odd, too out of context for the day. On the one hand, they expressed an odd sensibility lyrically, and in their overall musical thing, and they were so musically unusual that even people who later wanted to record some of our songs had a hard time, because the jazz elements or other harmonic elements were hard to pull off.'

'They have to be performed with a certain attitude,' adds Fagen, 'and we couldn't find the right singer when we started. I became the singer by default because I was the only one with the right attitude, essentially, even though I didn't consider myself a singer at the time.'

Covertly, the three New Yorkers began assembling a band, calling Denny Dias, Jim Hodder and Jeff Baxter over from the East Coast, and using ABC's money to buy equipment. Eventually, the label realised what was happening, but had enough faith in them to give the project the nod, especially since Becker and Fagen weren't exactly proving a raging success as staff song-writers. A deal was signed, in typical music biz fashion.

'We were like most people,' says Becker. 'When you start out, you get some horrible little deal, that no matter how many records you sell you could barely eke a living out of it and, when you get more successful, you gradually negotiate improvements in that deal. Our lawyer in the deal we originally signed with Jay Lasker was someone who'd worked for Jay until a few weeks before – he was in there with his boss and he came out and said, "I gotta tell you, guys, I got killed in there. This is a terrible deal; they didn't give me anything and they say you can either sign it or get the hell out of here!" So we signed it.'

'It seemed OK at the time,' adds Fagen. 'We were only kids, y'know?'

The first product by Steely Dan – the name was taken from that of a dildo in William Burroughs' book *The Naked Lunch* – hit the stores in June 1972. A single, 'Dallas', featured drummer Jim Hodder on lead vocal, Fagen still having qualms about his own capacities in that respect. The album which followed five months later, *Can't Buy A Thrill*, even featured another vocalist, the prissy-voiced David Palmer, on a couple of the softer tracks. More importantly, it also included two hits, both of which estab-lished Fagen's nasal sneer as the band's trademark.

The slinky mambo rhythm and electric sitar solo of 'Do It Again' proved surprisingly irresistible over the airwaves. Entering the singles chart in the last week of the year, it eventually peaked at No. 6, swiftly followed by the rockier 'Reelin' In The Years', which reached No. 11. Buoyed by the singles, the album hit the Top 20. All of a sudden, at long last, Becker and Fagen were a success.

Success, though, brings its own obligations. People want to see hit bands. More to the point, record companies want to see hit bands promoting their records, and the only way to do that effectively is to pack your bags, climb on board a bus, and traipse around playing gigs in places like Dogbreath, New Jersey.

For a while, it's fun. The camaraderie of the road, the in-jokes, the last-gang mentality, the acclaim and, of course, the music. But then it all starts to get a little sour. Denny Dias, for one, recalls touring with Steely Dan as 'kinda like going to war: hours of boredom, followed by seconds of terror'.

In the beginning, though, those seconds of terror brought their own reward: the follow-up album *Countdown To Ecstasy*, widely considered the group's best, profited greatly from the weeks spent honing the new material. 'That was the only album where the songs were developed on the road, in rehearsal and onstage,' explains Fagen. 'We were playing them before the album was recorded, so it had a more live, blowing feel about it.'

'Before we did the first album,' says Becker, 'we had written the songs and pretty much finished arrangements at the point where we presented them to the musicians. In the case of the second album, the musicians got to hear the songs and participate in developing the arrangements at an earlier stage. Because we knew what the band sounded like, we had a more developed conception of it and it became a more integrated framework.'

Consequently, where their debut album had seemed rather like a prefabricated pop marvel, this one presented Steely Dan as a great band, bursting with energy and chops, with the rare ability to build on each other's parts in a way that took the material to new heights. Not that ABC saw it that way, mind.

'When we finished that record,' recalls Dias, 'a number of executives came to the studio to hear it played back for the first time and nobody seemed to like it. They were so unhappy about it that there was hardly any promotion for it and it was disappointing commercially. We were trying to go higher and better and they were looking for something more saleable. They were used to AM pop stuff and what they heard was a little more sophisticated and they didn't know what to do with it.'

They didn't like the sleeve illustration either. A painting by Fagen's girlfriend of the time, it featured three forlorn humanoid forms sitting on chairs. Since there were five members in the band – David Palmer having by this time been issued with his P45 – the record company felt there should be five figures on the cover. Two extra figures were accordingly added, though in ghostly, insubstantial form. Few of the band realised it at the time, but this was to prove something of an omen.

Why were early songs like 'Charlie Freak' and 'Parker's Band' on your third album, rather than your first?

WB: See, that's touring for you. We did our first record: boom, they threw us out touring. We managed to get through our second record with mostly new songs, I think, but, by the time we had to go into the studio for our third record, we had to go through the files and pull out a bunch of old songs to fill out the record.

You didn't tour for very long, did you?

WB: Well, we didn't make any money touring. The only reason we could tour England was because the record company kicked in some money: it was a money-losing proposition and we were beating our brains out. We felt if we kept on doing this we would burn out very soon.

DF: And of course, the Beatles had not long before set the example of concentrating on records and not touring, and we were arrogant enough to follow their example.

But shortly after that they split up, didn't they?

DF: Well, we split up shortly after too. We were following their example to the letter! And now we're back together, just like they are. We never make a move without consulting the Beatle Chronology.

———

Though its inner gatefold sleeve features a photo of the same band as that on *Countdown To Ecstasy*, by the time the third album *Pretzel Logic* came to be recorded, Steely Dan was all but finished as a group. The LP was largely recorded using session players, with the actual group being used to present the songs live. Unfortunately, even that involvement didn't last much longer. A tour of Britain in 1974 was abruptly curtailed when Fagen fell ill, and that was that.

'Touring interfered with recording,' explains Becker, 'because you'd go out and trash your voice and your chops and everything and all the gear would be wrecked. Back from a tour, we wouldn't have any songs because we couldn't write on the road. That's why we broke up the band – the other guys couldn't for the life of them see why we didn't want to go out and tour and have the good times they'd been having: we weren't particularly having a good time, but *they* were!

'That's one of your big *Rashomon* situations there – in rock'n'roll bands everybody sees a slightly different version of what's going on, depending on their position in the organisation. And because they're all kids, usually you haven't developed your empathy to the point where you realise that the other guy's got something else he's dealing with. I think musicians in general are childish – in all the best and worst possible senses of that term.'

What did the other guys in the band think when you started to bring in session players to play parts they might have played?

WB: A mixture of bitterness and, er, hatred. Betrayal, a feeling of betrayal. Desire to strike back, to get even, perhaps. Actually, they were good sports about it, to the extent that they didn't quit or throw a screaming shit-fit right there on the spot, but it didn't really make sense to them that we wanted to do that. It was, like, contrary to the ethical understanding they had of the band.

From their point of view, they probably thought they'd be able to tour the album once it was made.

DF: Yes, we could see there was just too much of a lie involved at one point, so they had to go. It was too uncomfortable. They put two years in and we tried to be fair with them financially – they've always gotten full royalties from albums they've played on, and so on. So we've not had bad relations with them since.

And so, almost as soon as it had started, Steely Dan the band was finished. Guitarist Jeff 'Skunk' Baxter and keyboardist Michael McDonald (whom the band had drafted in as a support vocalist) took a free transfer to the Doobie Brothers and all the fame and gigs they could handle: drummer Jim Hodder disappeared to northern California, where nothing was heard of him until his death by drowning in June of 1990.

Denny Dias hung in longer than the rest, a reflection of his closer relationship with Becker and Fagen: unlike the other members of the band, who'd been introduced to them by Gary Katz, Dias was the duo's own choice.

'Denny was a very specialised kind of musician,' explains Becker, 'because he was neither a jazz guitarist nor a rock guitarist – he had the technical ability and training of a jazz guitarist, but he understood how to apply that to play over our chords. And there wasn't much else going on that he was a logical candidate for.'

'He was very devoted to our music,' adds Fagen. 'He's been asked many times to join various groups and, when we stopped touring, he just wasn't interested.'

Since ceasing work with the Dan, Dias did a little low-key music work with jazz pianist Hampton Hawes, but spent most of his time doing systems-level programming for database development environments: he now, however, confesses himself disenchanted with the corporate nature of the computer software world. When the Dan played Los Angeles' Greek Theatre on their reunion tours of 1993 and 1994, Dias sat in with them for a few songs and professes it's the most fun he's had in years. 'I just decided I had to get back into music,' he says, 'so I got a hard-disk recording system which I hooked up to my computer and I've been writing and recording, trying to develop a concept for a record of my own.'

For their part, Becker and Fagen holed up in studios for the rest of the decade, developing perfectionist LPs and a reputation to match. They became studioholics: Becker recalls trying to get an English engineer to work on Boxing Day and being told in no uncertain terms that that was not an available work day. 'We both liked recording studios,' he admits. 'As much as anything else, it was just the coolest place to be on a hot afternoon, sitting on those couches or wheeling around behind a console.'

They had already found themselves struggling against the limitations of their own and their band's abilities: as early as the first album, they had called in session players such as guitarist Elliott Randall, who played the solo on 'Reelin' In The Years' while, on the second album, dissatisfied with Hodder's less-than-metronomic pulse on 'Show Biz Kids', they had had to improvise an eight-bar loop of two-inch tape – which ran from the tape machine to an idler wheel outside the control room – to achieve the hypnotic effect they wanted. At every turn, they were determined to use the best and the most cutting-edge, whether that meant bringing in Bernard Purdie and Chuck Rainey to lay down a groove, or using the earliest digital recorders.

'In the '80s,' reflects Becker, 'hand-crafted, hand-played music was being overtaken by this increasingly mechanical, perfectionist machine music and we were just trying to get there first. They had all these disco records that were just whack-whack, so perfect, the beat never fluctuated, and we didn't see why we couldn't have that too, except playing this incredibly complicated music, and the drummer would go and play a great fill or something and come exactly back at the perfect beat at the same tempo, y'know? It seemed like a good idea.'

Gradually, the Steely Dan sound grew more and more refined

and, by the time of *Aja,* had come to be recognised as the very epitome of rock sophistication. 'We were interested in a kind of hybrid music that included all the music we'd ever listened to,' explains Fagen, 'so there was always a lot of TV music and other things, in there. It was very eclectic and it used to make us laugh: we knew something was good if we really laughed at it when we played it back. We liked the sort of faux-luxe sound of the '50s, there was just something very funny about it. I grew up in a faux-luxe household and it was a very alienating world, so for me it has the opposite effect: muzak is supposed to relax you, but it makes me very anxious. So in a way, I think I get it out of me by putting some of it in my songs. Then I start to laugh at it when I hear it.'

'In some ways, the early, rougher ones sound better now than the later ones,' believes Becker, 'whereas at the time it seemed like we were ever rising towards the light. I think because of the kind of music we were doing, it seemed to us that it should be really seamlessly put together and have a high level of polish to make it work. We didn't want it to sound like kids trying to play jazz – which I think it did pretty much sound like sometimes, and which now I kind of like the sound of. But at the time we thought what we were doing was so different to other things that were going on and our own harsh appraisals of our talents dictated to us that we work harder to make it really smooth and flawless.'

In Los Angeles – and in New York, when they returned there to make *The Royal Scam* – Steely Dan sessions took on a certain cachet among the session community: whose members were, in the main, relieved to be given the opportunity to stretch their talents a little further than the average soap-powder commercial. Sometimes, though, Becker and Fagen could be the most infuriating of taskmasters.

'A lot of times we didn't know what we wanted,' admits Becker. 'Donald and I would write a song on piano, or piano and guitar and sometimes we'd have a very primitive demo, but often as not we'd go in the studio and we'd be hearing the song played by a band for the very first time. And sometimes it didn't sound like what you'd thought it would sound like, and you had to try and figure out why that was, whether your conception of the song was wrong or who could change their part or how to rethink what you were doing to make it work. So a lot of times we didn't know exactly what it was we needed to do at a given moment to get things to be the way we wanted them to be.

'Other times we just wanted it to be better, so we'd keep trying for another take. We kept adjusting our standards higher and higher so, many days, we'd make guys do thirty or forty takes and never listen to any of them again, because we knew none of them were any good, but we just kept hoping that somehow it was just going to miraculously get good.'

Who was the most difficult session player to work with?

WB: To me, the most difficult guys – without getting down to specific names – would be jazz players who, if it wasn't a jazz date, would treat it just like another gig. They'd have a kind of contemptuous attitude, and they didn't like the fact that these young kids were running these sessions and trying to tell them what to do.

DF: It only happened a few times: the guy wanted the gig for the bread, but didn't like the music, essentially. Especially in the early '70s, 'cos there was still a lot of deep snobbism about rock'n'roll . . .

WB: ... and we assumed that, because we had these chord changes and everything, we'd be able to impress these guys and in some cases that didn't turn out to be so. It was all still bullshit as far as they were concerned.

Living hard will take its toll, though, and Becker in particular was living hard, making full use of the recreational drug opportunities afforded by the Los Angeles celebrity lifestyle. The city held little other appeal for them, however, and, by the time they finished their most sophisticated, jazz-inflected album so far, *Aja*, they'd both relocated back to New York. Keen to switch labels, too, they signed up with hotshot manager Irving Azoff, who used his industry muscle to make *Aja* their most successful album yet.

This, however, only served to put greater pressure on the duo to top its success with the follow-up, *Gaucho*. But a series of delays and disasters combined to slow its progress to a crawl. The New York musicians were not as used to their methods as the LA musicians had become and Becker was becoming less reliable because of his drug problem. Then, at the end of 1979, the first completed track for the album, a song called 'The Second Arrangement', was accidentally wiped by a studio engineer. The following month, Becker's long-time girlfriend, Karen Stanley, died in their New York apartment from a drug-overdose suicide. 'I could barely understand what was going with her, really,' he recalls. 'If you've ever known anyone that's chronically depressed like that, it's hard to appreciate what's going on: you're looking straight at it and you still don't get it because you've never gone through that.'

As if that weren't enough, in April 1980 Becker was knocked over by a taxicab, fracturing his right leg in several places. Luckily, recording was all but concluded, but the mixing sessions for *Gaucho* were severely complicated by the injury. By the time the album was released to mixed reviews in November, all concerned were thoroughly sick of it. It was time, they realised, to pull down the curtain on Steely Dan.

'Working together as long as we did,' says Becker now, 'Donald and I followed a certain line of thinking to its logical conclusion and then perhaps slightly beyond – that was what we realised when we'd finished *Gaucho*. It was not as much fun . . . it wasn't fun at all, really.'

Two years on from the demise of Steely Dan, Donald Fagen's solo debut *The Nightfly* was released, to widespread acclaim. Far from heralding a career rebirth, however, it seemed to put the cap on the entire Dan story. The follow-up, *Kamakiriad*, would not appear for another eleven years.

'I really put everything I knew into that album,' says Fagen of *The Nightfly*. 'I wanted to do an autobiographical album. And after that I really wasn't inspired to do anything. I fell into a bit of a depression for a while and I started going to therapy. I think that, like a lot of artists, especially in the music business, I was successful and young and I was basically still an adolescent. I was trying to get out of that with *The Nightfly*; it was kind of self-examination of my childhood. It took me a long time to go through a kind of transformation. Until, around '86–'87, I felt I had some energy and some new things to write about. I worked every day, but I didn't like what I was doing. I'd play the songs back next day and didn't much like them.

'I basically had to figure out how to have an actual life – I was a workaholic till the end of *The Nightfly*; the only life I had was in the studio. A lot of it had to do with my not wanting to address certain things that I had to address personally, and working gave me the chance not to do any kind of self-examination. I'm a very introspective person as it is, so always working is a kind of therapy in itself.'

While Fagen was having his mid-life crisis in New York, Becker had made what seemed a strange jump, moving to the Hawaiian island of Maui, where he cleaned himself up, drug-wise, and set about rebuilding his life.

'The last few years of the '70s got a little out of control around my place, and it really wasn't that much fun,' he recalls. 'The career was a good organising principle for something that was pretty chaotic in other ways. But eventually that didn't work either, and when the dust had settled it was 1980 and it was time to clean up my act, so I ended up coming here because I wanted a complete change of pace – and I must say I had a pretty good time of it: my son was born, I got married. So I spent a couple of years not doing any music or anything, just here in Hawaii trying to get healthy and adjust to the new regimen I was setting up for myself.'

––––––––

As the old Steely Dan LPs were given a new lease of life on CD in the '80s, providing a steady source of revenue, both men tried their hands at alternative, music-related jobs: Becker built a studio on Maui and became a producer for such artists as China Crisis and Rickie Lee Jones, and for new age/jazz labels Triloka and Windham Hill. Fagen, meanwhile, wrote a little film music, for the movie of *Bright Lights, Big City*, and for a while became the film-music correspondent of *Premiere*, the US film magazine. Then, in the early '90s, they hooked up again to produce each other's solo albums, *Kamakiriad* and *11 Tracks of Whack*.

'When I was about to go into the studio, I got kind of nervous about handling everything myself,' says Fagen, 'especially the idea of doing vocals and having to come in and listen to them myself. I realised I was really lonely in the studio by myself, without someone to bounce off. So I thought, Why break in someone else – if that's even possible – I'll just call in Walter. He was more than a producer, really, he was a collaborator as far as some of the music went. Especially in playing: he ended up playing all the bass parts and the lead guitar parts as well.'

From there, it was a short jump to reconstituting Steely Dan, at least as a touring entity: 1993 and 1994 saw them taking an expanded band on tour in America and Japan, the highlights of which are about to appear on their first live album, *Alive In America*. As slick and meticulous as you'd expect, the album features a broad selection of material, the old songs sometimes rearranged in the style of the later Dan records – most notably a 'Reelin' In The Years' reupholstered with spiffing horn arrangements. And while it's at a very early, tentative stage yet, there is actually talk of a new Steely Dan studio album in the works. Wheel turnin' round and round . . .

So . . . why did you decide to go back out on the road after nineteen years?

WB: Well, clearly it was a mistake. We see that now.

DF: Yeah. I'm gonna rescind the whole thing. Can we recall the summer tours of '93 and '94?

WB: We're gonna send all the money back. In fact, anybody who has been to one of our shows in the past two years, if you would be willing to send a stamped, self-addressed envelope to the offices of our business managers, we will cheerfully refund the price of your tickets. There is a hundred-dollar filing fee associated with our book-keeping costs, so make sure you include that.

Review of Show at Wembley Arena, London

Chris Ingham, *MOJO*,
November 1996

———————

They quit touring in '74; broke up in '80. Now the arch hipster auteurs of literate, cynical, smart-ass rock jazz – the creators of some of the most substantial, nourishing sounds of the rock era, the studioholics of the '70s – have looked to their pensions, and taken their greatest hits on the road.

The climb down from the dignified heights of non-reunion is notoriously inelegant but, hey, this is the Dan: Becker and Fagen with newfound live confidence and a kick-ass jazz-chopcentric band clipping into a song bag full of pearls. I mean, look at the set list. Isn't your mouth watering? How dull could it be?

Quite, I'm afraid. We'll only blame Walter and Donald insofar as their admitted moolah-related motivation persuaded them to be booked into arenas. This was a bad idea for two reasons. First, much of the Steely Dan magic lies in the pristine detail of the fine-tuned groove, the meticulous voicing of intricate harmony and the master-chef blend of texture. Tonight, everything is reduced to a lumpen Wembley mulch. The indistinct bass'n' drums chemistry means the usually irresistible lazy shuffle of 'Chain Lightning' and sprightly minimalism of 'Hey Nineteen' leaves heads curiously unbobbing. The sinister space and backing-singer snap of 'Babylon Sisters' is lost, the spine remaining resolutely unchilled. Fagen's menacing whine drifts in and out of the picture, totally indecipherable. Without these arresting particulars and the absence of any break-the-mood dynamics (no ballads, no acoustic numbers, everyone plays *all* the time) you end up noticing how many medium tempo, fat fusion-plodders Steely Dan do, which misses the point by a mile.

Second, arena gigs require big triggers to fire them and the Dan don't have many of those. Their customary rave-up 'Bodhisattva' is inexplicably absent, and potential singalongs 'Reelin' In The Years' and 'Rikki Don't Lose That Number' are re-riffed and re-harmonised, the latter given a cruel key change just before a chorus, just in case anyone is having too vulgar a time. Visually, the most that happens is Fagen leaving his keyboard, Ellington-style, to conduct the big-finish kicks. The Kings Of Cool in this space just look miserable. The Dan are so anti-stadium-gestures that when the lights get excitable near the end, you're embarrassed for them.

Of course, there are pleasures. 'Green Flower Street' skips and skims immaculately. 'Home At Last' benefits from the cavernous sonority, becoming darker and more vivid than the *Aja* version. There's a new Becker/Fagen song, 'Jack Of Speed' ('which we hope to have out sometime in our lifetime'), on first hearing an unremarkable minor blues thing; let's hope there's resonance to be enjoyed in time. Becker's guitar playing is a delight, tasty and thoughtful, a nice contrast to the mind-blowing jazz-metal of Wayne Krantz, and Fagen plays sparkly keyboard, consistently more interesting than the garrulous solos of 'Windham Hill Recording Artist' John Beasley.

And let's get the carping in perspective. The show's current incarnation may not add much to their legacy, but I listened to Steely Dan for four hours before the gig, two and a quarter during, countless since, and I haven't had nearly enough. Their oeuvre is as significant and rewarding as any. So perhaps we'll forgive them for not giving us the perfect gig as they once made perfect records.

Then again, at £25 a seat, more than half the price of their essential *Citizen Steely Dan* box set, perhaps we won't.

3

Review of
Two Against Nature

Ian MacDonald, *Uncut*,
March 2000

———————

There are two schools on Steely Dan: those who like the early
Poppier Stuff With Tunes: those who prefer the later, Purer
Stuff Without Tunes. Either way, it's all one continuous cool third
stream. This group (for, whoever its changing participants, it's
always a group) has consistently made the most urbanely expres-
sive popular music since we waved a resigned farewell to that
now nearly inconceivable Golden Age of Beatles, Dylan, Motown,
Beach Boys, Brill, Bacharach, and others too numerous.

Apart from its use for tour promotion and the *Alive In America*
album in 1995–96, the Steely Dan brand name has been moth-
balled since Becker and Fagen's most extreme voyage into
refinement, *Gaucho*, was registered on vinyl in 1980. Has there
ever, in this anxious business, been so prolonged a pause between
instalments? Has such a pause produced anything other than
disillusion at the far end? Not until now.

If the words 'extreme' and 'refinement' didn't turn your attention off, we can take it that you are prepared, at least, to entertain the proposition that *Two Against Nature* is the best thing Steely Dan have ever done, despite being a further twenty years along the blue horizon in their aforesaid journey into the rare. Which is to say: even later, even purer, *even withouter* Without Tunes . . . yet still just-below-room-temperature lens-flare-dazzlin'. Out there, Frontier. Looking Ahead, Binoculars.

So obliquely futuristic that at first it doesn't even seem to be here, this exquisite album reminds you of the older jazzman who, faced with the swiftness of Parker and Gillespie's bebop improvisations, admitted, 'Man, I can't *hear* that fast!' On the slick surface of its Thunderbird carapace, the Steely Dan ethos appears languid, often operating on something close to, but not quite, cruise-control. The speed is all inside: in the depth and detail of thought, the precision sensors beneath the sporting grace. Only deeper acquaintance with this sleek thing allows you to sense its specifications; until then you're slower than what you're hearing. It'll seem insubstantial. You may not quite catch it flashing by like the longest, lowest dragster on Bonneville Flats.

What's it about? The usual stuff, only this time with a new photo-realistic clarity and a warmer up-closeness. A twenty-year hiatus has failed to dent the continuity of the music Becker and Fagen make together. Knowing them apart through their solo albums, we can only marvel at how the synergy between them produces stuff not only a level higher than what they do alone, but also of a different character. When they collaborate as equals, the result is Steely Dan. Separate, neither can do this trick.

With Becker's down-in-the-gutter cynicism balanced by Fagen's looking-up-at-the-stars lightness, the gritty Zevon-esque dark-rock of the former's *11 Tracks Of Whack* meets the drolly glamorous soul/lounge/jazz pastiches of the latter's *The Nightfly* and *Kamakiriad* ... dissolving into *Two Against Nature*, an album so clean, clear and dry that it may seem sterile on first hearing. Indeed, some will say as much. Wrong.

Having said that, Becker and Fagen do tend to keep their drummers on too tight a leash. Example: the closer, 'West Of Hollywood', which might as well have been sequenced and whose final four minutes (a strivingly virtuosic Coltranian tenor solo over incessant modulations) beg for something more spontaneous. Apart from that, the inaugural impression of desiccation quickly fades as something else comes into focus: educated deftness of a lucidity rarely encountered nowadays. The life and humour in the music begins to shine as you learn your way around those initially arbitrary-seeming sequences and recognise the subtle aptness of the lyric-melodic fit.

Born genre-blenders, Becker and Fagen have long proved adept at pulling crafty card-sharp switches on styles, as evidenced by their less manifest reggae mutations ('Peg', 'Babylon Sisters'). Here, they do it again with the aerial grace of 'Negative Girl', swinging out on a tape-delayed Dean Parks guitar arpeggio almost as beautiful as Denny Dias's comparable figure on 'King Of The World' from all of twenty-seven years ago. But it takes a few hearings to spot that the spaced, entry-overlapping air-funk of the opener, 'Gaslighting Abbie', is their version of James Brown – or that the voodoo title track, despite being in 6/4, is also, under the bonnet, that old funk-soul, brother.

The traditional column-inch requirements of headline and photograph forestall discourse on further details. This being so, it behoves us to cite with honour Fagen's never-finer vocal phrasing and gorgeous horn arrangements, Becker's paradigmatic rhythm guitar, the soloists throughout, the wily backing vocals, the dual purpose yet pellucid lyrics, the crisp demonstration-quality mixes, and the general air of blithe nonchalance radiating from an album that fully deserves to be called a masterpiece. Four years in the making, *Two Against Nature* is so close to perfect that its passing flaws – a couple of overstretched fades, the low vocal mix on the title track, the not-quite-cooked 'West Of Hollywood' and what appears to be (gulp) an audible tape-edit at 4:27 in 'Cousin Dupree' – irk in a way they wouldn't on ninety-nine out of a hundred albums. Musicians and studio-buffs will love it to death and listen intently; fans, too. The unconvinced (and/or those who prefer it louder and shaggier) will remain so.

If Becker and Fagen can knock out one of these every four years until they retire, we'll get five more Steely Dan albums by the year 2020.

4

Hey Nineteen:
It's About Time

Wayne Robins, *Los Angeles Times*,
February 2000

'**W**hat record company are we on, by the way?' Donald Fagen
wants to know. 'I'm not kidding.'

You can excuse the Steely Dan man's disorientation. Fagen and
his partner, Walter Becker, last released a studio album of new
material as Steely Dan in November 1980, the month Ronald
Reagan was elected to his first term. And that one, *Gaucho*, had
been anguished over for half of Jimmy Carter's administration.

You could listen to *Gaucho* on your turntable at 33 1/3 rpm,
and maybe even on a portable cassette player (the Sony Walkman
had been invented the year before). But not on CD – the compact
disc was still in the research and development phase. Whether or
not to make videos was a non-issue for the stage-shy Fagen and
Becker: Cable TV was in its infancy, MTV yet to be born. But this
week they release *Two Against Nature*, an album that picks up
seamlessly where *Gaucho* left off.

In a large rehearsal studio, the Dan's large-ish band works through the new material in preparation for PBS and VH1 TV concerts and a soon-to-be-launched international tour, tentatively set to begin in Japan in May. Upstairs, in a small, cold, bare, dimly lit room suitable for interrogation by secret policemen, the question for Steely Dan is: twenty years? What's the hurry?

'We approached this record fairly deliberately,' Becker says with considerable understatement. 'We decided in 1994 or 1995 that we were going to do a record, in no small part because we wanted to continue to tour. We didn't want to be playing just old songs. We wanted to have new songs that had been released on records that audiences would be able to hear, songs that we had written recently, rather than just things we'd written in 1976. We wanted to feel like playing live and having a band was part of an ongoing aesthetic process, and not just a reprise of a career we had had at one time.'

———

The first time around they were allergic to touring, hardly ever played live after 1974 and dissolved as Steely Dan shortly after *Gaucho*. Fagen went back to New York; Becker retreated to Maui. During the endless interim of the '80s, Fagen made a solo album, *The Nightfly* (1982), while Becker intermittently produced records (Rickie Lee Jones, Michael Franks). Occasional Fagen tracks showed up on soundtrack albums and, in the late 1980s he wrote a column for *Premiere* magazine.

There were tentative gear-ups in the 1990s. Fagen made another solo album, *Kamikiriad*, produced by Becker. By 1993, Fagen and Becker were touring again as Steely Dan, but the record came ever so slowly. (Becker released his own solo album, *11 Tracks of*

Whack, in 1994.) 'We wrote and recorded a lot of things we didn't use and a tune or two we wrote or finished after the recording process started, so a lot of time was spent working on things that ultimately weren't on the record,' Becker says.

Like many Steely Dan albums, there's a thematic consistency to *Two Against Nature*, even if it is, as usual, a bit opaque. 'There wasn't actually any concept, but I think it's sort of like some of the other Steely Dan records, which were written in the same time period when we were thinking about certain things,' says Fagen, fifty-two. 'Whatever was in our minds at the time. But there was a commonality of themes: loss. Decay. Potential rejuvenation . . . '

' . . . however brief, however impermanent,' adds Becker, fifty.

Friends for nearly thirty-five years, Fagen and Becker often answer questions simultaneously, ending each other's sentences like a long-married couple that has survived rocky moments to emerge in a mutual comfort zone.

One of the provocative songs on *Two Against Nature* is 'What a Shame About Me'. As with many of the new tunes, it's set, like Fagen and Becker, in New York. A once-ambitious writer is now working in a bookstore, with no illusions left regarding fame or achievement. The sense of loss and decay, as Fagen put it, is palpable, although maybe not personal. 'I think it should have been called "What a Shame About Us", kind of a generational thing,' Fagen offers. 'It's about expectations.'

'Let's face it,' Becker adds, 'us '60s folks had pretty high expectations. It's not hard to imagine being disappointed in the end.'

There are also titillating touchstones to Steely Dan's past. In 'What a Shame About Me', an old college girlfriend – now a movie star – shows up and suggests getting it on for old times' sake, making believe they're 'back in our old school' – a fan-friendly reference to their 1973 track 'My Old School'.

WB: 'It's sort of an attempt to be somewhat self-referential . . . '

DF: ' . . . we're just trying to connect, you know . . . '

WB: ' . . . and trying to acknowledge our own position in all this.'

———

If 'position in all this' means figuring out where they stand in the pop pantheon of the last thirty years, the answers can be as contradictory and elusive as some of their lyrics.

After their first three albums, Fagen and Becker were singed by their candle-at-both-ends schedule of recording during the week and playing gigs on the weekend. Touring was the music business in those days, but Steely Dan ended as a road unit – and as an actual band – after the 1974 tour to promote *Pretzel Logic*, their third platinum album, which spawned the Top 5 hit 'Rikki Don't Lose That Number'.

The musical introduction to 'Rikki' – a deft appropriation of a phrase from jazz pianist Horace Silver's 'Song for My Father' – signalled the direction Fagen and Becker found themselves going. They'd become steeped in jazz as teenagers growing up in the suburbs around New York. Now they were going to mix it with their music. *Katy Lied* (1975), *The Royal Scam* (1976) and especially *Aja* (1977) and *Gaucho*, all million-selling albums, made Steely Dan's later music an accessory to the plush, yuppie, audiophile lifestyle.

The entire LA studio musician aristocracy was at Steely Dan's service then. The elusiveness of perfection might have tormented

Becker and Fagen on the road, but with these players in the studio, perfection was in reach. 'Their expectation from musicians was always very high,' Roger Nichols, the Dan's long-time engineer, says. 'They'd always come away sweating, playing at a hundred and ten per cent of their capability.'

Nichols has worked with Fagen and Becker since they were tunesmiths for hire, recording demos in the early 1970s for ABC-Dunhill Music. 'We were all hi-fi freaks,' Nichols says. 'They didn't have a record deal yet, but I liked the songs. I liked that they were perfectionists. They had a vision; they could see exactly what the finished product would sound like.'

Bringing polished jazz musicianship and impeccable arrangements to a pop song structure put Steely Dan in the vanguard of a movement they never wanted to join. Call it fusion or pop-jazz or whatever, but don't blame them. 'You can't always count on the devices, attitudes and conceits that stood you in good stead in 1972 or 1973 or 1978–79, to still have the same impact all these years later,' Becker says. 'It works in a musical way too: hearing virtuoso jazz stuff on a rock'n'roll record in those days had more of an impact. Then that got shunted off into an ultra-tame side of the musical world called smooth jazz, which can no longer be subversive.'

Cyber-novelist William Gibson clicked his mouse finger on the distinction a few years ago, telling a British journalist: 'A lot of people think of Steely Dan as the epitome of boring '70s stuff, never realising this is the most subversive material pop has ever thrown up.'

The trick, as Becker puts it, is simple: 'We try to write things that work on a variety of levels at the same time: A sleek exterior with a turbulent lyric.'

However you want to try to pigeonhole Steely Dan – always an unavailing task – there's no question that they are as remote from the mainstream of the record business today as they were back in their first prime time. 'Because,' Fagen suggests, 'our taste in music goes back so many decades more than most people in music does. We were like mouldy figs before we were born.'

Their deeply ingrained aloofness makes it all the more surprising that they've accepted (reluctantly) the promotional demands of today's music business, and embraced (wholeheartedly) connecting with their fans on a website (www.steelydan. com). 'We sort of looked at the website as an opportunity to publish some of the running gags,' Becker says. 'It's kind of neat. There's a sense of connection to people in your audience, where you can communicate with them directly in ways other than your artistic output.'

Can these once-cranky loners really be doing tours, TV and the internet, humming, 'Reach out and touch,' albeit in 7/4 time? 'We can't rely on radio to play us in any wide way,' Fagen says. 'We're trying to sell records that will let us make more records.'

'We were persuaded that the slightly irregular gap between this and our last studio album made it incumbent on us to do things we normally wouldn't consider,' Becker says. 'We want this to be a going thing for us. It's a really satisfying job to have in life and we recognise that. I think we want to make it so that people are aware we're doing this and give it a fair chance to be heard, and it's not likely that will happen unless we do a lot.'

Their label, by the way, is Giant/Reprise.

5

Steely Dan and Jazz

Chris Ingham, *Jazzwise,*
December 2000

───────────

Waiting for Walter Becker and Donald Fagen, a.k.a. Steely Dan, in their publicist's New York office, I spot two mouth-wateringly opulent 24-CD sets of *Duke Ellington: The Complete RCA Victor Recordings 1927–1973* on a shelf, still shrink-wrapped, 'one each for Walter and Donald,' the publicist explained. (The Dan's record company, Giant, is under the same BMG umbrella as the Ellington RCA archives.)

I enthusiastically point the sets out to Becker and Fagen when they arrive. 'Oh, yeah,' drawled Donald Fagen, not making a move to pick the box up; 'we already know most of that stuff.'

For many jazz enthusiasts, that is the essence of what makes Steely Dan the coolest of rock bands: they know most of that stuff.

Meeting in New York's bohemian Bard College in the mid-'60s, Becker (a bassist and blues guitarist) and Fagen (a 'mostly self-taught' jazz pianist, a hopeful saxophonist and reluctant vocalist) were a pair of hipster misfits who shared tastes in beat literature and jazz. They began writing rock songs with aspirations to Dylan-esque cryptic depth and melodic sophistication; 'classical and jazzical third stream,' assesses Fagen.

Answering an advert in the *Village Voice* that read, 'Bass and keyboard player required, must have jazz chops. No assholes need apply,' Becker and Fagen found themselves with a band. Between 1972–80, they released seven albums, the latter few of which remain among the most finely-honed and sophisticated in the entire rock canon.

Quitting touring in '74, subsequent output established that Steely Dan was not a band at all, just Walter, Donald and an ever-flowing tributary of top session musicians. Yet when they started touring again in '93 with hired jazz hands – and even on this year's triumphant comeback album *Two Against Nature* – they always produced the unmistakeable sound of Steely Dan.

'One thing people don't realise is that we never, ever went for a specific kind of sound, even in the '70s,' says Fagen. 'It's really a function of what we like to hear. A kind of rhythm and blues foundation with jazz harmonies and my voice and a few other points of style give you that sound.'

Becker attributes their sound to clarity and consistency of conception. 'I have a CD at home, an Impulse! sampler, all recorded over a period of four or five years in the early '60s for the Impulse! label by Rudy Van Gelder, produced by Bob Thiele. Cut to cut, all of these records sound like they were made on the same day. The sounds were consistent: Coltrane, the drums . . . it's really remarkable. And the reason is the engineer and the producer had a really clear idea of what they thought things should sound like. Same with Ellington. Granted there was consistency in his bands too which he fought for, but here was a guy who obviously had a vision of something and it didn't change a whole hell of a lot over time. He enriched it and added to his vocabulary, but it sounds like the same guy. Why wouldn't it?'

Fagen's jazz influences stem from an early rejection of post-Chuck Berry rock'n'roll, childhood exposure to Symphony Sid's jazz radio show and Red Garland's *Jazz Junction* album. Fagen: 'I bought it and ever since I've tried to imitate his style in the privacy of my own home.' They both cite 'the best jazz players from the '50s and '60s' as primary influences. Significantly, the DJ on the cover of Fagen's 1981 solo album *The Nightfly* has a copy of Sonny Rollins's *The Contemporary Leaders* to hand.

'You might say that Walter and I have a rather narrow spectrum of taste when it comes to that sort of thing,' Fagen once remarked. 'I like Sonny Rollins, John Coltrane up to the point where he self-destructed jazz. He got a little smart and ventured into realms where no man should ever tread. I also dig Mingus, Duke Ellington, Charlie Parker, Eric Dolphy, sax players in general and good rhythm sections. Also Miles's quintets.'

Both Becker and Fagen agree on the pre-eminence of Bird. A college pal remembers Becker and Fagen explaining world history to him thus; the planet formed, the Earth cooled, fire was discovered, the wheel was invented, Charlie Parker appeared and it was downhill from there.

Though the majority of their song structures have a pop/rock base and their grooves are mainly rooted in R&B and occasionally Latin rhythms, the harmonic element of their compositions became increasingly jazz-oriented with each album. Lacking confidence in themselves as players, they hired dozens of the greatest rock, jazz and session musicians to realise their singular compositions.

Having relocated to LA, they forged a close relationship with Brit-jazz wunderkind turned prodigious session man Victor Feldman, who appeared on keyboards and percussion on all of their '70s albums. 'Victor always treated us good,' remembers Becker. 'However, there was another generation of jazz musicians who resented the idea that young guys would be popularising elements of jazz music in their pop music. In the early '70s in LA, we would hire someone and not know whether that guy was going to show up and be as interested, amused and delighted as, say, Victor was, or angered and disgusted the way certain other musicians were.'

Fagen: 'They were probably mad at themselves for whoring out, as they saw it. It didn't happen very often. It happened once in a while – that was a typical interaction between rock people and jazz people in that period, though musicians our age and younger were used to playing in fusion bands from the middle '70s. A lot of black guys had played in R&B bands; it always used to be part of what goes into making a jazzman. Coltrane used to play in R&B bands.'

Many of the current generation of jazz musicians were brought up to revere the Dan (Fagen: 'Yeah, we're very big in classroom jazz') and, these days, playing for Steely Dan is one of the prestigious gigs for a musician-for-hire. Though the drummer's role in Dan is less flexible than that of a soloist, they still look to the best to do the job. Peter Erskine, ex-Weather Report drummer and recently leader of two beautiful ECM piano trio albums with John Taylor, was the first choice on the reunion tour of '93.

'I never knew how much fun it could be to play a bass drum on 1 and 3 and a snare drum on 2 and 4,' comments Erskine. 'Jeez, I felt that years have gone by and I've missed something that a lot of other drummers have known. And it's not easy to do . . . to get it to lay right. But it's just as satisfying as the inter-active jazz drumming that I like to do. And in some ways it's more satisfying.'

Erskine also tells a story about testing Becker's and Fagen's legendary obsession with tempo and groove by notching up the strictly prescribed tempo of a tune one night by a single beat-per-minute, just to see if they noticed. They did.

Part of the Steely Dan fable is the exacting, often perplexing personal standards they demand of the performances of guest soloists. There's a scene in the *Classic Albums* TV programme on *Aja* where they revisit some of the accomplished-sounding but rejected guitar solos of 'Peg', fading them up and down with ter-rifyingly dismissive comments. It's a fascinating glimpse of that select Club Of Two that's daunted so many musicians.

On *Two Against Nature*, Chris Potter is the latest in an elite pantheon of saxophonists (that includes Wayne Shorter, Michael Brecker, David Sanborn and Phil Woods) to have passed the audition. Becker: 'We just couldn't shake him. He seemed pre-pared to improvise soulfully and swingingly over any kind of chords we gave him. Jeez.'

Fagen agrees: 'We tried to stump him but no matter what we came up with it didn't seem to really matter to him. Also, he was essentially reading chords, running the changes usually at first or second sight.'

Perhaps they should have made him play by ear. Fagen: 'Without the chords in front of him? We're gonna do that next time. You know, once he'd played 'em once through, he sort of *was*, actually, ha-ha! He was kinda looking this way out the cor-ner of his eye.'

A proportion of their material, at least one track per album (two on *Two Against Nature* – 'Jack Of Speed' and 'What A Shame About Me') examines the altered possibilities of the blues. Fagen: 'Sort of in the Blue Note tradition of Horace Silver, Herbie Hancock, that tune they made a rap out of, "Cantaloupe Island". Blues up to a point. A lot of what we do is grappling with how to make the blues more interesting.'

Though Fagen is a pertinent pianist who, on the '96 tour, made second keyboardist John Beasley sound positively garrulous, he continues to shun the spotlight as a player. Fagen: 'We can't play as fast as those guys. Ha-ha!' However, on the blues-based tunes – indeed on most of *Two Against Nature* – Becker comes into his own as an affecting, effective, altered blues guitarist. Becker: 'Donald encouraged me a lot and I think it was more important to have a take on what the music is about than a lot of chops. A rhythmic attitude.'

Fagen: 'Walter plays in that Chicago pocket, that's why I particularly like it. It's hard to find younger musicians who can lay that far back, yank it around.'

Becker: 'There has been a rhythmic shift over the years that's caused us no end of difficulty, where people feel the centre of the beat in a different place than what we're trying to do. It was already starting to happen by the end of the '70s.'

Fagen: 'Yeah, people weren't hauling the groove around like they used to with that kind of confidence. You can hear it in Miles Davis's playing, Thelonious Monk, Muddy Waters.'

Becker has a lot of space in which to yank it around, the backings on *Two Against Nature* are very sparse. Fagen: 'We realised that things generally sound better with more air in the rhythm track. It's sort of fun when the sustaining instruments suddenly disappear and you're left with the rhythm track and you can hear the detail of what the rhythm players are doing. Not unlike Count Basie – the *best* thing about the Basie things, this huge band stripped down to a trio with the tiny Freddie Green guitar.'

As literate pop/rock writers with a jazz understanding, they're virtually in a genre by themselves. Does that satisfy them or would they have relished a little competition? Fagen: 'I would have liked it if it had worked out so that there was more combination of genres. Maybe some people who had more jazz background and who could play rhythm and blues, or understand what's good about that. There may have been more interesting or smarter genres, but it just didn't happen.'

Becker: 'The amazing thing for jazz fans is that more musicians don't like that kind of music [jazz]. Musicians just went in a different direction. It's not just that they're not interested, they actively dislike it. It's actually repulsive to them to move away from triads.'

Fagen: 'That's standard since the bebop era. You can still clear a room in downtown Manhattan by putting on a Charlie Parker record.'

<u>6</u>

Review of
Everything Must Go

Richard Williams, the *Guardian*,
13 June 2003

nique among contemporary musicians, the post-comeback
Steely Dan make records that are more fun to read than to
listen to. Like this: 'Now did you say that you were from the
Netherlands/ Or was that Netherworld?' But in all other respects,
this new set of songs fails to live up to such assured invention.

Thirty years on from their debut, Donald Fagen and Walter
Becker have reduced the musical content of their compositions to
a series of beautifully machined gestures, virtually devoid of the
bright hooks and bold flourishes that gave them such a vital role
in the wasteland of the 1970s and sent fans skipping down the
street humming snatches of 'Barrytown' or 'Deacon Blues'.

Time spent with the lyric sheet of *Everything Must Go* will not
be wasted, but only the hard-bop horns on 'Things I Miss the
Most', the slick guitar lick of 'Godwhacker' and the laconic strut
of 'Pixeleen' rise above the mood of well-heeled world-weariness.

7

A Droll Double Act

Gavin Martin, the *Independent*,
6 June 2003

I t is late afternoon before Walter Becker and Don Fagen greet their first interviewer of the day. The two men, who first fronted a band called Steely Dan in 1972, are lounging in a fifth-floor suite of the ocean-front Fairmont Miramar hotel in Santa Monica, California.

The venue, a midway point between Becker's home in Hawaii and Donald's upstate New York residence, has a faded grandeur perfectly in keeping with the Steely Dan canon, where musical opulence and a longing for a distant past are so often intertwined. Sat on the couch in front of me, Becker, at fifty-three the younger by two years, momentarily stops reading the morning paper to offer an amiable welcome. Fagen hovers uncertainly behind my chair, slurping from a bowl of raspberry sorbet. The singer/pianist has the most painfully ill-at-ease body language of any interviewee I've ever encountered.

Like Becker, Fagen has a rapidly receding hairline and middle-aged spread, visible beneath his rumpled sweatshirt. But his head has all but vanished deep into hunched shoulders, while his eyes dart furtively round the room like a trapped animal.

The new Steely Dan album, *Everything Must Go*, was made in a comparatively short space of time. Mostly recorded live, it is a stark and punchy counterpart to its predecessor, the four-Grammy-winning album *Two Against Nature*, released three years ago.

Though Steely Dan have seldom been considered an overtly political band, from its opening 'The Last Mall' to the closing title track, *Everything Must Go* is an unflinching look at venal greed, mindless consumption and ersatz realities. The album's recurring concerns are the debris of the capitalist dream (the impoverished divorcee on 'Things I Miss the Most') and the victims of counter-culture utopia (the junkies on 'Blues Beach'). Neither Don nor Walter is aware that Welsh agit-poppers the Manic Street Preachers have already used the record's title.

'So what, every set of words has been used by someone somewhere already, it's a common phrase. Anyway, I think capitalism has got everybody's goat, don't you?' grins Becker.

'Only for the last fifty years or so. Actually, I think you will find these same themes on our very first record,' argues Fagen.

Walter: 'If it wasn't capitalism it would be something else – we'd be complaining about whatever system was calling the shots.'

As Donald continues to slurp his sorbet, Walter returns to the paper to brief his partner on the issues of the day, namely current uneasiness in Europe over US foreign policy.

'The actor Vince Vaughn says we just have to try to remind Europeans about the Marshall Plan.'

'Oh, I see, so he's just like all the other scumbags,' moans Fagen, noticeably relaxing as he sits down at the opposite end of the couch to his pal.

Becker shrugs. 'Well, I suppose you can take historical details and twist them whatever way you want.'

Indeed. In the late 1960s Walter and Don were two smart, jazzy, savvy kids fresh out of Bard College in upstate New York. Their attempt to establish themselves in the Brill Building song-writing stable met with meagre success so they set about rewriting the pop rulebook in Steely Dan, a hastily convened group named after a steam-powered dildo in William Burroughs' junkie, sci-fi beat-era novel *Naked Lunch*. Burroughs, however, never became a fan.

Becker: 'I think he found we were marginally less unpleasant than other popular music, but no more than that.'

Apart from the striking appendage, did Burroughs' writing particularly inspire them?

Fagen: 'He brought something new into literature, but most of his work is unreadable. The way he influenced us was through his use of science fiction and the erotic, though his flavour of the erotic was not the same as ours.'

Walter: 'And the use of addiction as a metaphor for existence was very interesting. He wasn't just a bohemian joker; he had points to make.'

And so of course did the Dan. Between 1972 and 1980, Walter and Don were the unassailable hepcats of East Coast cool, subverting the West Coast mainstream with lyrical intrigue, dazzling crafted intelligence, their twitchy finger on the pulse of popular taste.

They wrote about gambling addicts ('Do It Again'), a stock market crash ('Black Friday'), cruel decadence ('Show Biz Kids'), drug dealers ('Kid Charlemagne'), fugitive gunmen ('With A Gun', 'Don't Take Me Alive'). Albums like *Pretzel Logic* and *Countdown To Ecstasy* presented a quintessential American songbook filled with characters that ranged from the seedy and desperate to vengeful dreamers ('My Old School') and lost romantics ('Midnite Cruiser').

Steely Dan has always been Walter and Don with an ever-changing line-up of the finest musicians that money and talent can buy. 'As musicians, we've had dream careers: just being in the studio or in the control room with those guys was all you could ask for, really,' reflects Becker.

Looming large in Dan mythology is Jeff 'Skunk' Baxter, the moustachioed guitarist responsible for some jaw-dropping solos. Bizarrely, as Becker explains how their former associate is now 'a self-instructed expert on numerous weapons systems', a military helicopter thunders up the coast rattling the windows of the hotel as it passes. 'See what you get when you mess with the Skunk, don't fuck with him,' exclaims Becker.

'His U2 plane will be along in a minute,' warns Fagen.

In 1974, before they'd recorded their biggest hits, Steely Dan ceased to function as a live band. Signs of studio exhaustion were evident beneath the meticulous design of 1980's *Gaucho* and, shortly after it was released, they ceased operations completely. For the rest of the decade they engaged in fitful solo careers and waged personal battles against tragedy and depression. Becker's girlfriend OD'd in his New York apartment and he struggled to conquer heroin addiction. Fagen had a breakdown and suffered a long period of writer's block.

Their comeback took time to blossom after the 1993 reunion tour, but they are now on a creative roll which even their deeply imbued cynicism can't stop. They've changed labels since *Two Against Nature*, but are quick to dispel any illusion that they are now independent guns for hire.

Becker: 'The idea that we're working for a different record company is purely an illusion – it's actually the same record company with a different name. I would say we are merely foot soldiers for a vast criminal enterprise where the names keep changing but the faces are always the same – namely, the music business.

'I think what we do artistically is subversive, but when it comes to marketing and that sort of thing, we're not interested, we settle for what is easiest. We talked over some options, we could put out our own record, do it over the internet, but it was all too much trouble.'

Fagen: 'We aren't really salesmen. Who wants to spend time and energy in the marketing business? I know there are some talented younger performers who use the internet and have no intention of getting a record deal . . . '

Walter: ' . . . or earning a living, buying a house or raising a family.'

Don: 'Yeah, they're young, they will learn.'

As they slip into their old repartee, it is hard to imagine how they coped apart from each other during their extended separation. Did they each feel they were only half there without their sparring partner?

'By that time, I was only half there,' laughs Becker, alluding to his drug problem, 'but I managed to get about thirty per cent of it back.'

The comment causes Fagen to guffaw uncontrollably – a weird whinnying sound that resembles a mule in traction.

Other artists who've undergone trauma and recovery favour personalised songs of survival, anguished and confessional interviews. That is not the Dan style. They admit that gallows humour has been an essential part of their survival mechanism, although past personal experience does feed into their lyrics, however obliquely.

Becker: 'We are constantly competing with the monsters from the id.'

Fagen: 'The unseen reptiles within.'

Walter: 'All the good things we tried to do and all the bad things we tried not to do, as James Brown once said.'

Becker and Fagen are many things – laconic revolutionaries, mischief-makers who seem irrevocably altered by past chemical intake, jazz buffs with a still-bright pop sensibility, and, perhaps most surprisingly, concerned parents too.

On the new album, 'Pixeleen' is born out of unease with present-day teenage reality.

Don: 'I have stepkids but Walter has had experience parenting teenagers; he contributed his knowledge of teenage mores.'

Becker: 'I think what television and videogames do is reminiscent of drug addiction. There's a measure of reinforcement and a behavioural loop. Even from a metabolic point of view, a person sitting on a couch watching television burns fewer calories than a person sitting on a couch. Though far be it from me to preach.'

'You mean you can lose weight just by turning off the TV?' says Fagen. 'That sounds like a good diet.'

Becker and Fagen on the Heavy Rollers tour, Rotterdam, July 2007.

Paul Bergen/Getty Images

SIX: Grey Eminences

'We're constantly competing with the monsters from the id.'

Walter Becker, 2003

1

Review of Fagen's
Morph The Cat

Geoffrey Himes, the *Washington Post*,
3 March 2006

How do you write a song about homeland security without sounding preachy or trite? On the other hand, how do you make honest music in 2006 without writing about homeland security?

Steely Dan's Donald Fagen solves this challenge on his terrific third solo album, *Morph The Cat*. He turns newspaper headlines into personal stories, sometimes twisted for humour and sometimes for paranoia.

On 'Security Joan', he has fun with the sexual connotations of a frisking at an airport gate; his slinky keyboards buzz like an x-ray machine as he purrs, in his faux-soul voice, 'Confiscate my shoes ... search me now'. 'The Night Belongs to Mona' offers a darker view of the same subject. Ever since 'the fire downtown' on 9/11, Mona is afraid to go out. She spends all her time inside her fortieth-floor Manhattan apartment, 'CDs spinnin',

AC hummin', feelin' pretty'. Is that pity or sympathy we hear in Fagen's voice?

Darker still is 'Mary Shut the Garden Door', with its eerie melodica and ominous images of government agents hiding behind the dark-tinted windows of Lincoln Town Cars as they point their headlights through the blinds of our windows. Even the romantic fantasy of 'The Great Pagoda of Funn', he admits, is an escape from the real world 'of psycho moms and dying stars and dirty bombs'.

No one was ever better at fusing jazz and post-Beatles pop than Steely Dan, and Fagen continues down that path with ambitious chord changes and elastic rhythms that hint at both swing and rock. He hires such gifted jazz musicians as saxophonist Walt Weiskopf, trumpeter Marvin Stamm and guitarist Wayne Krantz, and allows them to stretch out in solos within arrangements that more often than not extend beyond the six-minute mark.

2

At Long Last, Fagen
Puts The 'Cat' Out

Ira Robbins, *Newsday*,
1 March 2006

Donald Fagen makes and releases solo albums on a timetable
more familiar to comet-watchers than observers of pop's
hectic rush. Working in the off portions of Steely Dan's four decades of on-and-off-again existence, the Grammy-winning
singer-keyboardist from Passaic, NJ, has come up with three
albums in twenty-four years, and that's stretching it, since *Morph
The Cat* won't be out until next week. At this rate, the Fagen section in CD stores will not expand again until 2017.

Reached by phone during rehearsals for a March-long tour,
Fagen, fifty-eight, says the three albums form a trilogy.

'It's nothing premeditated. I tend to [make records] after I'm
in some other next phase of life and have something to say about
it. When I did my first album, *The Nightfly*, in '81, I wrote a
couple of songs and realised they were an adolescent's look at the
world, so I just kept writing songs like that. When I had enough

to fill ... forty-five minutes, because it was a vinyl record, I was done. The same thing happened with my second album, *Kamakiriad*, in 1993. That was really about midlife. At that point, I figured I should write a third album about the end of life. Only this time, I had to fill an hour because it's a CD.'

Stylistically, *Morph The Cat* doesn't stray far from Steely Dan's pretzel logic: exquisitely clear production of genial funk, jazz and soul stylings with wry, literate lyrics in narrative frames, fragments of short stories told from surprising points of view. 'What I Do', for instance, offers a young man's dialogue with the ghost of Ray Charles. 'Mary Shut the Garden Door' is a response to the 2004 Republican convention, and 'Security Joan' is about finding romance with an airport guard.

Indeed, Fagen says women are what differentiates Steely Dan from the solo albums he and his partner, bassist-guitarist Walter Becker, make. 'We both have families and wives and everything. Steely Dan is guys without girls. The collective persona we unintentionally developed is a guy who's talking to the guys, except once in a while, he breaks down and you get to see that he's unstable. Kind of like Dick Cheney. Every once in a while, he takes a shot in the bushes without knowing what he's shooting at.'

Becker, who produced Fagen's second solo record, has no role on *Morph The Cat*, but there's no gauging that impact. Fagen says, 'We started working together when we were young and developed a style together. On my own, I'll sometimes say, "Hey, Walter, what do you think about this?" and there's no answer. It's very frightening.' (Yet Becker found it lonely writing songs on a computer for his first solo project, *11 Tracks of Whack*. 'But it got a little better as I went along, especially after I started calling the computer Donald.')

While voters get the politicians they deserve, bands can attract audiences they don't always expect. 'When Steely Dan started out, we had a more normative band . . . So our fans were the usual bunch of psychos, just normal rock fans. The sort of psychos we have now are a much higher class of people.' A wry tone creeps into Fagen's voice. 'A lot of dentists. Every time I go to the dentist in any city, they've always got plenty of Steely Dan records to play while they're drilling your teeth and producing pain. Whole dental colleges run on Steely Dan music.'

He's kidding, and chuckles at a joke about the music's possible anaesthetic effects. He takes in his stride a suggestion that Steely Dan's marriage of jazz and pop could have – by the removal of irony and intelligence – mutated into smooth jazz. 'I'll publicly apologise for that if you want. It's certainly nothing we intended.'

3

Becker's *Circus Money*

Richard Cromelin, *Los Angeles Times*,
8 June 2008

———————

'Then you find you're back in Vegas with a handle in your hand,' goes a memorable line from Steely Dan's debut hit 'Do It Again'. Thirty-six years later, Steely Dan co-auteur Walter Becker is still positioning characters in front of the slot machines. Betsy Button sits with her cup of nickels, waiting for her break as Becker croons, 'She needs three bars, three cherries, three lemons, three pigs . . . '

Gambling, desperation and other basics of the human condition feed Becker's muse on *Circus Money*. Even though he wrote the songs with the record's producer, Larry Klein, rather than Steely Dan partner Donald Fagen, they embrace concerns and settings – bohemian haunts and showbiz retreats – that Dan fans will find familiar.

'I don't think we felt necessarily compelled to break new ground in that way,' says Becker, who will be reuniting with Fagen for a Steely Dan tour this summer. 'A lot of the material for the lyrics had to do with various LA and Hollywood-type scenarios that we would talk about. Larry is one of the seven native Angelenos, so he has a very rich and jaundiced – quite rightly in my view – take on it. It occurs to me as I listen to it that there is a sort of a lyric shape to the album. It had a romantic element and then . . . a certain nastiness or edginess came into it as it went.'

That might describe the bittersweet 'Downtown Canon', in which a youthful idyll goes wrong and leaves a persistent memory and such vignettes of venality and manipulation as 'Selfish Gene' and 'Three Picture Deal'. But there's another side. 'Paging Audrey', for one, taps a surprisingly tender vein of loss and regret, as the singer reaches vainly into the past searching for a vanished lover. 'It's the idea of what happens to people that disappear in various ways,' Becker says. 'You still relate to them as if they were present in ways that they may not actually be. I think it's a way of realising that some people who may not continue to exist as part of your life or otherwise may continue to exist in your mind.'

For the music, Becker and Klein (producer of Herbie Hancock's Grammy-winning *River: The Joni Letters*) groomed snug, swinging, small-combo grooves with such stellar musicians as drummer Keith Carlock, guitarist Jon Herington and keyboardists Ted Baker and Jim Beard crafting a less complex, more intimate version of Steely Dan's jazz-informed harmonics.

The wild card – and probably an insurmountable stumbling block for some – is Becker's voice. Limited in range and uncertain in intonation, it's a shortcoming he wrestles into submission, eventually finding a balance that allows the focus to fall on the tales rather than the technique.

For Becker it's a mixed blessing. 'The biggest drawback, of course, is the self-loathing that keeps me from doing things, because I feel as though it places an unfortunate ceiling on how good it can ever sound to me. As far as the strengths go, the only real strength is that I can sing things that I would not be able to explain to other people how to sing. And I can manifest the intention of the lyrics in some way, without having to be taken aback or angered or disgusted as any normal human being would be with most of the lyrics that Larry and I have written.'

4

Review of Fagen's
Sunken Condos

Adam Sweeting, *The Arts Desk*,
10 October 2012

———————

Donald Fagen's fourth solo album arrives thirty years after his first one, *The Nightfly*, though there can be no doubting it's the work of the same artist. The quizzical chord sequences, supple instrumental interplay and teasingly cryptic lyrics will be instantly familiar to students of his work, and indeed of the later days of Steely Dan.

Fagen and his partner Walter Becker have successfully rejuvenated the Steely Dan legacy by assembling a touring version of the group bristling with hyper-capable musical gunslingers, and Fagen has used several of them here, notably guitarist Jon Herington, bass man Freddie Washington and the so-called Steely Dan Horns. The result is a set of impeccably tailored grooves which wear their expertise with insolent nonchalance.

In 'Memorabilia', they click into a swingbeat-ish stroll, illustrated with cool-jazz muted trumpet and carefully blended vocal layers. For 'I'm Not the Same Without You', Fagen has opted for a sleek, streamliner-ish tempo that mirrors the ironic optimism of the lyric (the message is: 'You've gone and I'm delighted'), punctuating it with washes of brass, nimble guitar and harmonica in a post-Toots Thielemans vein. The harmonica is back on 'The New Breed', a jaunty jazz-pop strut where Fagen plays the wizened oldster rendered obsolete, in several respects, by a young computer geek.

Eight of these nine songs are originals, the exception being a Fagenisation of Isaac Hayes's 'Out Of the Ghetto'. Where Ike's 1977 original was raw and funky, Fagen has kept the funkiness and introduced a sardonic smirk, some woozy jazz voicings and a wailing klezmer clarinet, which must be what he meant when he described the track as 'an Ashkenazi recasting'. The punchy directness of the track makes it one of the disc's most instantly memorable moments, since Fagen's own compositions generally take a bit more time to sink in, even if the intro of 'Miss Marlene' sounds uncannily like the opening of 'Deacon Blues'.

One exception is 'Weather In My Head', a gravelly blues powered by a lowdown guitar riff and lit up by some searing lead playing from Herington, whose guitar dips in and out of an ongoing dialogue with the brass.

This album probably won't provoke a stampede of new Fagen enthusiasts, but it should slip down a treat with the initiated.

5

Donald Fagen

Bruce Pollock, *Songfacts*,
7 November 2012

A t the keyboards, Donald Fagen was the smoky voice and songwriting co-conspirator (with Walter Becker) on all of Steely Dan's classic hits, from 'Reelin' In The Years' to 'Rikki Don't Lose That Number' to 'Peg' and 'Deacon Blues' and 'Hey Nineteen'.

Carving perverse lyrics into cryptic and sardonic storylines, wound around a sampling from the literature of pop-rock-jazz-blues melodic constructions, the Dan's output also included some of rock's most memorably ragged character portraits, among them 'Charlie Freak', 'Rose Darling', 'Kid Charlemagne', 'Pearl Of The Quarter' and 'Dr Wu'. Charting the inevitable comedown from a decade of street theatre, Fagen and Becker swung from the chandeliers while the roof was caving in.

Now removed from such turbulence, and approaching his songwriting midlife alone, Fagen contemplates the glittering, standard-strewn byways that led him to this juncture in a much more measured fashion. In the last thirty years, he has produced but four solo albums, including the 2012 release *Sunken Condos*.

As befitting his reclusive reputation, Mr Fagen agreed to this interview only if he could answer all questions in writing.

Songwriting style and the early years

'I don't think Walter and I were songwriters in the traditional sense, neither the Tin Pan Alley Broadway variety nor the "staffer" type of the '50s and '60s. An attentive listening to our early attempts at normal genre-writing will certainly bear me out. It soon became more interesting to exploit and subvert traditional elements of popular songwriting and to combine this material with the jazz-based music we had grown up with.

'In college, we were both intrigued by certain humourists of the late '50s and early '60s, such as John Barth, Joseph Heller, Kurt Vonnegut, Thomas Berger, Terry Southern and Bruce Jay Friedman (I've since cooled on a lot of these writers). Walter read a couple of novels by Thomas Pynchon.

'We both thought the predicament in which popular music found itself in the middle '60s rather amusing too, and we tried to wring some humour out of the whole mess. We mixed TV-style commercial arranging clichés with Mersey beats, assigned nasty-sounding, heavily amplified guitars to play Ravel-like chords, etc. The fairly standardised rock instrumentation of the original group added to the schizy effect. We never tried to compete with the fine songwriters of the era (Goffin and King, Lennon and McCartney). We were after a theatrical effect, the friction produced by the mix of music and lyrics – the irony.'

Work habits

'At this point I can't really remember who wrote this verse or that chorus, but the way it often worked out was like this: I would come up with a basic musical structure, perhaps a hook line and occasionally a story idea. Walter would listen to what I had and come up with some kind of narrative structure. We'd work on music and lyrics together, inventing characters, adding musical and verbal jokes, polishing the arrangements and smoking Turkish cigarettes. Of course, the musicians would kick in with arranging ideas, bass lines, etc. when we got into the studio.

'Working without Walter was shocking to begin with, but I got used to not having somebody to bounce ideas off. It wasn't that difficult coming up with the music, because I basically used to come up with the musical material anyway. But the lyrics were quite difficult. I think I was lucky to be able to draw on my own background for some semi-autobiographical songs.

'Lately I work mostly in the daytime, in a small sunny room. I own a few pieces of electronic gear, but I work at the piano, for the most part. I compose almost every day, usually five or six hours on average. I also make time to play some standards and jazz tunes and maybe run some scales. I used to be a workaholic (what a terrible word that is) – up all night, running to the piano before breakfast, that sort of thing. Nowadays I sometimes stop to smell those proverbial roses. These days I listen to very little music. When I do, I play old jazz records, Ray Charles, Chicago blues, some French composers and, once in a while, with shutters drawn, I sneak a listen to my crackly copy of *Highway 61 Revisited*. A goal I have now is to one day write a really terrific song and hear it in a movie theatre.'

Studio musicians

'When Walter and I decided we weren't cut out to be leaders of a touring band, we started looking for a more mature (some

257

might say slicker) sound. Our original players went their separate ways and studio players were just the ticket. Because the cost of rehearsal time with studio players was (and is) high, we began to prepare fairly detailed charts before going into the studio, sometimes with the help of one of the musicians on the date. The players would run down the tune a few times and then we'd start recording. With luck, we'd get an early take. More often we'd do quite a few. Solos were usually overdubbed and judged on flow and originality; however, a player with a nice touch could get by easily on blues alone.

'Larry Carlton played on quite a few of our records. He's a real virtuoso. In my opinion he can get around his instrument better than any studio guitarist. He's also quite a good blues player. He did the solos on "Kid Charlemagne". The middle solo he did in two takes and we used parts of both. The last solo was straight improvisation. Sometimes a player would come in and rip off a solo like that. Other times, if they were playing something we didn't think was stylistically consistent with the song or if they were just having trouble getting any idea, we might suggest a stylistic or melodic idea to get them started.'

Covers

'Because most of our tunes were written to be performed only by Steely Dan, they don't lend themselves very well to cover renditions. The lyrics are not the sort that would inspire singers to cover them. And most of the melodies are instrumental-type lines, and not songs in the usual sense of the term. By that I mean that a real song, it seems to me, has a kind of melody which is, first of all, very easy to sing. It has a natural flow, usually in a stepwise motion, with consecutive notes, simple arpeggios and so on. That's a quality a lot of the great songwriters had. You can sing the melody without any chordal background and it'll still sound good. The melody is not dependent on the harmony; it's just a really good melody.

'I think our songs were derived more instrumentally, more in the way – not to make a comparison in quality – that Duke Ellington would write. I think his songs in fact don't work that well as songs. He wrote for the people in his band, the specific players. He wrote lines he thought they could play well. And although we weren't writing for instrumental performers – we were writing for my voice – I think our background, because it mostly comes out of arranging and jazz, made us lean toward melodies that had that kind of structure. They're more chordally situated.

'When I hear the occasional cover I almost always experience what I've come to think of as the Bill Murray Effect – i.e. Buddy Greco doing "Born To Be Wild".'

6

Review of Fagen's
Eminent Hipsters

Ian Penman, *City Journal*,
16 January 2014

In January 1974, Joni Mitchell released the exquisite, deceptively sunny *Court And Spark*; two months later, on the penultimate day of March, the Ramones played their first gig. The year obviously had some fine diversions and big surprises in store for the clued-up rock fan. But if you had to identify a dominant trend that year, it was huge stadiums echoing to the roar of monumentally heavy boogie. A lot of endless, finesse-free jamming. A lot of stack-heeled get-down. A job lot of stretched thin, double-live albums. A brutalised twelve-bar blues without end.

Donald Fagen and Walter Becker sat uneasily in this world of earnest sentiment and antediluvian riffing. An impassively odd couple with encyclopaedic jazz smarts and a glowering, gnomic mien, in some ways they sat exactly midway between Joni and the Ramones: pin-up idols of the urbane Los Angeles studio scene but with bags of spiky, shades-after-midnight New York City attitude.

Dorm buddies who met at Bard College in upstate New York, Becker and Fagen started out in a band called the Bad Rock Group, with Chevy Chase – no less – on drums. They were over-literate beatniks with midnight-cafeteria tans and their own hinky, beat-derived argot. Their second band found its name courtesy of William Burroughs: Steely Dan III is a garrulous sex aid, a minor player in the fizzing mind/body loop of *Naked Lunch*.

Musically, the Dan were more jazz-inflected than rock-driven, filled out by a movable feast of session musician pals. For their debut single they picked 'Do It Again', a baleful lament about finding nothing new under the sun. At a time when sitars played as prettily exotic signifiers of limpid bliss, they amped one up for a biting, nerve-jangled solo. At a time when *Rolling Stone* ran long, fawning Q&As with addled vocalists and when the counterculture was sold on faux-revolutionary emblems, Becker and Fagen essayed a light samba to declare that it was all bunk: 'A world become one, of salads and sun? Only a fool would say that.'

Putting the hook up front, taking things easy, capering along to the prevailing ethos – none of this was the Steely Dan way. Even so, 1974's *Pretzel Logic* seemed like the oddest work of an already odd career. The front cover gave little away – a monochrome shot, school of Winogrand or Arbus, of a New York street-food vendor. The title track is a surreal roadhouse blues, which switches lanes into an awed reverie on Napoleonic hubris. Other songs are gossamer light, over in a minute or two, like demos that a more popular act rejected for being too spectral, morbid, tart.

Becker and Fagen started out as songwriter hacks for hire, pale ghosts in the all-business Brill Building. 'Through With Buzz', 'Charlie Freak', 'With A Gun': a rough sketch of how hit singles might sound in some spooky alternate universe. Chart hits that got lost in a notorious park one night or missed civics class to stay in bed and read Henry Miller.

As if to prove the point, Steely Dan then scored the biggest hit of their career with 'Rikki Don't Lose That Number', a hesitant, mnemonic in-joke, strung around the card-shuffle chord changes of jazz pianist Horace Silver's 'Song For My Father'. To date, it remains the only chart smash that kicks off with an unaccompanied, twenty-three-second marimba solo.

But the strangest confection on a strange menu may have been their retooling of Duke Ellington's 1927 composition 'East St Louis Toodle-Oo'. It sits at the end of what we used to call side one, as the real-life East St Louis sits on one side of the Mississippi, facing the slightly tonier St Louis. Ellington's original is a lilting chameleonic vamp, perfect accompaniment for a pleasure cruise down the river Styx. It starts out mournful as recollected sin (you can see the bowed heads, the black frocks snaking behind a stately hearse), but then the dark clouds disperse and the band starts to raise everyone's knees, as if to prove that succour and sunshine were hiding under the heart-sore funk all along. It sounds in two minds – sad and ornery, yet elegantly drunk – and ends where it began, Bubber Miley's trumpet growling like a hungry bear.

Becker and Fagen take their own 'Toodle-Oo' at a slightly brisker clip, as though they're downing cheap champagne on a fast train home from the funeral. They usher in some unexpected guests to the wake: willowy pedal steel, gravelly wah-wah guitar, and tingling stride piano replace the two-toned horns of the original. 'Toodle-Oo' II shouldn't work, but does; shouldn't swing, but really does. It feels deeply affectionate, not glib. Steely Dan were later sampled, in their turn, by thrusting young hip-hop acts: wheel turning round and round. Nothing on *Pretzel Logic* is over-stressed or over-played; it's seriously hip but devilishly playful. 'Parker's Band' may slip in clever nods to certain Charlie Parker titles ('You'll be groovin' high or relaxin' at Camarillo'), but primarily it duplicates the joy of being floored by a polyphonic bebop rush for the first time. The drums are a rising heartbeat; when a multi-tracked squall of saxophones blows in without warning, you may want to rise and offer your own syncopated hallelujahs.

Still, many pop/rock fans were suspicious and remain so to this day. For the doubters, Steely Dan personified the infamous Terry Southern put-down: 'You're too hip, baby! I just can't carry you.' Even Dan fans started to read the work as if it was one big put-on – a prophylactic, perhaps, against the real pain and melancholy that some of these songs contained. Maybe all along, it was the audience that was too hip, not the band; there was definitely a stripe of intellectual snobbery among would-be acolytes like my teenage self. Other spoiled rock superstars maybe 'didn't give a fuck about anyone else' (in the words of 'Show Biz Kids') because they were empty-headed snots; if Becker and Fagen also didn't, we Dan fans agreed, it was coming from a far better, or at least a wiser, place – or maybe a far crueller place.

Some of this cognitive dissonance may be attributable to the fact that the more critics fawned over Steely Dan, the more the duo responded with markedly blasé gratitude. It may also be due to the palette they were drawing on – precedents such as Broadway theatre, soundtrack scoring, West Coast jazz. These were traditions in which a big production number didn't necessarily mean what it said; smiling major chords disclosed drooling wolf fangs; and a desolate blues prepared the soil for subsequent flags of triumph. It's hipness of a different order – tone and texture matter as much as, if not more than, what is explicitly said or sung. (In an early interview, Fagen claimed that he was amazed that anyone liked his singing at all, when it sounded, he averred, like a 'Jewish Bryan Ferry'.) The Dan's variety of minor-chord legerdemain went against the prevailing mid-'70s grain, an ethos where every precious singer-songwriter word was presumed to be heartfelt.

But then, Steely Dan went against the grain in a number of ways. They relocated to Los Angeles in pursuit of superior recording technology, but they didn't really fit the local scene. In a press shot for 1980's *Gaucho*, the duo look like creatures just emerged from a long and difficult hibernation; their flesh has the same gray, drained plasma hue as the bony hands of the album's cover art. Becker could be a backstreet physician, on the lam in a cheap hippie wig; Fagen looks like the anorexic, smart-ass kid brother of Jeff Goldblum's *Fly* guy.

Rumours began to surface of Steely Dan giving Fleetwood Mac a run for their per diem, as far as deep water dysfunction and high-end narcotics went. The difference was that the Dan's decadence felt more oblique and therefore more tantalising – these were chord-progression wonks, not boogie ogres! There was an added frisson in the idea of these two cerebral New Yorkers adrift in scented-candle Lotusland, like a modern-day Bird and Prez. Soon enough, they did both crash and burn, in discrete ways, and a long sabbatical followed. They packed up and left Los Angeles. Becker negotiated a divorce from his five-fathom drug habit in sunny Hawaii. Fagen returned to New York and, by his own account, embraced a long-postponed, full-bore breakdown.

There was never any point when Dan devotees felt: here are two guys who might open up and let us in on the odd-couple arrangement, all the extracurricular accidents and emergencies. They were never at the top of any list you'd draw up of people who would one day pen heartfelt memoirs about their lives in music. And while I can't see it getting an approving Oprah sticker, the big surprise about *Eminent Hipsters* is that it turns out to be, after a fashion, just that: Donald Fagen's heartfelt memoir.

Sure, he hides the fact behind a spunkily disingenuous 'it just fell together' introductory gloss, but it's still more flesh-and-blood affecting than even the craziest Dan-watcher might have dreamed. This being Donald Fagen, he doesn't come right out and solicit for big redemptive group hugs; the more tender lines are well hidden behind his deceptively offhand writing style. The first half is a suite of essays rooted in the late '50s and early '60s concerning 'artists whose origins lay outside the mainstream': forgotten singers, arrangers, sci-fi crazies, ahead-of-the-curve DJs and tastemakers. This brief takes in the overlooked Boswell Sisters; the under-praised – and arguably over-demonised – Ike Turner and the quietly influential real-life nightfly DJs Mort Fega and Gene Shepherd. Fagen also offers a few personal reflections on his late teenage years. The second half, 'With the Dukes of September,' is a diary he kept in 2010 while touring with Boz Scaggs and Michael McDonald.

While the essays present a fascinating prospect, the tour diary looks like it might be a bad goof, a parody of old-time, rock-star self-indulgence. Who needs it, even from one-half of Steely Dan? Do we want cool guys to spill? Doesn't our fascination rest precisely on their flinty, recessive nature? But 'With the Dukes' turns out to be one of the laugh-out-loud funniest things anyone ever penned about the workaday woes of being a pro musician.

It's such outrageous fun, in fact, that it threatens to overshadow the less showy virtues of the essays. Structurally, the book doesn't quite hang together: it feels like two different pitches jammed together to make one awkward hybrid. If *Eminent Hipsters* was a film, you can imagine a weave of the two strands: jaded, lost-in-America Donald has a series of flashback reveries while spaced out along the tour, recalling just how it was that young Donny got here and who inspired him to light out this way.

There are moments when, exploring twenty-first-century America, Fagen has cause both to revisit his own chequered past and re-evaluate some of his heroes. There's a mildly tragicomic episode where Fagen realises that he is to play a local auditorium named after Count Basie. His mood brightens – and then darkens after he realises that none of the audience seem to know, or care, who this blow-in foreigner Count Basie is, anyway. Fagen doesn't belabour the point, but it might be a good topic for a social studies class: What is the point of civic commemoration if you're commemorating a blank?

Eminent Hipsters may itself be Fagen's way of throwing a greasy spanner into the works, at a moment when Steely Dan seem to be settling nicely into rock's own nostalgic industry. Fagen scans the American hinterland and wonders what he's doing and whether a creaking, picky New York homebody should be doing it at all at his age. Do the 'TV babies,' as he calls younger consumers (a phrase out of Allen Ginsberg via Gus Van Sant's 1989 *Drugstore Cowboy*), even know why he's honouring the old R&B pioneers whose ghosts he calls up nightly? Has the public conversation gone stone-cold dead?

Fagen doesn't want to come across like one of those testy old cranks who get aggrievedly reactionary with age ('Hobbesian geezers' – a nice bit of phrase-making), but he doesn't want to kid himself that all is right with the world, either. What he wants is some kind of safe, hallowed, but still-testing middle ground. He recalls the oft-derided era of the early '60s as a time with its own sense of verve, jest, and decorum. Of that era's TV: 'Lots of swell black-and-white movies from the '30s and '40s, all day and most of the night. No soul-deadening porn or violence. Decent news programmes and casual entertainment featuring intelligent, charming celebrities like Steve Allen, Groucho Marx, Jack Paar, Jack Benny, Rod Serling and Ernie Kovacs.' (So far, there have been no signs of a reality TV series in which Becker and Fagen audition session musicians for a new album and tour.) And for a flinty old cynic, he can be persuasively rhapsodic: 'And I'll start thinking about a late summer sun setting over fifteen hundred identical rooftops and my family and bop glasses and Holly Golightly, about being lonesome out there in America and how that swank music connected up with so many things.'

It's a portrait of the artist as an embryonic Florida retiree: grumpy, fidgety, fond (his hotel room iPod plays nothing but old Verve jazz or Stravinsky), ungrateful toward fans, snarling at managers, leering at young poolside babes, spiteful to hotel staff. Fagen doesn't skirt the risk of deep mortification. He leads us round 360 degrees of his touring profile: petty, grouchy, backward-looking, too smug by half. And yet, while it appears to be an entirely truthful account, all the time part of me was thinking: Is this actually the equivalent of a well-crafted Steely Dan character? 'Deacon Blues' on Prozac? As I said to a friend and fellow Dan obsessive, *Eminent Hipsters* is essentially *On The Road* with Alvy Singer. In Woody Allen's *Annie Hall*, his OCD doppelgänger Singer loathes Los Angeles, but work and romance install him there for months at a time. Allen initially wanted to name his feel-good film after a bleak psychiatric diagnosis: anhedonia, a condition that also seems to cover how Fagen now feels about touring: 'The inability to experience pleasure from activities usually found enjoyable.'

Like Allen, Fagen seems deeply versed in the language of shrinks and footnotes from the *Physicians' Desk Reference*. In the missing years between *The Nightfly* and resumption of his partnership with Becker, Fagen had a real Freudian schlep of therapy, and much (legal) pharmaceutical rewiring. While you still wouldn't call him a little ray of sunshine, these efforts seem to have done a lot to revamp his subsequent life: marriage, uninterrupted work, a relative cessation of hostilities towards the media. While the other Donald might conceivably have *written* a tour diary, you can't imagine he would have allowed it to be published.

Today, when we identify a hipster, it carries entirely different connotations from the word's original, darkly lustrous charge. 'Hipster' is now a slight, because hipsters now are slight – not so much a soulful tribe as a fly-eyed pose looking for somewhere to land. Hipsters move into your locale and, before you know it, brittle quotation marks are strung everywhere. Hipsters have become little more than an advance guard for the arcadia of 'hip capitalism'. Once, though, it truly mattered how hip you were.

In Fagen's day, things were different. Born in 1948, he belongs to a baby-boomer generation for whom the benediction of hip was most devoutly to be desired. It was a dark and uncertain thing, an arduous rite of passage, almost a spiritual gamble. Lewis MacAdams, in his 2001 overview, *Birth of the Cool: Beat, Bebop, and the American Avant Garde*, recalls how New York bohemian Judith Malina (later cofounder of the Living Theatre) found herself briefly jailed following a mid-Manhattan protest march. A nice middle-class girl under it all, she's shocked to find herself sharing space with honest-to-goodness streetwalkers. 'I like you,' declaims one prisoner to Malina, 'but let's face it. You're a square.' MacAdams supplies a subtle but powerful sense of where hip's true cargo originates. If it's at street level, the street is on the other side of town. Hip was, most of all, a black phenomenon, 'cool in its slavery-born sense, where attitude and stance is the only self-defence against overwhelming rage'.

New York was the seed bed of hip: Harlem's Apollo, Birdland, the Cedar Tavern, the *Village Voice*. Hipness was arcane. If you had to ask, you were nowhere. MacAdams: 'Everything had to be understated, circuitous, metaphorical, communicated in code.' It was a time when drugs of any kind, interracial dalliance, homosexual love, could all earn you serious jail time. Then, as the '60s loomed, hip crawled into the mainstream light: it began to be discussed, analysed, advertised. A lot of blame should probably be placed at Norman Mailer's door. True hipsters would let slip one pithy phrase or exit inside a ringing Zen ellipsis; Mailer blathered on at great length and made hipsterism seem verbose, fraudulent, a cheap thrill for bored socialites. He missed the unmissable point, which was: never explain or sermonise. There was an art to betraying nothing in public – not anger or fear, approval or approbation. Cool manners were a shield for those who were allowed few weapons of self-defence, a ghetto hijack of Kipling's 'If you can keep your head when all about you are losing theirs', both mask and recompense for folks who had a justified feeling that all sweet ideological promises tended to leave them in the same hole, holding the sharp end of the stick.

Fagen's roll-call of hipsterdom doesn't promote some overfamiliar cast of scurvy beats and angry savants, bemoaning the plastic tragedy of conformist Amerikkka. Fagen *likes* plastic. He digs people who straddle the divide between hep and square, margin and MOR, a no-man's zone where apparent squares take on the prompts of hip and parlay them into a wider audience. 'The concept of hip had exploded into the culture in a new manifestation.' Fagen is very good on artists from that time (Basie and Ellington, Erroll Garner, Billy Eckstine and Sarah Vaughan) who, abandoned by the hipster cognoscenti, worked their way into less cool but far more secure and remunerative positions. Most were in the early autumn of long careers and, while they weren't up for stretching any more boundaries, they could still knock out work of devastating economy and depth.

Fagen's paradigm is not the supposedly world-changing works like *Howl* or *On The Road*, Ornette Coleman's *Free Jazz* or Stanley Kubrick's *Dr Strangelove* – it's concertedly in-between stuff, bronchial guys in airless studios fussing over augmented chord progressions. Fagen is lyrical about his idol Ray Charles – hobbled by racism, blindness, and addiction, but a canny operator who smooched the mainstream with roughed-up textures, surprising combinations, dissimulated taunts. In another lovely tribute, 'Henry Mancini's Anomie Deluxe,' Fagen explains how the eponymous arranger used jazz idioms and jazz players in his TV and film work. 'He utilised the unconventional, spare instrumentation associated with the cool school: French horns, vibraphone, electric guitar and – Mancini's speciality – a very active flute section, including both alto flute and the rarely used bass flute. Instruments were often individually miked to bring out the detail... there was a lot of empty space. It was real cool.'

Mancini gave a bop edge to such TV bagatelles as *Peter Gunn* and *Mr Lucky*, just as Quincy Jones would later score *Ironside* and pianist Lalo Schifrin would rework the unforgettable *Man from U.N.C.L.E.* theme. (Both Schifrin and Jones were graduates of the Dizzy Gillespie touring band, and Jones was mentored early on by Ray Charles.) Mancini titles such as 'Dreamsville' and 'A Profound Gass' (*sic*) inspired Fagen to learn more about jazz and, 'out of these fragments of hip and hype I constructed in my mind a kind of Disneyland of Cool'.

For a moment, we're dropped into the adolescent Donald's reverie about a Mancini recording session: 'Everybody's smoking Pall Malls or some other powerful non-filter cigarettes. Hank hands out the parts. When they run down the chart, a thick membrane of sound flows forth and hovers in the room. It sounds incredibly plush.'

It's rare to read a musician who writes well about the recording process. Shelves of books are devoted to unearthing the fugitive 'meaning' of pretty song lyrics, yet often it's some forgotten scrap of melody that cracks us apart; an old sitcom theme from decades ago can deep-six us more effectively than most big-name, chart-topping tracks. Becker and Fagen knew all about the occult effectiveness of tone and texture. The more studio time they could afford, the more they explored this world of sonic spacing, layering, and counterpoint. Across *Aja* and *Gaucho* and Fagen's own *The Nightfly*, musical grain counts as much as buffed-up words. Listen again to 'Black Cow' from *Aja*: a moony relationship, bogged down in slackness and routine. Recrimination rears its snapping-turtle head and break-up is surely imminent: 'I can't cry anymore.' The rhythm uncurls like someone under deep anaesthetic. Plod, plod, plod, through a big black cloud. Then ('just when it seems so clear') we turn a corner and the music perks up, becomes almost punch-the-sky joyous, a homecoming parade of high-five bass and pungent roadhouse sax.

Or try 'New Frontier' from *The Nightfly*, which opens with an ear-popping surge of forward motion. Drums skip and skim like speedboats leaving a summer jetty; the electric piano nudges you with a conspiratorial grin. The chorus rises and falls like sun motes on a holiday balcony. But there's something else here, under all the mist and spray – a strange hesitant guitar fill, like a nagging second thought, fussing away throughout the song. The major-chord whole is so effervescent and pulls you along in such a happy trance that it's only in retrospect that you realise what a difficult balancing act Fagen pulls off. In 'New Frontier', he distils the secret fears slumbering under the aquamarine repose of hot summertime fun. Fagen sounds upbeat, like a Supremes 45, but 'the key word is survival on the new frontier'. Take that how you will. In isolation, it has a ring of tooth-and-claw realpolitik. But survival is living, too, and in the end, 'New Frontier' is a low-down limbo shimmy, celebrating a new-dawn limbo time.

The song's title is an uncharacteristically candid reference to an antecedent text: John F. Kennedy's speech accepting his presidential nomination at the 1960 Democratic convention. The onset of the decade ahead: Camelot dawning and Kennedy eternally young and forever tan in blinky monochrome footage. When the women behind him applaud, all you can see is a blur of white dress gloves. The 'New Frontier' was a tiny-nugget phrase that set free outsize reverberations. From 'I. G. Y.', which launches *The Nightfly*: 'Standing tough under stars and stripes/We can tell: this dream's in sight'. But consult the speech in question, and you find that it has a surprisingly ashy, cold war taste. Rather than the expected sound-barrier boom of celebration, the message is more like: ignore this advice at your peril.

The speech's rhetorical march falls on a series of hesitant downbeats: 'unknown', 'unfilled', 'uncharted', 'unsolved', 'unconquered', 'unanswered.' It's full of pinched undertones, as much provocation as celebration. Are you up to the trek ahead? Have you got the bright stuff? Do you relish the idea of uncharted space, unfilled time? As much as he was looking forward, celebrating American know-how and optimism, Kennedy was also speaking against unacknowledged failings: prejudice, poverty, everything that held the American Dream out of reach for many sections of post-war US society. On the page, if you Magic-Marker those via negativa *unwords*, it looks like the grand bummer of all 'New Tomorrow' speeches, and a less capable speaker might have stumbled and missed his moment. (JFK had a rather nasal, whiny voice but, boy, he could deliver a lyric. He was the Bob Dylan of '60s' political oratory.)

Fagen's original hipster era is now as old-world distant and faraway as a Victorian player-piano or, indeed, the urtext that Fagen swipes his own title from: Lytton Strachey's 1918 study, *Eminent Victorians*. Strachey caused a big stir with his discreetly anti-hagiographical work, but he saw this slim volume as a resource as much for future readers as for his own contemporaries. Lytton was a bit of a proto-hipster himself – beardy, polysexual, equally at home with Maynard Keynes or sheaves of fussy French symbolist poetry. Where Strachey was out to puncture received wisdom about the era in question, Fagen wants to rescue a misunderstood time. Just possibly, Fagen has something similar in mind to Strachey's idea of a biographical time capsule – he may be writing against his time, as much as for it. (The diary form is a useful means of raising serious concerns in a deceptively airy manner.) Looked at in this way, the essays seem less of an ad hoc grab bag. A quick glimpse at the table of contents may suggest that Fagen's essay choices are flagrantly, even perversely, personal; but they add up to an overview of a specific historical moment. As MacAdams puts it in *Birth Of The Cool*: 'Before, there had been many individual acts of cool. Now Cool – a way, a stance, a knowledge – was born.' Previously, what was hip had been the preserve of certain underground cliques, signalling among themselves in the darkness. Most of all, black American culture in general and jazz culture in particular were the choppy currents that fed into societal sea change.

Hip now found itself working backup for – not the Man exactly, but close enough. Fagen is spot-on identifying hip's undercover dispersal through phenomena like TV cop shows, the film version of *Breakfast at Tiffany's* and Sinatra's pals in the Rat Pack. Here were 'street-wise swingers' who were palpably hip, 'but they could operate in the straight world with existential efficiency'. This birthed a tradition of what you might call 'straight hip,' exemplified by the one guy Lalo Schifrin worked for more than anyone else: Clint Eastwood. Starting with his own nightfly DJ character in *Play Misty For Me*, through the imperturbably cool (and sharply dressed) Harry Callahan, Eastwood embedded discreetly hip tones in precariously conservative settings, right up to *Bird*, his controversial 1988 biopic of original hipster Charlie Parker.

Perhaps none of this should surprise us. The conventional wisdom about the success of something like *Mad Men* is that it plays to our cloudy nostalgia for a time before political correctness and the culture wars, a time when we were positively encouraged to smoke and exist on a diet of highballs, one-night stands, and diet pills. Everything free and easy, no constant checking of guide-lines (and emails).

But isn't this nostalgia less for a lax, ring-a-ding time than for a lost grid where every moral choice was mapped out? Where every-one accepted the existence of common rules? After all, frontiers are places where things end as well as begin. It's all about a pleasurable tension between strict rules and raised-eyebrow rule-breaking. Think of Eastwood as Callahan. He's got swell loafers and perfect shades, but he's thin-red-line to the core. He swings – but not in front of the children or on the streets or for public consumption. I suspect that, in decades to come, people will be absolutely baffled by the high-colour moral variegation of the *Dirty Harry* series.

Rule breaking is only worthwhile when the rules you break have real meaning. Fagen is funny but acute on that moment in our teenage years when we snub parents and dismiss all author-ity figures but simultaneously initiate a desperate search for persuasively hep figures, people to tell us exactly what we should listen to, view and read. What to *dig*. The mainstream culture of that early-'60s era may get a bad rap for being queasily pater-nalistic, but sometimes we need experts to teach us the art of making fine distinctions and keeping valuable traditions alive. Our twenty-first-century snake-oil promise of 'more choice' often devolves into homogeneous slop, a moraine of thin and stony repetition. In the current YouTube moment, we're told that we have a limitless look-see option on everything there ever was, laid out right before us – but at the price, perhaps, of a complete absence of critical chiaroscuro. Look up Steely Dan's wistful 'Hey Nineteen' on Wikipedia and you find: 'See also: age dispar-ity in sexual relationships'. Which is nearly straight-face inapt enough to be a Becker/Fagen in-joke.

Hipsters these days have to use all their desperate wiles just to stay one step ahead of the local TV news; but back in Fagen's youth, sources of alternative info were next to zero. It's easy to sneer at the old idea of 'in the know' hepcats, but hipsters once really were those who lit out for terra incognita. I have deeply ambivalent feelings about the over-canonised Beats, but it's easy to forget the reason they were elected figureheads in the first place: they sallied forth into the unknown and set about indexing the whole of American dreaming, not just a few choice sanitised cuts. Some of their takes on black culture may now strike us as risible and patronising and some of the quasi-religious, holy-fool sub-notes feel a bit self-hypnotised (and on, and on) but, at the time, they were navigating wholly without maps.

There are times on his grand tour of the US in 2010 when Fagen wonders if a whole lot has changed over the preceding fifty years. There may be a black president, but whole swaths of culture are in danger of being re-forgotten, belittled or neutered in divisive 'culture wars' (with errors of taste and scale on both sides). He's alternately combative and perplexed: a sixty-three-year-old singing the golden notes of his youth and struggling to work out if they still mean anything – if any songs do. Suddenly, hip seems less like a faded hobbyhorse for a middle-aged malcontent and more like a lively topos.

In the end, Fagen is hip enough to know that you can't run from your own adult quandaries. There are deeply affecting passages here about family and marriage, loss and aging – things the younger Donald might not have copped to: difficult negotiations, real blues. When you've spent your life using Cool to hold an untidy, insensate world at bay, how do you manage the rough stuff when it rears up and blindsides you on the street where you live, one fine day?

He's good on his parents – both 'the father thing' and a mother who was a more than capable lounge singer, far more creative than she let on (and thus emblematic of many women from that era with curtailed dreams). Fagen Senior was someone who sincerely believed in the promise of the American Dream but found himself knocked to the canvas by real economic jabs. There was the rhetorical fandango of JFK's New Frontier, and then there was how it played out in work places, bank accounts and parental bedrooms. Also, you begin to see where the askew texture of Steely Dan lyrics may have found some of its every-day inspiration: his parents lived in a 'nightmarishly bland apartment, which was in a high-rise building on – wait for it – Chagrin Boulevard'.

Finally, Fagen's hipster is not what Anita Brookner, in a lovely spearing of Baudelaire, called a propagandist of the *pauvre moi*. What's revealing about the scattered reflections in *Eminent Hipsters* is that, in the end, the claim that Fagen makes for these marginal eminences is that they were *good people*. Good for art, good for the social fabric, good examples for one and all.

In those long-gone, fake-ID years, the other Donald longed to be a night-blessed pulp-fiction character with a cynical blonde on his arm and big thoughts in his nodding head. 'That shape is my shade/There where I used to stand.' Well, he got his dream. In the same way that Bob Dylan slowly became one of those gravel-voiced old troubadours he started out imitating, Fagen is now a prickly old jazzer, languid and bittersweet. Still on the road, still making for the border, still so hip it hurts. Next March, it will be forty years since *Pretzel Logic*: the same interval as between Ellington's merciful 'Toodle-Oo' and the Dan's own fizzing but seemly tribute. Some frontiers never grow old.

7

Icon: Donald Fagen

Dylan Jones, *GQ*,
February 2014

NOTE: *This is an edited version of a piece that Jones, the magazine's editor, wrote for British* GQ.

'Like most bands from before my time,' says Mark Ronson. 'I discovered Steely Dan through rap music, specifically because "Peg" had been sampled by De La Soul on *3 Feet High and Rising*. That was about twenty years ago, and I'm still discovering new things every time I put on a Steely Dan record. I'm still even discovering songs for the first time. No other band managed to let groove and intellect coexist as seamlessly. The most incredible rhythm sections with the most captivating narratives and these crazy chord changes.'

You can tell almost all you need to know about a person by asking them what sort of music they like. And although that's the sort of question usually only asked (and answered) by boys between the ages of twelve and eighteen, I was asked it a while ago by someone I'd never met before. It felt like a childish thing to be asked, but even though I could have easily beaten it back by saying something flippant – the last One Direction single, the next Jake Bugg album – I was stumped.

The American writer Chuck Klosterman said that – having for many years experimented with a litany of abstract responses when asked this question – he started to say, with some honesty as well as accuracy, 'Music that sounds like the opening fourteen seconds of Humble Pie's "I Don't Need No Doctor", as performed on their 1971 album, *Performance: Rockin' the Fillmore*.'

Now, never having heard this record, I couldn't comment – although it certainly sounds like the sort of thing I wouldn't like at all – but apparently it has the desired effect, the reply having the added bonus of significantly changing the conversation, or (preferable, this) ending it entirely. Usually, the answers to questions like these are either endearingly banal – 'Oh, the usual, you know, Jay-Z, the Beatles, a bit of Coldplay' – unbearably pretentious – 'the first five Fall singles and pretty much nothing before or since' – or, in the case of most politicians, simply lies.

Having thought about it myself, I've decided to adopt Chuck's policy. Initially I thought of just saying 'Steely Dan', because it not only shows confidence (by any modern definition of the term, they're not really what anyone would call cool), but like Marmite, they are an acquired taste and, unless you're an aficionado, you'll probably hate them.

However, like Chuck, I've decided to be annoyingly specific and, while I thought about singing the praises, yet again, of their sixth album, *Aja*, the next time someone asks me what kind of music I like I'm going to say, having first locked them in with my most sincere stare, 'Music that sounds like the second guitar solo in "Green Earrings" [from Steely Dan's fifth album, 1976's *The*

Royal Scam], the one that arrives after two minutes and seven seconds, the one that makes you feel as though you're cruising over the Florida Keys' Seven Mile Bridge in a rented Mustang.'

And if I were asked what the best album of all time is? Well, it isn't *Nevermind*, isn't *Revolver* and isn't *Pet Sounds*. Strangely it isn't even *Rumours*, *London Calling* or *The Ramones Leave Home*. No, the best album of all time was released at the end of August 1977, just as the sweltering Summer of Hate was beginning to wilt, a record that has nothing to do with the Sex Pistols, the Clash or the Jam (who all released classic LPs in 1977), and which has no affinity with the estuarial guttersnipe squall of punk. In fact, this record is as far away from the insurgency of punk as Southern California is from the Westway.

Steely Dan weren't just up my street; they were, to paraphrase Nick Hornby, knocking on my door, pressing the intercom and peering through the letterbox to see if I was in. Which I was, crouched over the B&O, devouring the pop-art dystopia that was the DNA of the Steely Dan brand (available in different forms on *Can't Buy A Thrill*, *Countdown To Ecstasy*, *Pretzel Logic*, *Katy Lied*, and more).

Aja was their high-water mark. You can keep your *Zuma*, your *Neon Bible*, your *Back To Black*, your *Parachutes* or your *OK Computer*. You can even keep *The Chronic*. They might all be straight from the heart, but Steely Dan's *Aja* offers the delights of a world uncharted by pop groups, past or present.

Those who hate the band call them sterile, surgical, cold. Which is sort of the point. Becker and Fagen – fundamentally sociopaths masquerading as benign dictators – like to give the impression they're being as insincere as possible, the very antithesis, frankly, of almost everyone else in the music business.

The aforementioned *Aja* is as gentrified and as anal a record as you'll ever hope to hear. Donald Fagen and Walter Becker's masterpiece is an homage to passive-aggressive studio cool, even though they were as disdainful of the palm tree and flared-denim world of Los Angeles as the whey-faced urchins from west London. The band's nihilism is plain for all to hear, disguised as FM-friendly soft-rock. Their lyrics are dispassionate, the architecture of their songs often labyrinthine, the guitar solos ridiculously sarcastic. And yet, on *Aja*, they made some of the most sophisticated, most polished, most burnished music ever heard: 'Black Cow', 'Deacon Blues', 'Home At Last' and the rest.

Aja is also the record that many musicians rate as the personification of musical excellence. Technically and sonically it is beyond compare. (The late *New York Times* critic Robert Palmer – no relation to the late singer – said that Steely Dan's music sounded like it had been 'recorded in a hospital ward'.)

You rarely meet a musician who doesn't love some aspect of *Aja* and whenever I've interviewed a rock star at their home, I've often seen a CD copy around the place somewhere. It used to be played constantly in those places where you went to buy expensive hi-fi equipment and can still be heard in the type of luxury retailers who understand the notion of immersive wealth. Having heard the album's 'Deacon Blues', Ricky Ross named his band after it, while 'Peg' would become widely known because of De La Soul's sampling of it on 'Eye Know'. Three years ago, it was deemed by the Library of Congress to be 'culturally, historically or aesthetically important' and added to the United States National Recording Registry. Get them!

At the time, Becker and Fagen were hard taskmasters in the studio, and would hire dozens of session musicians to record the same guitar solo or drum fill until they felt they had something approaching what they had imagined. They were obsessive perfectionists who spent millions of dollars relentlessly torturing the dozens of grade-A guitarists who apparently weren't 'yacht-smooth' enough. Musicians would spend hours, sometimes days, in one of the many Los Angeles studios that Steely Dan used to record *Aja*, only to find that their work had been jettisoned in favour of someone else's.

At the time of *Aja*, Fagen and Becker were New Yorkers on location in LA and, although they revelled in the recording facilities and the abundance of great musicians, seemingly on tap – they spent their days getting studio tans as opposed to any other kind – they found the city faintly ridiculous.

'Becker and Fagen are interesting characters, sort of isolationists by nature,' one of their session musicians, Elliott Randall, said at the time. 'They live in these houses in Malibu, not near anybody, and I have a feeling LA helps them keep their music going on a certain level – they're almost laughing at the people in their songs.'

Almost?

Still, they weren't above sentimentality. There was always a kind of skeuomorphic feel about Steely Dan records, in that they imbued a certain kind of nostalgia, even though the songs themselves were incredibly modern.

Aja was a case in point. Released at a time when both punk and disco were experiencing their own apotheoses, it seemed completely at odds with anything else. As a testament to that, the record was remixed thirteen times in the five months before its release. Becker and Fagen were scathing about the hard-rock world – finding groups like Led Zeppelin, the Eagles and Bad Company preposterous – and were far more interested in the construction of old jazz records. For them, the only correct response to the entire culture of 'rock' was to be dismissive about it. They were occasionally, and unfairly, compared to the soporific jazz-rock that seeped across US radio in the '70s, as their obsession with technical proficiency was mistaken for musical indolence.

Fagen and Becker were far more radical than that and, although they expressed the same disdain for punk and disco as they felt for the hegemony of mainstream rock, they enjoyed the fact that both were rebelling against the orthodoxy of FM radio. Not only that, but Fagen always seemed to be singing with one eyebrow raised.

Nevertheless, *Aja* oozed detached sophistication, its highly polished surface disguising awkward time signatures and extra-credit guitar fills. 'We're actually accused of starting smooth jazz, which I don't think is exactly true,' Fagen told *New York* magazine in 2006. 'A lot of the effects we got were intended to be comic, like "Hey Nineteen". We were in our thirties and still saddled with these enormous sex drives and faced with the problem that you can no longer talk to a nineteen-year-old girl because the culture has changed. That's set against an extremely polite little groove. And then the chorus is set to jazz chords and when you play them on electronic instruments there's a flattening effect, a dead kind of sound. And it's scored for falsetto voices, which adds to the effect. To me, it's very funny. Other people think it's nauseating.'

Like a lot of those obsessed by recondite impulses, both Fagen and Becker were as intimidated as they were dismissive about the popular and the cool.

At the time, Fagen said, 'We write the same way a writer of fiction would write. We're basically assuming the role of a character, and for that reason it may not sound personal.'

White-hot chops and black humour, more like. Yet Steely Dan were actually cooler than anyone. Maybe not on a haberdashery level, but cool all the same.

As the band didn't project their personalities, determined instead to tell their tales of dissipated, sun-bleached, '70s California angst, they became faceless. 'This is what happens when you don't construct an archetypal persona,' says Chuck Klosterman. 'If you're popular and melodic and faceless, you seem meaningless. [Look at] Steely Dan, a group who served as the house band for every 1978 West Coast singles band despite being more lyrically subversive than the Sex Pistols and the Clash combined. If a musician can't convince people that he's cool, nobody cool is going to care.'

As a personality, Fagen is an acquired taste these days – if you were to take an inventory of prominent men, you would have to scroll down quite a way before you found him – but then he always was. He never warmed to the weave of the sleeve, and, like his music, was always perhaps a little too cool, dry and fastidious. In this sense, an important sign of legitimacy has been missing, but then this is what makes Fagen who he is: someone who doesn't need validation. Yet he and his band are revered.

'Years ago, I flew out to LA to visit a girlfriend who dumped me as soon as I arrived,' says Mark Ronson. 'I couldn't change my ticket so I had to stay in LA, miserable, for five days. I bought the Steely Dan song book and a cheap electric piano and stayed in my room for the duration of the time, teaching myself those songs. I don't often think of the girl, but I use those amazing chord voicings nearly every day.'

The Farrelly brothers based an entire soundtrack on the band, as eight of their songs were covered by the likes of Wilco, the Ben

Folds Five and the Brian Setzer Orchestra in their 2000 movie *Me, Myself & Irene*. 'Only one person turned down our request to do a cover and that was Jonathan Richman,' says Peter Farrelly. 'I called him up and said, "Look, will you do a cover of a Steely Dan song?" He called back and said, "Uh, Peter, I'd like to do this, but the lyrics – I don't know what they mean. I never understood what they were saying." When Jonathan sings, he puts his whole heart into it, so he passed.'

They have another film fan in Judd Apatow: 'I don't think I have listened to any band more than Steely Dan,' he says. 'They are a bottomless pit of joy. The songs are gorgeous, the lyrics are mysterious and witty. When I was young, I used those records as a gateway drug to learn about a lot of great jazz performers. I would read the credits and buy the albums of all the people who played on their records. That led to thousands of hours listening to the Brecker Brothers, Larry Carlton, Phil Woods, Wayne Shorter and countless others.'

Blackpool's Rae Morris, who has toured with Bombay Bicycle Club, Noah and the Whale and Tom Odell, is something of a fan, albeit begrudgingly. 'I was exposed to a lot of Steely Dan when I was little,' she says. 'I hated it [then, but] now I'm starting to think it was a good musical influence.'

Other fans include Phoenix and Daft Punk. The latter have made no secret of their fondness for the band, while their influence can be heard all over last year's *Random Access Memories*. 'If people still went into stereo shops and bought stereos regularly, like they did during the era Daft Punk draw from, this record, with its meticulously recorded analogue sound, would be an album to test out a potential system, right up there with Steely Dan's *Aja* and Pink Floyd's *Dark Side of the Moon*,' wrote

Pitchfork's Mark Richardson. 'Daft Punk make clear that one way to "give life back to music" is through the power of high fidelity.'

The band are a sampling smorgasbord, and have been grazed by Beyoncé ('Black Cow' on the J'Ty remix of 2004's 'Me, Myself and I'), Ice Cube ('Green Earrings' on 1992's 'Don't Trust 'Em'), Hit Boy featuring John Legend ('The Boston Rag' on 2012's 'WyW'), Naughty by Nature ('Third World Man' on 1999's 'Live or Die') and dozens more. Kanye West famously sampled their 1976 hit 'Kid Charlemagne' for his 2007 single 'Champion', although not without a lot of heavy lifting.

'From time to time, we get requests for a licence for hip-hoppers to use part of an old song or something,' says Fagen. 'We usually say "Yes", but we didn't like the general curve of the way that one sounded . . . Kanye actually sent us a sample of his tunes and, frankly, Walter and I listened to it and although we'd love some of the income, neither of us particularly liked what he had done with it. We said, "No" at first, and then he wrote us a hand-written letter that was kind of touching, about how the song was about his father and he said, "I love your stuff, and I really want to use it because it's a very personal thing for me."' Surprisingly, the plea worked.

Somewhat perversely, Fagen and Becker were the winners of the 1999 award from the American Society of Composers, Authors and Publishers (ASCAP) for the most-played rap song, 'Deja Vu (Uptown Baby)', by Lord Tariq and Peter Gunz, who'd used a refrain from 'Black Cow'.

'ASCAP sent us these handsome plaques, but they told us we shouldn't come to the ceremony,' said Becker. 'They said there was some violence the year before and we should stay at home. So I did.'

The rappers, who had originally used the song without a license, managed to irritate P. Diddy too. According to Fagen, 'They were angry because the sample had already been licensed for Puff Daddy and Mase. We actually heard that Puff Daddy was riding around in a limo with Lenny Kravitz and went crazy when he heard it. He said, "They stole my sample!"'

———

Last year, Donald Fagen became a bona-fide author, albeit tentatively, with his memoir, *Eminent Hipsters*. As an eminent hipster himself, Fagen is more than adequately qualified to write about cool, although the book was a lot less expansive than it could have been. He is not what you would call loosey-goosey and in recent years has been described as behaving like a college professor trying to get fired.

The first half of the book is a collection of portraits of the cultural figures who influenced Fagen growing up in New Jersey in the early '60s, including Gene Shepherd, composers Henry Mancini and Ennio Morricone, and Ray Charles. The second half of the book is a kind of geriatric *Diary Of A Rock'n'Roll Star* and catalogues in exhaustive detail the trials and tribulations of touring in your sixties.

As you would expect from someone who has been one of the most consistently mordant voices in rock, Fagen can write. Here he is describing Blake Edwards' TV detective series, *Peter Gunn*: 'Edwards' camera eye seemed to take a carnal interest in the luxe and leisure objects of the period, focusing on the Scandinavian furniture, potted palms, light wood panelling and sleek, shark-finned convertibles. It was, in fact, all the same stuff my parents adored, but darkened with a tablespoon of alienation and danger.

Sort of like seeing a smiling Pan Am pilot climb out of his 707 with a copy of *La Nausée* sticking out of his back pocket.'

Eminent Hipsters is full of such gems, although for those who have silently worshipped Fagen from afar for too, too many years, perhaps he could have dug a little deeper into his psyche, and described some of the personal and professional motivations that have contributed to one of the most important and influential bodies of work in all pop.

But then perhaps that wouldn't have been cool.

Contributors

Nick Coleman wrote for *NME* for a year during the mid-'80s before becoming music editor of the London listings magazine, *Time Out*, in 1987. From 1994 until 2006 he was arts and then features editor at the *Independent* and the *Independent on Sunday* before leaving to go freelance. His memoir *The Train in the Night* was published in 2012, while his novel *Pillow Man* appeared in 2015.

Richard Cromelin has covered the pop music world since the early 1970s, primarily on the staff of the *Los Angeles Times* for more than 30 years. As a freelancer, he wrote for a range of music publications, including *Rolling Stone, Creem, Circus, Phonograph Record* and *New Musical Express.*

Daryl Easlea worked in music retail between 1979 and 1997, leaving to take his degree in American History and International History at Keele. He began writing professionally in 1999, becoming deputy editor at *Record Collector.* His work has also appeared in *MOJO*, the *Guardian*, *Uncut*, *Dazed & Confused* and the *Independent*. His books include *Everybody Dance: Chic & The Politics of Disco* (2004) and *Without Frontiers: The Life and Music of Peter Gabriel* (2013).

Andy Gill has written for *NME*, *Q*, *MOJO* and numerous other publications. He is a regular album reviewer for the *Independent* and author of *Don't Think Twice, It's All Right: Bob Dylan, the Early Years*.

Mick Gold photographed musicians and wrote about music from 1968 to 1978. His work appeared in *Let It Rock*, *Melody Maker*, *Sounds*, *Creem* and *Street Life*, but he threw it all away to produce and direct documentary films for TV. He lives in London with his wife and two daughters. His hobbies include spending too much money on books about rock music.

Geoffrey Himes has written about pop music on a weekly basis in the *Washington Post* since 1977 and has been a contributing editor to *No Depression* magazine since 1998. He has also written about pop music for *Rolling Stone*, the *Oxford American*, *Musician*, *Crawdaddy* and many other outlets. He has been honoured for music feature writing by the Deems Taylor/ASCAP Awards and by the Music Journalism Awards.

Barney Hoskyns is co-founder and editorial director of Rock's Backpages, the online library of pop writing and journalism. He is a former contributing editor at British *Vogue* and US correspondent for *MOJO*. He is the author of the bestselling *Hotel California* (2006), the Tom Waits biography *Lowside of the*

Road (2009) and *Small Town Talk* (2016), a history of the music scene in and around Woodstock, New York. His most recent book is *Never Enough: A Way Through Addiction*.

Chris Ingham wrote for *MOJO* and *Uncut* until there was nothing left to say, authored *Rough Guides* to The Beatles (2003) and Frank Sinatra (2005) and fed his family by producing/composing, lecturing in jazz and pop at Anglia Ruskin University, Cambridge and gigging as a freelance jazz pianist.

Jonh Ingham was born in Australia to English parents and grew up in Australia, Canada and the USA. While still at college his work appeared in *Rolling Stone, Creem* and other contemporary magazines. Moving to London in 1972, he was a freelance writer for *NME* and other UK music magazines. As a *Sounds* staff writer from 1975 to 1977 he wrote high-profile interviews with major rock artists and was one of the first journalists to champion punk, subsequently managing Generation X and the Go-Go's.

Dylan Jones has written twenty books on subjects as diverse as music and politics and fashion and photography. He has been an editor at the *Observer,* the *Sunday Times, i-D, The Face* and *Arena,* a columnist for the *Guardian* and the *Independent* and is currently the editor-in-chief of *GQ.* He has won magazine editor of the year eleven times and been awarded the prestigious Mark Boxer Award. His book on the former British prime minister, David Cameron, was shortlisted for the Channel 4 Political Book of the Year. He was awarded an OBE in the Queen's Honours List in 2013.

Mark Leviton had his first review published in *Rolling Stone* while still in high school and has written on music, film and books for over three decades, with hundreds of credits in *Fusion*, *Phonograph Record* magazine, *UCLA Daily Bruin*, *LA Weekly*, *BAM* magazine, *Music Connection*, the *Los Angeles Times* and many other publications. From 1979–2004 he was with the Warner Music Group in Burbank, overseeing the release of over a thousand compilation albums and box sets. He currently divides his time between Los Angeles, the San Francisco Bay Area and Nevada City, where he can be heard broadcasting his '60s-themed radio show *Pet Sounds* on KVMR-FM.

Ian MacDonald was the author of the acclaimed Beatles book *Revolution in the Head* and of the collection *The People's Music*. He was assistant editor of *NME* in the early '70s and contributed regularly to *Uncut*. Ian died in August 2003.

Gavin Martin published *Alternative Ulster* in Ireland's punk rock summer of 1977, joined *NME* as a freelancer the following year and has written about music and movies ever since. He now freelances for a wide range of publications and was the music critic for the *Daily Mirror*.

Charles Shaar Murray is the Ralph J. Gleason Music Book Award-winning author of *Crosstown Traffic: Jimi Hendrix and Post-war Pop* and *Boogie Man: The Adventures of John Lee Hooker in the American Twentieth Century*, short-listed for the same award. The first two decades of his journalism, criticism and vulgar abuse were collected in *Shots from the Hip*. A founding contributor to *Q* and *MOJO* magazines, he made his print debut in 1970 in the notorious 'Schoolkids Issue' of underground magazine *OZ*, becoming a frequent contributor to *IT* and *Cream* magazines before joining *NME* in 1972. His first novel, *The Hellhound Sample*, was published in 2011.

Robert Palmer was the chief pop music critic for the *New York Times* and also wrote for such publications as *Rolling Stone*. His books included *Deep Blues* and *Rock'n'Roll: An Unruly History*. He died in 1997. 2009 saw the publication of *Blues And Chaos*, an anthology of Palmer pieces edited by Anthony DeCurtis.

Ian Penman wrote for *NME* in the late '70s and early '80s and has subsequently written for *The Wire*, the *London Review of Books* and other publications. A collection of his best pieces, *Vital Signs*, was published by Serpent's Tail in 1998.

Bruce Pollock has written for such publications as the *New York Times, Saturday Review, TV Guide, Entertainment Weekly, Musician, Family Weekly, USA Today, Playboy*, the *Gannett Westchester Newspapers* and the *Village Voice*. He is the author of seven books on music, including *Working Musicians, The Rock Song Index, Hipper Than Our Kids* and *In Their Own Words*, as well as three novels.

Ira Robbins discovered rock music when his big sister made him listen to the Beatles on WABC-AM in 1963. Robbins' first published piece of music criticism was a Doug Sahm record review in *Good Times* in 1972. He continued by writing album and concert reviews for *Zoo World*, then *Circus, Creem* and – laterstill – *Spin, Entertainment Weekly* and the *New York Times*.

He co-founded *Trouser Press* magazine and kept it going for a decade, drifting from a writing/editing role to a writing/publishing role. Since 1997, he has been employed in syndicated radio.

Wayne Robins has been writing about rock since 1969. In the '70s he wrote for the *Village Voice* and *Rolling Stone*, but especially *Creem*. He subsequently wrote for *Newsday* and *New York Newsday*. He lives with his wife and two of his three daughters in Queens, NY.

Steven Rosen has written for dozens of publications, including *Guitar Player*, *Guitar World*, *Rolling Stone*, *Playboy*, *Creem*, *Circus* and *Musician*. He is the author of such books as *Wheels of Confusion: The Story of Black Sabbath*, currently in its third printing, and acts as West Coast editor for the Japanese magazine *Player*.

Bud Scoppa's multifaceted, four-decade career has encompassed writing about pop music, editing music mags and working in the music business, primarily in an A&R capacity. He has contributed to virtually every major music publication, including *Rolling Stone*, *Creem*, *Rock*, *Fusion*, *Crawdaddy!* and *Phonograph Record*. When not writing about music, he was helping to create it at the Mercury, A&M, Arista, Zoo, Discovery and Sire labels. His outlets include *Uncut* and *Paste*.

Fred Schruers' writing has appeared in *Rolling Stone*, *Circus*, *Premiere* and *Entertainment Weekly*. He wrote a business blog about the entertainment industry at Portfolio.com, in addition to being one of *Premiere* magazine's most loved-and-feared figures (he wrote the annual power list).

Sylvie Simmons writes for *MOJO* magazine and is a contributor to the *Guardian*. Since she first started writing about music in 1977, her features and reviews have appeared in countless publications and books worldwide. Like her 2001 study of Serge Gainsbourg, *A Fistful Of Gitanes*, Sylvie's 2012 biography of Leonard Cohen – *I'm Your Man* – was widely acclaimed.

Rob Steen's first flirtation with music writing came in a Kentish Town tower block as editor of *Ikon-UK*, a fanzine fuelled by a slavish devotion to Todd Rundgren. He began reviewing gigs and records: first for a Watford freesheet, then *Record Mirror, No.1, The Hit, Mix, City Limits* and any other long-forgotten publication prepared to publish his quirky offerings. As editor of *The New Ball*, cricket's *Granta*, he contented himself with providing the planet's finest forum for sporting agitprop.

Adam Sweeting is a former features editor for *Melody Maker* and wrote for *Q* in its early days. Currently he writes regularly for *The Arts Desk*, the *Guardian* and *Uncut* and other magazines.

Andrew Tyler wrote for *Disc & Music Echo* in the early '70s and then for *NME* from 1973 to 1980. He was subsequently news features editor with *Time Out*. As a freelance writer, he contributed regularly to the *Observer*, the *Independent*, the *Guardian* and others. He was the author of *Street Drugs*. From 1995 until September 2016, Andrew was the director of Animal Aid, Europe's largest animal rights organisation and one of the first in the world. Andrew died in April 2017.

Penny Valentine was one of the first UK pop writers of note, writing in the '60s for *Disc & Music Echo* and then later for *Sounds, City Limits* and many other publications. She was also the first female pop writer in the British press. She co-wrote (with Vicki Wickham) *Dancing with Demons: The Authorised Biography of Dusty Springfield*. Penny died in January 2003.

Chris Van Ness was a music journalist based at the *Los Angeles Free Press* (where he also served as editor), making regular contributions to the *NME* and to CBC Radio in Canada. Most active from 1967 to 1975, he profiled artists from Billy Eckstine to Yoko Ono – plus two guys named Becker and Fagen. He is currently completing *Orange Marmalade*, a book-length essay on his years trying to make sense out of what was loosely known as 'the counter-culture'. Van Ness is retired in the wilds of Connecticut.

Richard C. Walls contributed extensively to *Creem* magazine in its '70s heyday and subsequently reviewed for *Spin, Rolling Stone* and other publications. Based in Detroit, Walls reviewed movies for the city's *Metro-Times*. He died in May 2017.

Michael Watts was *Melody Maker*'s US editor for much of the 1970s. He's since been an editor at the *Financial Times*, the *Independent*, the *Evening Standard* and *Esquire*. He now writes for *Wired* and anyone else who'll have him.

Chris Welch joined *Melody Maker* in 1964 as reporter and features writer and became features editor in 1970. He stayed with the *MM* until 1979 and became assistant editor of *Musicians Only*. During the 1980s he was a reviews editor and feature writer for

Kerrang!, writing about Iron Maiden, Judas Priest and Megadeth et al. He has written thirty or more books including *Hendrix: The Biography* and *Ginger Geezer: The Life of Vivian Stanshall* (co-written with Lucian Randall).

Richard Williams is the former editor of *Melody Maker* and chief sportswriter for the *Guardian*. His books include *Out Of His Head*, about Phil Spector and *The Man in the Green Shirt*, about Miles Davis. *Long Distance Call* collected some of his best music pieces.

Index

Note: page numbers in **bold** refer to information contained in captions. Song and album titles appear under their artists/bands.

INDEX